ENVOY EXTRAORDINARY

ENVOY
EXTRAORDINARY
A Most Unlikely Ambassador

Horace Phillips

The Radcliffe Press
London · New York

Published in 1995 by
The Radcliffe Press
45 Bloomsbury Square
London WC1A 2HY

In the United States of America
and Canada distributed by
St Martin's Press
175 Fifth Avenue
New York
NY 10010

A full CIP record for this book is available from the British Library

Library of Congress Catalog card number: 95–067459

A full CIP record is available from the Library of Congress

ISBN 1–85043–964–8

Copy-edited and laser-set by Selro Publishing Services, Oxford
Printed and bound in Great Britain by WBC Ltd, Bridgend, Mid Glamorgan

Contents

Illustrations

Acronyms and Abbreviations

ANZAC	Australian and New Zealand Army Corps
ARAMCO	Arabian-American Oil Company
ASEAN	Association of Southeast Asian Nations
BEF	British Expeditionary Force
BP	British Petroleum
CENTO	Central Treaty Organization
CIA	(US) Central Intelligence Agency
COMET	Committee for Middle East Trade
DOT	Department of Trade
DP	Democrat Party
DTI	Department of Trade and Industry
EOKA	Ethniki Organosis Kipriakou Agonos (National Organization of Cypriot Struggle)
FLOSY	Federation for the Liberation of South Yemen
FO	Foreign Office
GHQ	General Headquarters
HQ	Headquarters
IMF	International Monetary Fund
IRA	Irish Republican Army
JP	Justice Party
KCMG	Knight Commander of the Order of St Michael and St George
MP	Member of Parliament
NASAKOM	nationalism/religion/communism
NATO	North Atlantic Treaty Organization
NLF	National Liberation Front
OECD	Organization for Economic Cooperation and Development

Acronyms and Abbreviations

OPEC	Organization of Petroleum Exporting Countries
PLO	Palestine Liberation Organization
RAF	Royal Air Force
RPP	Republican People's Party
SAVAK	Security and Intelligence Organization (secret police)
TRNC	Turkish Republic of Northern Cyprus
TUC	Trades Union Congress
UN	United Nations

Acknowledgements

I am grateful to Dr Lester Crook of the Radcliffe Press for his encouraging reception of my draft and his helpful discussions with me leading to publication. And my thanks are due to Mrs Selina Cohen for her careful copy-editing of the manuscript and her helpful comments and recommendations which did much to improve it.

Finally, I acknowledge gratefully the permission given to me by the *Wall Street Journal*, New York, to reproduce occasional material from articles I wrote some years ago for the *Asian Wall Street Journal*, Hong Kong, with the encouragement of Melanie Kirkpatrick, editorial features editor; and in particular Chapter 23 (Slow Train to Hong Kong) in its entirety.

Although I have in this work referred to situations in which I was officially involved, the views I have expressed are my own and are not to be taken to reflect those of Her Majesty's Government.

Foreword
Sir Denis Wright

Sir Horace Phillips was born in Glasgow in 1917, one of seven grandchildren of humble Jewish immigrants from eastern Europe. His autobiography, *Envoy Extraordinary*, is an unusual and happy story of a talented, determined and ambitious man who, against all odds, succeeded beyond his wildest dreams in a career on which he had set his heart as a youth. By the age of 48 he had become one of Her Majesty's ambassadors and a few years later received the accolade of knighthood from her hands. In retirement, too, his story is an unusual one — not the non-executive directorships and consultancies of some retired ambassadors but a full-time job for nine years drumming up business for one of Britain's leading construction and engineering firms, in Tehran, Hong Kong, Bahrain and Peking, followed by three years of lecturing on international affairs in Turkish universities. *Envoy Extraordinary* is an absorbing account of a full and varied life of achievement and political drama.

Horace began his working life at the age of 17 as an Inland Revenue clerk in Glasgow. Inspired by books of foreign travel and adventure he attended night classes with a view to entering the consular service by the back door if not the front. His big chance came at the end of the Second World War (during which he rose from private to major and saw active service in many countries), when he passed the Foreign Office entrance examination for ex-servicemen and in 1947 was appointed vice consul at Shiraz in south Persia.

Envoy Extraordinary

Thereafter, thanks to ability, personality, a remarkable gift for mastering foreign languages and the support of his wife, Idina, whom he had married in India during the war, he moved rapidly up the FO ladder. When I arrived in Tehran as ambassador in April 1963 and met him for the first time Horace was counsellor there — that is, he was my deputy, and an excellent one to boot. Until then, apart from two years in London, he had served entirely in the Muslim Middle East and Afghanistan, his Jewish origins having been no obstacle to success or promotion. However, in 1968 when the *Jewish Chronicle* proudly drew attention to his appointment as HM Ambassador to Saudi Arabia (where he had already served and spoke fluent Arabic) the Saudis felt obliged to withdraw the *agrément* they had already given to his appointment. Mercifully Horace's career was not affected by this bitter personal disappointment. There followed two important and difficult posts, as high commissioner in Tanzania and ambassador to Turkey, in both of which he made his mark before retirement and turning to other fields.

Horace's story is a credit both to himself and to the FO, which recognized a good man when they saw him.

Preface

An ambassador can expect to be visited at his post by a long series of politicians, businessmen, journalists, representatives of the arts, and others, all anxious to exchange views with him on the local scene. The visitors may be interesting, dull or tiresome. But the ambassador does well to remember that his reaction to them will be seen as a reflection not only of his personal manner but of the attitude of the diplomatic service in general to such visitors. For my own part I behaved towards them in my usual informal way, which at times, to some with a preconceived, often prejudiced notion of an ambassador, may have been not quite what they expected.

Among my visitors when I was high commissioner in Tanzania was a reporting team from the BBC whom I received without reserve and entertained hospitably. This, and the interview that I gave, seemed to have so impressed the young woman heading the team that in her advance notice of the interview in the programme magazine she flatteringly described me as a most unlikely ambassador. Perhaps, in the sense that she had in mind, unusual would have been a more accurate adjective. But, looking back, I think it true enough to say that unlikely does correctly describe my ambition of getting into the diplomatic service, then my advancement in it — given the obstacles and setbacks which I have spelled out in this account of my career, spanning nearly 60 years from the age of 17.

It is an account based largely on memory, helped by reference books for some dates and events. In my 30 years as a diplomat I kept no official papers or copies of them, nor records of conversations. My purpose in writing this book has not been to comment on controversial political or diplomatic situations; where I have referred to these I have done so simply as matters of fact in which I was involved in my official capacity. Nor has my purpose been to disclose information which came my way about the personal attitude or behaviour of leading figures I had to do with. In a word, this is a chronology of reminiscences written from personal experience — an autobiographical record, not a political memoir. It is an experience that covers, before my diplomatic service, my years in the home civil service and the army, and, after it, two further, short, careers in completely different fields.

Among my coreligionists there are some who have made the point that I seem to have been the only one among the few Jewish career diplomats in Britain who has risen to be a senior ambassador; and they have tried to put this forward as evidence of discrimination in the Foreign Office. But the fact is that no entrant to the diplomatic service is asked about his religion: it is sufficient that his parents were born here (no matter where theirs were) and that he has passed the highly competitive entrance examination. That very few Jews compete is simply a reflection of the fact that in their circle there is no tradition of diplomatic service: they tend towards business or the professions.

Jewish criticism of the Foreign Office has sometimes gone so far as allegations that officials there who deal with the Middle East are biased in favour of the Arabs. It seems to me that these allegations are based on nothing more than the fact that there are naturally more Arab desks in the Foreign Office than Israeli ones, and more Arabic than Hebrew speakers in the service. Added to which, two centuries of association with the Arabs have given British officials a tradition of relations with them of a kind which a few decades of relations with Israel have not yet established.

For the rest, I can only say that my own Jewishness did not become a matter of concern to the Foreign Office, and of interest outside it, until the traumatic occasion of my abortive appointment as ambassador to Saudi Arabia in 1968, which I have described in these pages. The Foreign Office could not have been more sympathetic and supportive, and when the dust settled I was given another appointment, at least as substantial, and went on from there to the higher reaches of the diplomatic service. My career gives the lie to any suggestion that there is discrimination in the service. And it provides evidence that as a result of the reforms introduced by Anthony Eden 50 years ago the way to the top is open these days to any candidate who can pass the entrance examination, irrespective of his social, financial or religious background. I myself never looked over my shoulder at my background. I regarded myself simply as a British ambassador.

H.P.

1

Origins–Ambitions–
Civil Service

S uwalki, in the northeastern corner of Poland about 20 miles
from the border with Lithuania, is not much of a place. A
small slow-paced agro-industrial town, it straddles the main
road two-thirds of the way between Warsaw and Kaunas, capital
of the independent Lithuania of the 1920s and 1930s. It is undis-
tinguished by anything; stereotyped in its communist way of life
until the changes of the Gorbachev era.

In the latter part of the nineteenth century it was even less of a
place. It lay in that part of Poland which, in over 100 years of
successive partitioning by Russia, Prussia and Austria, had fallen
to Russia. A comparatively neglected part of the tsarist empire, far
from the major centres of population, it was a place where some
of Poland's five million Jews had come to feel they could live in
peace. In 1860 there were between 6000 and 7000 of them in
Suwalki — nearly half the population. They lived mainly in the
related market town of Sejny, some miles to the east near the
border with Lithuania, its former imposing synagogue now a
museum and cultural centre.

Some 300 miles to the northeast, in Latvia, lies Daugavpils. For
over 200 years from the middle of the sixteenth century Latvia
had been ruled by Poland, before falling to Russia in the eighteenth century. In the nineteenth it became largely the fief of the so-
called Baltic barons, Germans in Russian service. Until near the
end of the century, when the Russians changed it back to Dvinsk,

Envoy Extraordinary

Daugavpils was known by its German name of Dunaburg. But to the Jews there it was always Dvinsk, which rendered itself easily into Hebrew and Yiddish. By 1880 there were around 30,000 of them — as in Suwalki, nearly half the population. The Great Synagogue was a focal point. The *yeshiva*, or seminary, produced rabbis and cantors, some of the most eminent of whom were later to hold distinguished office in Western Europe and the United States.

By the middle of the nineteenth century the whole of this corner of the tsar's empire of that time was a flourishing centre of Jewish learning where religious leaders were trained and children educated in the ways of their fathers. Not only in Suwalki and Dvinsk, but in Kovno (now Kaunas), and 100 miles east of there, in Vilna (Vilnius), sizeable Jewish communities maintained tradition and culture without undue interference from their Gentile neighbours. They were shopkeepers, pedlars, butchers, tailors, carpenters — poor communities, but devout.

With a few favoured exceptions they were confined to the so-called Pale of Settlement, a restricted area established by Catherine the Great in 1791 to prevent the Jews in Poland, brought under her rule by the first partition of that country, from spreading into central Russia. In principle the Pale covered 25 specified provinces, but its actual boundaries varied over the years with the changes in intensity of persecution that the Jews suffered under successive tsars. Alexander II alleviated some of the hostile decrees of his father Nicholas I. But on the assassination of Alexander in 1881 in popular revulsion at his despotism, his son Alexander III's ministers represented to him that the anti-imperial agitation had been fomented by the control that the Jews had gained of trade and small industry and by their acquisition of land within the Pale.

As a result, new harsh laws against them limited their possibilities for business and education. They were driven out of rural into urban areas and forbidden to move from any one town to another. Communities established for generations now found themselves uprooted and forced to leave their villages. Some were fortunate enough to be able to sell their property and chattels, if only for a song; others had to abandon nearly everything. But all found themselves refugees in long lines heading for the nearest

2

towns, carrying their few remaining possessions on foot or in handcarts — a poignant picture described by the Yiddish writer Sholem Aleichem in his play, *Tevye the Milkman*, later produced in the West as *Fiddler on the Roof.*

The conditions attending the flight of these refugees varied from time to time and from district to district. In some cases expulsion was directed by not unfriendly officials; in others it was enforced violently by squads of mounted Cossacks who often beat and looted. The resettlement resulted in the overcrowding of Jews in towns and the creation of ghettos there, with the blocking of economic opportunities. It was a situation that eroded the earlier tolerable relations between Jews and their Gentile neighbours. In many places the latter now used the hostile official attitude to the Jews as an excuse to harass and persecute them in one way or another, while the authorities did nothing to stop bands of Cossacks from carrying out fierce pogroms.

To add to this oppression, military conscription bore down on Jews more harshly than on the rest of the population. Jewish communities had to supply a certain number of recruits each year between the ages of 12 and 25, whose service lasted anything up to 15 years from the general conscription age of 18. They were trained at special institutions outside the Pale and then often sent to serve in Siberia and other distant regions in the east. They could not become officers, and they were under constant pressure to convert to Christianity. Inevitably Jewish youth sought every opportunity to evade service. The severe punishment for this if they were discovered and could not pay a bribe, together with increasingly oppressive treatment of them in general, turned the thoughts of scores of thousands of Jews to fleeing the country. By the latter years of the nineteenth century the ports of Riga and St Petersburg saw a steady stream of refugees making for the West. Among them, two couples unknown to each of them leaving at different times, were my four grandparents.

In the Suwalki synagogue on 1 May 1866, Rachel Markiss married a master tailor later to be known as Bernet Phillips. What he was called at that time cannot now be ascertained, since the synagogue records no longer exist. On 8 May 1883, in the Great Synagogue in Dvinsk, Barnet Yaffie, also a tailor, had married

Katya Krakinowski. By 1870 the Phillipses, and by the late 1880s the Yaffies, had had enough of the tsar and his ways, and with their first children they made for a ship to the West, probably from Riga. Perhaps, like thousands of others, they thought they were taking themselves to what they called the golden land of America, land of freedom, justice, opportunity — and no pogroms. But they got no further than the east coast of Britain, the Phillips family to London and the Yaffies to Edinburgh.

By 1874 the former had moved to Glasgow, brought there by a London company to fill a need for master tailors. In 1889 Bernet Phillips was listed with others in an enquiry by a House of Lords Commission into sweated labour, but came out of it without blame. Meantime, soon after the Yaffies arrived in Edinburgh, an organization that had been set up by the small local immigrant Jewish community, dating from the early nineteenth century, directed them across the country to Glasgow where the handful of Jews who formed the first community in the 1820s had by 1880 increased to nearly 1000. In due course the children of both families, the majority born in Glasgow, grew up and met there — among them my parents, who were married in the city's second synagogue under a traditional covenant in Hebrew, followed by civil registration.

Phillips was my paternal grandfather's name as shown on my father's birth (1888) and marriage (1916) certificates in Glasgow. Presumably he decided after his arrival in Britain that he must take a name appropriate to his adopted land. He might well have been called originally Filipowski, a common enough name in his home community — and one not entirely unknown in Scotland. The *Jewish Encyclopaedia* lists one Hirsch Filipowski who also bore the name Phillips, a mathematician and Hebraist who arrived from Russia in 1839 and, after some years in London, worked in Edinburgh. He died in 1872, which was about the time my grandfather arrived in London and a few years later settled in Glasgow; and it is just possible that someone suggested the name Phillips to him. But, equally, changes of outlandish names of East European immigrants were often the result of a British immigration officer's phonetic or simplified interpretation of them, which he then put on record.

4

Origins–Ambitions–Civil Service

My parents quickly produced me, in May 1917, the first of what were eventually to be seven children. We were brought up as an Orthodox family associated with what by now was the city's leading synagogue, Garnethill, of which I am still a member. We received our secular education at local schools and attended in addition the synagogue evening classes for Hebrew and religion, which prepared me for a pass in the Jews' College first-grade examination. The virtues of hard work were dinned into us by parents and teachers and we never hankered after material things which we knew we could not have. We accepted that our parents, intelligent and educated, were not well off: my mother had no money of her own and my father wandered in and out of a succession of mediocre jobs as commercial traveller, retail salesman, finance house manager. His situation was plagued by recurrent illness, and in 1935 at the age of 47 he died of cancer. My mother, then 39, was left with seven children and no money.

* * *

It was always our parents' wish to see us fully educated, and in my case they had planned that after finishing at Hillhead High School I should compete for a bursary to take me to Glasgow University. But in view of my father's death it became clear to me that this was a luxury that could not be afforded, and that I would have to find a job and support the family. My mother was doing her best by baking and sewing for sympathetic friends in the Jewish community, who realized that paying for work that she did for them was acceptable to her where charity would not have been. We could never have afforded to buy one, but I won a bicycle in a competition in the weekly magazine of the Boy Scouts (I was a member of the Garnethill synagogue troop), and every Friday evening, before the Sabbath, I would ride round delivering my mother's handiwork to her customers.

But meantime I had decided what to do to help. Towards the end of 1934, at 17, having obtained the Scottish Higher Leaving Certificate, I sat the competitive examination for entry to the civil service clerical grade. Since it would be some months before the results were announced, I answered an advertisement for a clerk in the Imperial Tobacco Company office in Glasgow. After a competitive interview I was accepted, and found myself responsible for processing the orders obtained by the company's travelling salesmen in the north of Scotland. I gradually came to know by heart the names of all the villages north of a line from Dingwall to Ullapool and the prices of every brand of cigarette and tobacco from Wild Woodbine to Navy Cut. As a non-smoker (to this day) I gave my colleagues my free ration of cigarettes.

* * *

Early in 1935 I learned I had passed the civil service examination and been appointed to one of the income-tax offices in Glasgow. With some trepidation I asked the tobacco company manager to release me after only a few months in his employ. To begin with he was fairly caustic and accused me of using the Imperial Tobacco Company simply as a stepping stone in my career. I could only reply that all I had done was reinsure myself against the possibility that I might not pass the civil service examination, in which case I would have said nothing and remained with the company. (Though I doubt if I could have carried on for long in such routine work.) In the end he softened and wished me luck.

I regarded that civil service appointment as only a first step. I was determined to work my way up — but through further competitive examination, and not by waiting for possible internal promotion. After the day's work in the income-tax office I spent the evenings in the Mitchell Library studying for the executive grade examination in three years' time. The syllabus for this was much more advanced than for the clerical, and I found myself short of one in the minimum number of subjects that I had to offer from a given list. To fill this gap I set about learning Spanish by a correspondence course. In 1938, just before I was 21, I passed high in the examination.

By this time I had a good knowledge of French, German and Spanish, and I had become interested in reading about famous travellers and proconsuls of the past, particularly in the Middle East — Blunt, Burckhardt, Niebuhr, Doughty, Burton, Stratford, Canning and others. I was familiar with the history of the Levant

Company since its foundation in the reign of Elizabeth I and with the experiences of early ambassadors and consuls in Turkey and Persia. Fired by this reading, I wanted a career that would take me abroad, preferably to the east. The consular service seemed the way (the diplomatic service being well out of my reach). I realized that this meant passing a stiff competitive examination for which I might not be qualified. But I believed that if I could once get into the Foreign Office at a lower level I could take things from there.

I knew that executive grade posts in that department were not generally operational but were concerned mainly with organization and establishment matters and personnel and finance. But I thought there might be some eventual internal process of selection of executive officers for junior work in consulates. I therefore put the Foreign Office at the top of my list of choices of appointment following my success in the executive grade examination. But the only vacancy in that department was given to a clerical officer already serving there who had also passed the examination. My second choice was to remain in the Inland Revenue, and in the summer of 1938 I found myself transferred from Glasgow to the personnel and administration department in Somerset House in London.

But I regarded this as simply another stopgap, a temporary stage on the way to my ultimate goal; and I wrote to the civil service commissioners, with some details about myself, for information on the conditions for direct entry to the consular service. I received a reply in the stiff formal style of the time — the writer (my 'obedient servant') being 'instructed by the commissioners' to inform me that without the prescribed educational qualification (an honours degree) I would be unlikely to pass the entrance examination; and to add, for my information, that candidates were expected to have some private means, so that if they passed the entrance examination they could maintain themselves abroad for a year of advanced study of a foreign language before being appointed to a consular post. For these reasons the commissioners could not even admit me to the pre-examination selection interview. I swallowed my disappointment and settled down for the time being to my duties in Somerset House, wondering how to get round the problem.

2

War–Marriage–On the Viceroy's Staff

O ne of these duties a year later, when war threatened, was to process the departure of Inland Revenue officials in the armed services reserves who were being called up. The process included provision for guaranteeing their right to return to the department after the war, and for paying them or their dependants the difference between their civil service pay and their armed service pay if less. In due course, in January 1940, I found myself processing my own departure for the army. Shortly afterwards I received a postal order for four shillings (two days' pay) and a travel warrant to Dorchester where at Top o' Town Barracks I became, at 22, a private in the Dorsetshire Regiment. I could never have believed then that it was the start of what was to be seven and a half years in the army. By April, after basic training which included learning how to fall off a powerful motorcycle without actually breaking any bones, I found myself in a field security section in the British Expeditionary Force in France. It was, I think, my ability to ask the way of French farmers and interrogate the odd German prisoner, rather than my prowess as a spy-catcher, that put me there.

My unit was in reserve in Paris, where we were billeted in apartments in the Boulevard des Batignolles, near Sacré Cœur. We naturally, proud of our French, cultivated some of the young ladies of the neighbourhood. By and large they responded prettily; but the more acute among them asked pointedly how it was that we were enjoying Paris in the springtime while their fathers and brothers were facing the discomfort and danger of the Maginot Line. While perhaps not over-anxious to see an early end to the phoney war, honour required us to say in reply that one day if required we would be there with them. That day came sooner than we had expected: early on the morning of 10 May 1940, following the German parachute landing in Holland, we were ordered to pack up and form a convoy ready to drive north. As these preparations got under way some of the girls rallied round to say goodbye — and we felt glad to be vindicating the good name of the British army by going off to what looked like being a real war.

But of course it turned out to be a very one-sided one. We had barely crossed the frontier into Belgium at Tournai when the main body of the BEF, which had advanced beyond Brussels in an attempt to stem the German attack on Belgium through Holland, began to be forced back westward through Brussels and eventually into France. There my unit was caught up in the retreat and, under heavy air bombardment by the Germans while their ground troops closed in, we joined the thousands of the BEF moving towards the coast of France, the only escape route: Roubaix, Lille, Tourcoing, Armentières, Hazebrouck, Cassel, to the beaches of Dunkirk. These were littered with abandoned trucks under which we at first misguidedly took cover from the bombing and strafing of the Luftwaffe. When, as they obviously learned to, the Germans concentrated on these vehicles, we dispersed on the beaches as best we could, gratified that bombs exploding in sand caused fewer casualties than might have been expected. After several days of waiting, with only intermittent sleep and little to eat or drink, I was taken off with others in a small boat and ferried out to a destroyer offshore which gradually filled up to bursting point, all of us standing the whole way to Dover packed so closely that we supported one another.

Having arrived there in the early hours of the morning, we staggered on to the quay across two submarines moored alongside, to be greeted warmly by Women's Voluntary Service helpers with tea and something to eat before being loaded into a train waiting at the marine station. We slept through the slow night journey until the train stopped at a place I had never heard of —

Andover — where we were taken to a light training regiment depot. The armoured car hangars had been emptied, and laid out in them were scores of palliasses and blankets. After a long sleep and good food we quickly recovered. It was 31 May, my twenty-third birthday, and with some others — all of us now bathed and shaved at least — I decided to see what Andover was like. We were given virtually the freedom of the city: bus conductresses refused to take fares, restaurant snacks were on the house, cinemas let us in free. From having wondered if the field advances of pay given to us in the depot would be enough, we now returned from town with the money still jingling in our pockets.

Dunkirk was a magic word and the sentiments of the man in the street were heartfelt. But clearly the holiday could not last forever, and it was not long before we had to parade before the depot sergeant major who, after some caustic references to the privileges we had been enjoying, ordered us to get cleaned up, polish our boots, and begin to look like soldiers again before going on short home leave. With a rail warrant for Glasgow in my pocket, and several weeks' pay, I was looking at a jeweller's window on my way across London, wondering whether I could afford a new cheap wristwatch to replace the one broken on my way to Dunkirk, when an old cockney woman asked if I had just got out of there and proffered me half-a-crown. It was clear that she needed it more than I did, and I gently rejected it. But she insisted that I must take it; we had all done so much for people like her and this was the least she could do in return. I tried to argue, but I could see that she was going to be offended, perhaps thinking that I was turning down her offer because it was so small; so I accepted it with her blessing. I was very touched.

There was no telephone in our house in Glasgow so I sent my mother a telegram about my arrival, hoping she would not fear the worst when it was delivered. And this might well have been the case, since she had had no news not only of me but of two of my brothers: one in the navy and the other an air-gunner in the RAF — who a year later was shot down and missing until some time afterwards we learned he was one of only two survivors and had been picked up out of the Bay of Biscay by a German patrol boat and taken prisoner (not released until the end of the war).

10

My mother of course had no idea that I was in the retreat to Dunkirk; she had hoped that with my knowledge of French I would be in some military office in Paris. At any rate, for the next 18 months she saw me from time to time on short pass from various places in the south of England where the field security section I was in was taking part in tactical exercises, protecting sensitive installations and keeping an eye on aliens and suspicious characters.

In November 1941 we moved to Birkenhead for posting overseas: not allowed to know exactly where — though we guessed where after khaki drill uniform had been issued. And to encourage us on our way we were visited by the first general I had ever seen, who was to command the newly formed IV Corps in which we would be serving. About this time my sergeant major received instructions to detach me from the draft and send me to an officers' training school. I told him I would rather go with the unit as the plain corporal I now was (with the prospect of my first contact with the Middle East), and after some exchanges with higher authority this was agreed to.

In winter weather the convoy of thousands of troops set sail across the Atlantic. For the most part we were transported in liners not yet converted to troopships: while men were accommodated in hammocks slung above mess tables in crowded holds below the water line, officers had cabins and ate in the regular dining rooms furnished with the shipping company's silver and linen and attended by its stewards. As if this was not contrast enough with the miserable conditions below deck, the regimental band which was in the draft had to play at the officers' dinners. It seemed incredibly short-sighted to me. But it says much about society and the attitude of soldiers 50 years ago that, apart from some mutterings, we took the situation for granted.

The convoy had little or no escort until it picked one up off the Canadian coast and then sailed south off the east coast of America. In view of the danger there was of course a complete blackout at night in all ships, and for the week across the Atlantic we had to remain fully clothed at all times, including the night. The weather was foul and did not begin to improve until we were further south, finally changing course eastward for Freetown in

11

West Africa and a short stop there. By that time the blackout had been lifted and it was bliss to be able to lie on deck in the sun. It was a pleasure only marginally dimmed by envy at the sight and sound of officers dancing in the evening with nurses on the deck of one of the other liners of the convoy in harbour.

The next stage of the voyage, during which we heard the news of Pearl Harbor, took us round the Cape to Durban. There, for the first time in weeks we were able to stretch our legs for a few days on dry land — many of us in the company of South African families (Boer and English alike) who sought us out in town and entertained us in their homes with great hospitality during our stay. In the camp, where we were accommodated in bell tents and fed lavishly, I had my first taste of the warm south with its starry skies and chirping cicadas.

We were soon at sea again, and only now told that we were bound for Iraq as part of Paiforce (Persia and Iraq). Rashid Ali Gilani, the pro-German rebel leader in Baghdad, had been defeated by British troops in May 1941. But there was still concern about the danger that in their advance on the Russian front the Germans might break through the Caucasus to threaten the oilfields of northern Iraq; and troops of Paiforce were deployed in the Kirkuk/ Mosul area at the beginning of 1942 for the defence of these. My unit moved up there from Basra on our motorcycles as part of a convoy. Once in the north, for protection against the desert winter cold we dug down into the sand and bivouacked under tent roofs.

After having been disrupted by a Russian offensive, the German advance resumed in the spring and went on as far as the foothills of the Caucasus. But an attack in force through that barrier did not seem imminent in view of the fierce Russian resistance (culminating at Stalingrad in November 1942), so it was possible meantime to reduce the British defence force in northern Iraq. Elements of this, including my unit, were hurriedly withdrawn down to Basra and shipped from there to reinforce the Indian frontier with Burma, which the Japanese had overrun by May 1942, posing a threat to India. From an assembly camp near Bombay we drove for days across India in convoy up to Jhansi, then down the Grand Trunk Road and on to what was to be our base at Imphal in Manipur State, on the Burma frontier. We were still IV Corps troops, now part of the 14th Army (later to be known as 'The Forgotten').

I was now an acting sergeant and was detailed to position myself in a hide on the frontier with a small Indian escort for protection, to try to sort out Japanese infiltrators in the stream of Burmese refugees making their way into India along jungle tracks. Because of the difficulties of recognition and language a Chinese-speaking officer from the American China–Burma–India theatre headquarters brought in a squad of Chinese soldiers from Chiang Kai-shek's army who were to help me. They could manage basic communication in Japanese and Burmese, but knew no English. The American therefore wrote out for me a phonetic transliteration of Chinese words and phrases I would be likely to need in order to speak to them. Not that there was much to say. They knew the purpose of the operation — though so far as I can recall it did not net any Japanese. Those who did infiltrate into India tended to do so further north, to make contact with Indian Congress elements then actively opposing and sabotaging British rule.

Late in 1942 my sergeant major told me that the papers relating to my selection for officer training in England (which had been shelved when I told him in Birkenhead towards the end of 1941 that I preferred to remain with my unit) had been taken down and dusted off; I was now to present myself at the Officers' Training School in Belgaum in western India, south of Poona and near Goa, to be prepared for a commission in the Indian Army. And this time it was an order. I had no option, for that army had to be expanded for eventual operations against the Japanese. I arrived at Belgaum to find it untouched by war, apart from an increase in the number of officer cadets. The officer instructors had their families living with them in quarters; everyone (including cadets) had Indian servants immaculate in white; mess and club nights continued the formal tradition of the years. To me it was a completely new aspect of living — in contrast not merely to my army experience up to then, but to my whole upbringing in Glasgow.

At the end of the training course, which included instruction in Urdu, obligatory for all Indian Army officers, I was in January 1943 commissioned as a second lieutenant in the 1st Punjab

Regiment — advanced shortly afterwards to lieutenant after I had passed the examination in Urdu. After Intelligence training in Karachi I was posted to the School of Japanese Instruction, which had been set up in Simla by GHQ India to provide six-month full-time courses in the language to a succession of about a dozen British officers of all three services who were linguists. The purpose of the course was not to turn out fluent interpreters and translators: these already existed in a specialized American-led centre elsewhere. Our Japanese was to be for use in the field, to exploit enemy operation orders that might be captured and to listen in to clear language wireless messages between Japanese units. In six months of punishing day-long study we learned enough for that, taught by a couple of Korean internees and several Japanese domiciled in India, including wives of British officers in the Indian Army who had met them in Japan while they were studying for army interpreterships before the war.

Pressure on us was high and at the end of the day's study we would relax in one or other of the (not very sophisticated) haunts of Simla. The town had the added attraction for us of an English girls' boarding school, some of whose young teachers and senior pupil teachers we got to know. At a school concert I went to with an RAF officer on the course with me I was attracted by the back view of a young woman in a yellow dress sitting at a grand piano opposite another one where a grey-haired woman, her teacher, sat; they were playing Weber's Invitation to the Dance. I contrived to be introduced to the girl, who had finished school and was acting as a pupil teacher, and we went out and about together for the next couple of months.

✻ ✻ ✻

Towards the end of 1943, just before the Japanese course ended, we were standing one evening on the Ridge, a high point in Simla, looking across at the snow-covered foothills of the Himalayas shining in the moonlight. I told her I would soon be leaving, with no idea, until I reported at the 1st Punjab Regiment at Jhelum, in that province, where I would be posted. And who knew? We might not meet again. Her reaction was non-committal — not, I

14

liked to suppose, because she was positively unconcerned, but because she was unsophisticated enough not to want to appear to be pressing the issue.

I decided to press it myself, encouraged by the fact that she was also leaving Simla shortly, also by happy coincidence to Jhelum, where her family knew a number of the officers there. Her Irish father, a traffic inspector on the Indian Railways, had, like his father before him, served in the army then stayed on in India. (The family left India on its independence in August 1947 and settled in London.) I did not formally propose to the girl. I took her by the hand, hurried down to the jeweller on the Mall just as he was closing, and asked him to show me some engagement rings. I fingered them and turned the tags over with growing dismay until he reassured me: these were catalogue numbers, not prices. We selected one that I could afford on my pay; put it on her finger there and then; somewhat overwhelmed at the speed of things, she agreed to marry me. She was 19; I was 26. We were married soon afterwards at the regimental depot under an archway of swords — a marriage that despite inevitable ups and downs has lasted generally happily these 50 years.

Given my Orthodox upbringing, I instinctively questioned myself about marrying a non-Jewish girl. But any doubts I might have had were outweighed by my mother's acceptance of her in reply to my letter (and affection for her when they eventually met) and by the absolute certainty of myself to remain always a practising Jew — which has in fact been the case. After a short honeymoon in Kashmir and a few weeks in married quarters in Delhi while I was attached to GHQ, now a captain, my wife returned to her family in Jhelum and I went on active service again, not to see her until after the end of the war, by which time she had borne our first child, a son. I found myself at Army Group HQ in Ceylon, working to piece together the Japanese order of battle throughout Southeast Asia from often fragmentary intercepts of their headquarters and field unit wireless messages. The picture built up was surprisingly accurate: after the eventual Japanese surrender we were able to give some of their own formation head-quarters the location of field units which had lost touch with them. Meantime I was in July–August 1945 shipped out in the

15

force that set sail for a seaborne invasion of Malaya. But, before we could land, the atomic bombs had been dropped early in August and the Japanese had surrendered. Nevertheless, the force went ahead with the planned landings in the southern part of the west coast of Malaya in case there were still Japanese units there which had not obeyed the order to surrender. One of the main landings would have been a disaster had it been opposed, since the beach proved to be soft and unable to bear the weight of armour and vehicles, which sank to their axles in the sand and would have been sitting ducks for the Japanese.

The ship I was in was among a number diverted from the landing, and it sailed up the Singapore river to that city, where we began the roundup and eventual repatriation of the Japanese garrison and reserve troops. There, on 12 September, Mountbatten took the formal surrender of all Japanese forces throughout Southeast Asia. At the end of May 1946 he returned to London on the winding up of Southeast Asia Command.

✻ ✻ ✻

Out of the blue in Singapore in mid-1946, by which time I had been promoted major, I was ordered to London to join Mountbatten's personal staff there. I had never met him and had no idea what my job would be. I was still an officer in the 1st Punjab Regiment and was given permission to go to the regimental depot in Jhelum to collect my wife and baby son and take them with me in the troopship to Britain. When I arrived in London Mountbatten told me he had asked for me as someone who knew Japanese and was familiar with the campaigns in Southeast Asia: with special reference to the Japanese role in these I was to assist Peter Murphy, his close friend from Cambridge days, who was drafting Mountbatten's dispatches — his 'Report to the Combined Chiefs of Staff on Operations in Southeast Asia'. I was happy to be doing something constructive, and worked with Murphy in Mountbatten's offices opposite the Ministry of Defence. In addition, I acted for some time as the latter's aide-de-camp and came to know him quite well and to appreciate the qualities that had made him such an able and well-liked young 'Supremo' in Southeast Asia.

3

Diplomatic Service
Reconstruction–Obstacles
in My Way

By this time I had been six and a half years in the army, and although I knew that release from the Indian Army was later than from the British, I had begun to plan for my return to civilian life. I was still bent on a consular, if not diplomatic, career, and the war had brought an unforeseen development which gave me more hope than I had been left with in 1938: namely, the reforms initiated in 1943 by Anthony Eden when foreign secretary. Basic to these was the amalgamation of the Foreign Office, diplomatic service, consular service and commercial diplomatic service into a single foreign service. This widened the range of choice for all posts, broke down the social barrier between diplomat and consul and the professional barrier between political and commercial work, and opened the way for a wider intake of candidates. It was designed to destroy the impression that British diplomacy was dominated by the caste prejudices of certain public schools and universities. (The continuing high intake from these places is not now a matter of caste, but of their traditional emphasis on the studies best suited to prepare candidates for the diplomatic service.)

In this unified service, however, an important division across the board was planned. There would be a senior branch (Branch A) for entrants of civil service administrative calibre who, subject to

17

merit, could progress right up the ladder to the top ranks of ambassador. And a junior branch (Branch B) at civil service executive level, which would not lead to these heights but could provide a satisfactory career (generally to consul-general level). From time to time, in exceptional cases, there would be the possibility of a sideways transfer from Branch B to Branch A.

Before the Eden reforms candidates for what would henceforth be known as Branch A had to have an honours degree, second class at least, and pass a severe entrance examination in French, German, European history and a number of optional subjects. The high language qualifications demanded penalized candidates not able to afford expensive language study, especially abroad, after three to four years at university. But now the academic examination system was to be less rigid; much emphasis would be placed on selection boards following a simpler examination. Foreign language study, now at public expense for selected entrants, would be arranged in their first year or two in the service.

Calculations at that time forecast a future annual intake of around 20. But during the war the normal flow of entrants had been completely suspended: entry on a temporary basis was made on the strength of personality and record assessed by *ad hoc* selection boards. So it was estimated that to resume regular recruitment in the first years after the end of the war there would be a one-off requirement for anything up to 200 new entrants, most of whom were expected to be men (and some women) who had served in the armed forces. Since these would have had no opportunity for study during their service, the long prewar academic examinations were replaced by a series of short qualifying (so-called Reconstruction) examinations designed to test a candidate's knowledge of, and skill in the use of, English; his numeracy, general knowledge and intelligence; and an examination in a main European language, or proof of aptitude for foreign languages.

Those who passed the qualifying examination (and however successful in other subjects, failure to qualify on the language requirement led to rejection) would go through a two-day residential course to determine their intellectual, psychological and practical fitness; then, if up to standard in that, they would appear before a stringent final selection board. The overall pass mark would be 80 per cent. These Reconstruction examinations for entry to the senior branch (A) would be open to all ex-service personnel of whatever rank, up to the age of 29, irrespective of social, financial or formal educational background. Intelligence, personality and a candidate's war record would count for a lot; his or her potential would be closely considered. These would be the criteria of success. The only academic stipulation was that if a candidate did not already have an honours degree from before the war or through a university grant after it, he had to prove that he could have attained one, in second class at least.

A War Office circular brought this opportunity to the notice of serving personnel of all ranks and I of course applied. In 1946, while still serving in Singapore, I appeared for preliminary interview before a board set up for servicemen in the Far East. There I was questioned on the subject of an honours degree. With some foreboding I explained the family difficulties which had made it impossible for me to go to university.

Meantime, however, I was allowed to take the qualifying examination — which I did in London in November 1946. I passed, but was not listed in the table of results because my eligibility to compete had not been established: it appeared that my old school could not confirm that I would have been able to get an honours degree had I gone to university.

I went at once to Glasgow in uniform to see the headmaster (a new one since my day). He said that the school's report to the civil service commissioners had been based purely on my examination records; but now that he had seen me and spoken to me as I now was ten years on, seven of them in the army, he believed it to be right to amend the report in my favour. Accordingly, in due course my pass in the qualifying examination was listed and I was eligible to go forward to the tests in the two-day residential course and after that, if successful, to the final selection board.

However, it was not known when the next of these would take place. And I of course could not be sure that I would pass. Yet I desperately wanted to get into consular work somehow, and not go back to the Inland Revenue. I therefore went unannounced (still in uniform) to the Foreign Office personnel department to state my case and find out about possibilities outside the Recon-struction examination that I had sat. I was warmly welcomed and, after a discussion in detail, I was delighted to learn that they could accept me in my existing (i.e. prewar) grade of executive officer on cross transfer from the Inland Revenue into the equivalent grade in the junior branch (B) of the diplomatic service for training in consular duties, irrespective of the eventual outcome of the Branch A examination. But the Inland Revenue had to agree to release me.

* * *

I went at once to Somerset House and explained my plan to the under-secretary for personnel. He was not happy about it: the department was short of staff and was only waiting for the return of men like me, who he said could look forward to early promotion. But I persisted — stressing that the war had taken me to many places in many different circumstances, and I would not be happy to sit in London for the rest of my life. And surely I would be of little use to the Inland Revenue if my heart was not in my work? It crossed my mind to tell him that if he was not willing to let me go I would feel obliged to resign. But I refrained from this: he might call my bluff; and if I were not actually in the civil service the Foreign Office might not accept me in the informal way it had done. Moreover I would forfeit the 12 years' pension rights I had accumulated since my first entry into the civil service in 1935 — war service reckoning in full for prewar civil servants. So I pursued my argument strongly until the under-secretary finally agreed to my transfer to the Foreign Office.

This was at once processed pending my release from the army, which I hoped would be soon — depending on the progress on Mountbatten's still unfinished dispatches on which I was working hard with Peter Murphy. But by 1947 it was clear that these would not be ready for some time yet, and in February Mount-batten told me that he would be going out to India as viceroy the following month and would be taking a small personal staff with him, which would include Murphy and myself (with War Office approval), and we would continue to work on the dispatches. When I expressed some concern that this further deferment of my release from the army might prejudice the appointment to consular duties I had secured, Mountbatten wrote personally to the permanent under-secretary of state at the Foreign Office, who assured him that my appointment was firm whenever I was released from the army and that I might be posted to Persia.

About this time I unexpectedly received a letter from the War Office inviting me to let the writer know if I would be interested in being considered for civilian employment after I was eventually demobilized. Being curious to know what was involved, and still only past the first stage of the examination for the senior branch of the diplomatic service, I replied that I would be; whereupon I was instructed by phone to report for interview at an apartment near Victoria station. There I was received by what was obviously a senior armed services officer in civilian clothes who sized me up and enquired closely into my background and my experience before and during the war. He did not specify the appointment for which I was being interviewed, but did say that it was in the field of Intelligence and would require that I serve abroad. After quite a long interview, he asked me to come back in a few days when I would hear further; and meantime I myself could think it over, saying nothing to anyone.

I duly returned, to learn that I could be offered an appointment in what I later realized was the secret Intelligence service, initially at a post in the Far East. My interlocutor was aware that I was a candidate for the diplomatic service, and that his offer would require me to decide which of the two services to choose. I knew in my own mind where my preference still lay, but if I failed the final stages of the diplomatic service examination his offer might be an acceptable standby instead of the consular post that was already available to me.

It was an offer, however, that I decided to turn down before things went any further, since I now learned that the appointment would not be regarded as a continuation of my 12 years in the civil service and army, but that I would have to resign and start afresh, with no possibility of carrying forward my pension rights of these years. Moreover, the appointment would be on two years' probation — so if I failed this I would be out in the cold at the age of 32 at least. This was too much of a risk. Even if I did not get through the senior diplomatic examination I always had the assurance of a place in the junior branch, which would be a continuation of my existing service; and it would have been foolish to give this up given the question mark over the Intelligence appointment, however attractive it might seem.

4

Transfer to Diplomatic Service (Junior Branch)–Consul in Persia–Failure in Examination for Senior Branch

S o with the Foreign Office assurance of a place in Branch B when demobilized, I flew out to Delhi in March with Mountbatten and his staff and lived and worked with them in Viceroy's House, Lutyens' most spectacular work. I was of course not involved in the independence negotiations, but as a matter of general interest I was at a couple of meetings where I had an opportunity to meet Nehru and Jinnah, each in his own way a powerful personality. For the most part I worked with Murphy through to completion of the dispatches, just after independence in the middle of August 1947, then sailed to England with a batch of copies of them in an officer's uniform trunk for delivery by hand to the Ministry of Defence. That done, in September I rejoined my wife and by now our second child, a girl, in London; and then reported to a demobilization depot at Woking, where my seven and a half years in the army ended.

Shortly afterwards I was summoned to the second part of the diplomatic service (senior branch) entrance examination — the residential course tests — followed by an appearance before the final selection board. The results would not be announced for a couple of months. But meantime I was on my way out (alone at this stage) to south Persia as acting vice-consul at Shiraz. It was a small step that would not of itself take me to great heights. But it was a start. At 30 I had finally achieved my teenage ambition: I was in, at least; and with the senior grade in my sights, depending on the eventual outcome of the examination I had sat. At that time air passages were not easy to get, but I learned that General Ismay, formerly Churchill's Chief of Staff, whom I had known in Delhi as the viceroy's chief, was flying out there with the RAF, and he gave me a lift as far as Habbaniya, the British air base about 50 miles west of Baghdad.

From there I shared a taxi to Tehran, 200 miles to the east, with two Persian merchants, one of whom spoke fair English. By the time we made a night stop at a resthouse just short of the border with Iran, I had told them where I was ultimately going and why. At this they asked me if I would help them lighten their load through customs the next day — since I had comparatively little baggage of my own — by carrying one of their bags. Having no intention of jeopardizing my career before it had really begun, I refused — which was as well, since it turned out that the bag was full of watches. But they did not hold it against me that my refusal had cost them a substantial bribe to the Persian customs officer to let the consignment through. They were friendly throughout the uncomfortable journey along the unsurfaced road, and after a further night stop at Kermanshah (where I stayed at the British consulate) we went on to Tehran.

There my travelling companions insisted that I should go with them to the house of one of them, where both their families were waiting to welcome them back; and it would be a welcome for me also to their country. It could not have been a warmer one — traditional down to the sacrifice of a sheep on the steps of the house. It was my first unforgettable taste of the life I was embarking on, and I went on to the embassy in high spirits to report my arrival. After a few days I was on my way south by bus over an atrocious 600-mile unsurfaced road, boneshakingly corrugated for most of the way, with an overnight stop halfway at Isfahan.

Next evening, Shiraz — over 5000 feet high, home of the great poets of the Middle Ages Hafiz and Sa'adi, famous for its gardens, roses, nightingales, carpets and wine — surely one of the most desirable of consular posts. There was a favourite story about a consul in earlier times who had astounded the Foreign Office by asking to be transferred after only a couple of years there. When asked why, he is said to have replied that by day the scent of the roses kept him from working, by night the song of nightingales from sleeping. *Embarras de richesses* — he had to get away.

The streets — like the main roads — were still not paved: and there were no taxis, only droshkies with drivers in appropriate Russian-style peaked leather caps. I shall never forget that evening in November 1947, in the slanting pink light of the setting sun, riding in a droshky, my baggage beside me, to the consulate. There was only one consulate in Shiraz and nobody used the word British: it was simply the *konsulgari*. The great wooden doors (built to withstand the attacks of tribesmen at the turn of the century) were opened to me and I went up the driveway through the magnificent Persian garden to introduce myself to Frank Ogden, the consul. I had to wait until he finished his ablutions in a great zinc tub hand-filled by the water carrier with water boiled in four-gallon petrol tins over a kerosene fire. He then welcomed me warmly; and was to become a good friend.

A few weeks later I was joined by my wife and our two young children, all of whom had endured a three-day airport-hopping Dakota flight from London to Tehran, then to Shiraz by hired car. It was the first of many foreign journeys she was to make to and from my posts over the next 40 years. She has shared the interest and pleasure that I have found in my career, and has been my constant support — in difficult as well as easy times. She quickly set up house in a bungalow at a picturesque address alongside the consulate — the Sheikh's Garden in Butterfly Lane, which many years before had been the residence of the British officers from India who supervised a section of the British-built Indo-European telegraph line.

❋ ❋ ❋

Meantime I had been getting down to work. In the mornings I began to gain experience in consular duties; in the afternoons I sat

Envoy Extraordinary

under the great mulberry tree in the garden (until it got too cold to be outside) learning Persian from a retired Iranian official of the oil company that was eventually to become BP. From my army study of Urdu (a related language) I knew the Perso-Arabic script, and the grammar and syntax of Persian came easily enough to me. I have never lost my knowledge of it — a situation helped by having to use it again in later years. Although I was learning about traditional consular procedures — to do with passports, visas, registrations, notarial acts and the like — there was not in fact much of that in Shiraz, where there was only a handful of British and no tourists. The consulate existed, as it always had done, for political purposes: to observe and report on local events in the south, particularly in tribal areas.

Foremost among these were the Qashqai, a Turkic group transported to the southern province of Fars (of which Shiraz is the capital) by Reza Shah in the 1920s from their lands in Persian Azerbaijan when they unsuccessfully challenged his abolition of their traditional autonomy. As late as 1946 they revolted against his son Mohammed Pahlavi, who had succeeded to the throne in 1941 after the Allies had forced his pro-German father to abdicate when he refused to cooperate with them. The Qashqai wanted greater representation in the National Assembly for the province of Fars, representation intended to include their own leaders, whom I came to know well. Believing that Britain still had its traditional influence in Tehran, emissaries from the tribes would come to the consulate to press for our support to obtain seats in the assembly for them. The fact was of course not only that that influence was disappearing but that it was our policy not to continue to interfere in the internal affairs of Iran.

During the Second World War the northern half of the country was for strategic reasons (among these the transport of arms from the Persian Gulf to the USSR) occupied from August 1941 by the Russians, while the British occupied the southern half — all this under a tripartite treaty of alliance with Iran. In January 1943 that country joined the Allies and in September declared war on the Axis powers. With the coming of peace the British left at the beginning of 1946 in accordance with the treaty, but the Russians delayed, meantime setting up a puppet communist government in

26

the country's Azerbaijan province. The young Shah supervised personally an operation by his army to restore the situation, whereupon the Soviet ambassador in Tehran urgently requested an audience of him. When the Russian appeared he began to speak in threatening terms, protesting that the Iranian military moves in Azerbaijan 'were endangering world peace'. In the name of his government he demanded that the Shah, as commander-in-chief, should order his forces to withdraw.

The Shah told the ambassador that on the contrary it was the situation until then prevailing in the province that endangered peace, and he rejected the Russian demand. He then produced a telegram from the puppet regime's governor-general designate, informing the Shah that the rebel forces offered their unconditional surrender. The ambassador appeared to be stunned, having not yet received that news. Unable to think of anything to say, he departed. Shortly after, in May 1946, the Russian forces pulled out of the country. The young Shah had shown his mettle for the first time. For Britain to have now shown any signs of interfering again in Persian affairs would have given Moscow an excuse to resume its own activities. I had therefore to be firm in rejecting the approaches made for support to obtain seats in the assembly.

The Shiraz consulate was essentially a legacy of British policy up to the Second World War to ensure the defence of India. Persia afforded a route for enemy attack overland, while a hostile power in the Persian Gulf could threaten the sea lanes to the sub-continent. London and Delhi had therefore early in the century begun to establish a chain of consular posts and political agencies in south and east Persia and the Gulf. Even when I arrived there were still about a dozen such posts in place, though many would be closed following the independence of India. Eventually all of them would disappear in 1952 when diplomatic relations between Britain and Iran were broken (resumed at the end of 1953) following nationalization of the Anglo-Iranian Oil Company by Mossadegh when prime minister.

Before this development, however, London had had to consider the future of the British Political Residency in the Persian Gulf, at Bushire on the coast south of Shiraz. This had been opened in 1763 as successor to the East India Company establishments in the

Gulf dating from the seventeenth century, and was staffed from Delhi by British officers of the Indian Political Service. Although based in Iran, the Residency's responsibilities lay on the other side of the Gulf, in maintaining relations with the string of Arab states from Kuwait to Muscat. Except in the sovereign state of Muscat, these relations were governed by long-standing protectorate treaties, which gave Britain responsibility for defence and foreign affairs, thus effectively keeping any other foreign influence out of the area.

Later (in 1971 when these protected states had progressively over the preceding decade attained full independence and the seven smallest of them had at the end of 1971 federated as the United Arab Emirates) the Residency would be closed down. Meantime, in 1946, although there was then still a need for it, it was becoming clear that Bushire was no longer an acceptable site. To have maintained such a relic of Britain's imperial past on Iranian soil would have given the Iranians a pretext for asserting that we were still interfering in their internal affairs. And it would have weakened our effort to persuade them to oppose any renewal of Russian influence in the country. Consequently, in 1946 the Residency was, with the agreement of the ruler of Bahrain, moved across the Gulf to that state, one of those under British protection. On the independence of India in August 1947 control of the Residency and subordinate posts elsewhere in the Gulf, until then the shared responsibility of London and Delhi, passed to the Foreign Office.

✳ ✳ ✳

Early in 1948, still a vice-consul, I was sent to Bushire for some months to close down the consular post there and to discuss with the local authorities the disposal of the consulate and Residency buildings to them. I went with disappointment at news from the Civil Service Commission at the end of 1947 that I had narrowly failed to pass the final selection board, the last stage in the examination for entry to the senior branch (A) of the diplomatic service. But it was open to me to make a second attempt, and I of course entered myself for this.

Meantime I set about the work in Bushire, where my wife and two young children were with me. Bushire has a notoriously foul climate, especially hot and humid in the summer, which it now was. In those days there was no air-conditioning and the local electricity supply was erratic, so we could not even count on having fans all the time. To get cooler air at night we slept in the garden on Indian rope beds under mosquito nets, with a rubber groundsheet on top of the frame of the mosquito net to prevent the moisture in the air from dripping on to us.

In the middle of one such night I awoke with an acute pain in the abdomen, so constant that I got up and, with my wife, drove round to the local doctor; he diagnosed appendicitis but could not operate because his instrument sterilizer was out of order. I could only go back to the consulate and lie still in bed while my wife made ice in the kerosene refrigerator (a slow process) and packed it on the affected area.

Next day she telegraphed the consul in Shiraz (there was no telephone link), who authorized me to return there by the next scheduled plane. This was two days later, but it was out of the question for me in my state to try to beat this delay by driving over the tortuous 150-mile mountain road. In the event the plane from Shiraz was delayed a further two days beyond its schedule because of fierce sandstorms at Bushire; however, by then my wife's efforts seemed to have calmed down the appendix. By that time also the consul had received instructions from London to send me there to appear again before the final selection board for admission to Branch A. It was therefore decided that I should not undergo an operation at the Christian Missionary Society hospital in Shiraz, but in London, after the board. So in August 1948 I flew to Tehran, then London. The very night I arrived there, however, I was taken acutely ill and moved by ambulance to hospital for immediate operation to remove a dangerously infected appendix.

5

Success into Senior Branch
–Diplomat in Afghanistan–
Foreign Office

I t was clear that I would not have recovered by the scheduled
date of my second appearance before the final selection board.
After visiting me in bed, a Foreign Office welfare officer called
in by the hospital at my request arranged with the Civil Service
Commission for me to appear later when I was fit. I duly did this
and looked forward to the outcome in the next week or two.
Meantime the Foreign Office included me in a weekend course at
an Oxford University college on some aspect of international
relations. In the train back to London I found myself beside a
member of the Foreign Office personnel department, whom I did
not know. We introduced ourselves and I mentioned my situation.
At this, he said he had a contact in the Civil Service Commission
from whom, if I wanted, he could probably get the result of my
final interview in advance of the formal notification to me. I
accepted the offer and went with him to his office and sat down
beside his desk while he phoned his contact. I remember vividly
my trepidation at that moment: my whole future was hanging on a
phone call. There was a minute or more of silence while someone
at the other end went to find out. There was a reply and my
colleague smiled widely into the phone. I was through, with 80 per
cent, into Branch A, one of less than 200 who had passed, out of
nearly 3000 candidates. October 1948, the end of ten years of

disappointment, effort and hope; now the way to the top was open and I meant to get there.

The immediate reaction of the personnel department was to want to keep me in the Foreign Office for a couple of years to learn the ropes there. But I argued that I had already learned a lot at the consulate in Shiraz, my family was there, and I was well into the study of Persian and would be sitting the first examination in it the following year. In any case the new grade I had just attained also included vice-consuls — which is what I was in Shiraz. The department finally agreed that I could go back there — which I did a few days later before they could change their minds.

I soon got down to work and study again, and was for a time in charge of the consulate at Isfahan, 300 miles north, while the consul there was on leave. Finally, in April 1949, I myself was promoted consul in charge of Shiraz; and I passed the first examination in Persian.

✳ ✳ ✳

Six months later, on transfer to Afghanistan as a first secretary in the embassy at Kabul, I was switched from the consular to the diplomatic stream. With my family I drove down to the coast at Bushire to embark in a small ship to Kuwait, to pick up a bigger one there for Karachi. Then by train to Peshawar and from there over the Khyber Pass in snow to Kabul, my wife and children by embassy car and myself by the weekly supply truck. We were housed, with the rest of the staff, in the compound of the magnificent embassy (built about 1920 after Afghanistan had become fully independent) which Curzon, as foreign secretary at the time and always alive to the imperial significance of India, intended should be 'the finest building in Central Asia'.

Until the independence of India the embassy in Kabul (like that in Katmandu, Nepal) had been administered from Delhi as being in the area of interest to the then government of India. These embassies were thus part of the assets of the latter and, as such, were for division between the successor states of India and Pakistan by mutual agreement. With the consent of Pakistan, the

Katmandu embassy was made over to India; but the latter would not agree that Pakistan should have the Kabul buildings. These therefore remained in the hands of the Foreign Office in London so long as the two countries could not reach agreement — which they eventually did in 1994, when Pakistan took the buildings over.

Pashtu, the language of the Pathan tribes of Afghanistan and of the northwest frontier province of Pakistan, had in 1936 displaced Persian as the official language of Afghanistan; but Persian was still widely used. Knowing that language, I was designated oriental secretary (a dying breed in the service) and one of my duties was to read the local Persian-language press and keep the embassy informed. For the rest I had to develop what Persian-speaking contacts I could, keep abreast of local developments, and advise the ambassador on things Afghan in general. The country was then an absolute monarchy, which even in those days had no more success in keeping the peace among a diversity of tribes than the later communist dictatorship was to have. Added to this was the ambition of the Pathan tribes in the south of the country to link up with the Pathans in adjoining Pakistan and form an independent state to be called Pakhtunistan. Since this gambit was calculated to disrupt Pakistan it was for obvious reasons encouraged by India. And India's main external support came from the Soviet Union, while China, soon to be at odds with the Russians, supported Pakistan.

* * *

After 18 months in Kabul I was transferred to the Foreign Office at the suggestion of my ambassador, John (later Sir A. J.) Gardener. He was a man who initiated me expertly and patiently into the diplomatic method — but the hard way. He would sometimes talk over an aspect of Afghan affairs, particularly in the context of relations with Pakistan (which it was my job to follow), then outline the form of a dispatch on whatever he proposed to send to London, and ask me to write a first draft. If to his thinking I did not get it right I would have to do it again. If occasionally it was still not to his liking I would go back to my desk with the unspoken thought that it would perhaps have been better if he had done the draft himself. But as an ambitious young diplomat I quickly stifled such a rebellious idea. In any case Gardener was always prepared to hear me out if there was something on which I disagreed with him — provided I could put a convincing enough argument across. He was a stickler for this: he would not put up with mere verbiage.

He was one of the small number of men originally in the prewar Levant consular service who had risen to be ambassadors — an occurrence a senior Foreign Office man once described as a romance of the service, like the promotion of a porter of Baghdad to be grand vizier. That service owed its origin to the nature of the British embassy in Constantinople before the twentieth century. Ottoman diplomatic exchanges with European governments were almost invariably conducted in Turkish. British, like other diplomats, did not normally know that language and therefore had to rely on locally recruited interpreters and middlemen for communication with the Ottoman authorities. These employees, known as dragomen, a corruption of the Arabic and Turkish words for interpreter, were generally Greek or Syrian subjects of the sultan and, as such, could not always be relied upon to represent faithfully the interests of the governments that employed them.

It was a situation that became more and more unacceptable to the Foreign Office in London, which in 1877 set up its own dragoman school in Constantinople, training young British diplomats as student interpreters in Turkish. In the course of time this cadre, with others trained in Arabic and in Persians, formed the core of a Levant consular service, founded in 1903 and so called because it supplied the specialists in the languages and local affairs of the countries around the eastern Mediterranean and beyond, where the sun rose — in French, *lever* — the Levant. As well as being consuls or consuls-general, members were also appointed to embassies in the role of what were known as oriental secretaries or counsellors. Few ever expected to become ambassadors.

Gardener was also a considerate man. He told me he had proposed my transfer to London because he thought it essential to my future career that I should learn how the Foreign Office worked — an opportunity I had missed by being appointed abroad straight away on my entry to the service. But he went on to say he realized that to rent accommodation in London and keep a wife and two children on my salary of £1000 a year would not be easy; and he wanted me to know that he would always be ready to help me with a loan if I found myself in difficulty. I was very touched, but hoped I would not have to call on him. In the event, however, after a year in London I did have to, and with great diffidence wrote to him. By return I received a warm letter and a cheque for £400 with no conditions attached — only an invitation to take as long as might be necessary to repay it. I began to do this in instalments the following year, when I was posted abroad again. This gesture of Gardener's, and the friendship shown to my family by him and his wife, both long dead, are an abiding memory.

In the Foreign Office from March 1951 I was a first secretary in the department covering Southeast Asia. Here I continued to deal with the problem of relations between Afghanistan, Pakistan and India, and with the attempt at so-called Pakhtunistan, the union of the Pathan tribes of southern Afghanistan and northern Pakistan. This involved constant consultation with the Commonwealth Relations Office (a separate department until merged with the Foreign Office in 1968), which was in an adjoining building reached through what was called 'the hole in the wall'. Among other things the Southeast Asia Department handled negotiations with the government of Nepal for political clearance for the expedition that conquered Everest in May 1953. I remained in the Foreign Office for two years, my only tour of duty in London in 30 years of service. This was quite exceptional, and due, I could only assume, to the fact that as my career developed I became known to personnel department as someone they could transfer from difficult post to difficult post without complaint.

In point of fact I did prefer these to what the Americans called striped-pants embassies: I never served, or wanted to, in Europe or the Americas, and at the end of my career I could look back with satisfaction at a meaningful pattern of service in the East which could not have been more enjoyable. I would have felt it pointless to be shunted indiscriminately — just to complete a chain of transfers in a personnel department programme — from, say,

Vienna to Seattle to Rio then back to Europe, and so on; or to be posted to the Foreign Office every few years. Colleagues did sometimes warn me that not to be posted there from time to time meant being out of the mainstream when it came to consideration of senior appointments; and I occasionally worried about this. But I never sought any specific posting or begged my way out of one, and in the event everything worked out all right for me in terms of both career development and job satisfaction.

Towards the end of 1952, while I was still in the Foreign Office, it was decided to widen my scope for service in the Middle East by adding Arabic to my Persian. The Foreign Office paid for me to attend evening classes in the language for about six months, which gave me a good grounding in it. Knowing classical Hebrew from my early years, I did not find Arabic strange. And I was soon to begin to put my elementary knowledge of it to practical use.

In February 1953 Egypt and Britain, as condominium rulers of Sudan, signed an agreement to grant that country the right of self-determination after a three-year transition period. Anticipating that the outcome would call for foreign diplomatic or consular representation in Khartoum (depending on whether the Sudanese chose independence or union with Egypt), Britain decided at short notice to set up an embryo post there in the shape of a trade commission. The man chosen to head this was on leave from Jedda in Saudi Arabia, where he was first secretary and consul, number two to the ambassador. Instead of returning there he was switched to Khartoum — which left the Jedda post to be filled at short notice; and it was proposed that I should be appointed to it.

6

A Jewish Diplomat in Saudi Arabia–The Buraimi Problem

N ow, for the first time since I had entered the diplomatic service, the question of my origins arose in the Foreign Office in view of the Saudi hostility to Jews. The Office was anxious to send me out notwithstanding. But the undersecretary who interviewed me was quite frank: while it was felt that I was the best man for the job, at the same time the problem of appointing me was recognized and I would have to be prepared to go along with this if I accepted. It was not proposed to disclose the facts to the Saudi authorities, who would be expected to regard me simply as a British diplomat. Whatever qualms I might have had were outweighed by the challenge of the appointment, and I accepted it without reservation. The only step taken by the Foreign Office to ease the situation was to remove the distinctly Jewish middle name Hyman from my entry in the annual *Foreign Office List* from that year onwards.

So in April 1953 began three and a half years in Saudi Arabia marked by a series of crises in Anglo-Saudi relations. These centred on two disputes: ownership of the Buraimi Oasis; and Saudi attempts to extend exploration for oil in the south of the country beyond what Britain regarded as the northern frontier of the Aden protectorate. This latter dispute, when from time to time it arose, could generally be calmed down by discussion between myself and American officials of the country's Arabian-American Oil Company (ARAMCO), with whom l became friendly and who would convey to the Saudi authorities the facts obtained from me regarding the frontier. But the first dispute was deep-seated, bitter and ongoing.

* * *

Buraimi is an oasis of several villages at the base of the triangle that makes up the Masandam Peninsula, thrusting north into the Strait of Hormuz, entrance to the Persian Gulf. The area was at that time undemarcated but was claimed historically in agreed shares, despite repeated Saudi incursions and occupation in the nineteenth century, by Abu Dhabi and Muscat & Oman, for whose defence and foreign relations Britain was responsible. The only oasis in a notorious desert, it was traditionally regarded as an important staging post nexus on caravan routes between Oman and the Persian Gulf. Towards the end of 1949 Saudi Arabia had after more than 80 years revived its designs on it. It was generally held to have done so on learning of promising oil-drilling tests in nearby areas of Oman; and it was encouraged in its action by ARAMCO. On behalf of Abu Dhabi and Muscat & Oman the British government contested the Saudi claim but got nowhere; and towards the end of 1952 a Saudi armed party suddenly arrived in the oasis and settled in.

The Sultan of Oman began to collect a force to eject the Saudis, but was persuaded by Britain to accept a standstill agreement with them pending negotiations. After much diplomatic haggling all the parties agreed early in 1953 (about the time I arrived in Jedda) to refer the dispute to an international arbitration tribunal. There followed often acrimonious argument between Britain and Saudi Arabia over the composition and procedure of the tribunal. Finally, in the middle of 1954, agreement on this was reached and a year later the tribunal met in Geneva. But it soon broke down after Saudi attempts to — as the Foreign Office euphemistically put it — tamper with the impartiality of it (by in fact trying to suborn one of its neutral members to support the Saudi case). Thereupon the Saudis were driven out of Buraimi by a force under British command consisting of elements from Oman and Abu Dhabi and the British-led Trucial Oman Scouts.

In addition to encouragement of the Saudi claim in the first instance, which was given by ARAMCO, the latter had provided logistical support for the 1952 incursion. And its research division formulated the legal arguments for the Saudi delegation on the subsequent abortive tribunal. ARAMCO would clearly have stood to gain if the Saudis had been able to hold the oasis. This seemed to it a more promising area for success than its southern exploration area where there was a frontier which the British would defend by force if necessary.

It was not surprising that in this atmosphere of contention I found myself in early 1953, as first secretary and the ambassador's deputy, plunged at once into ongoing disputes with Saudi officials. One of their favourite assertions to me was that, had Britain not divided the Arab world into a series of artificially-created states after the First World War, there would today have been a single unified Arab nation — by tacit implication under Saudi rule — and so no difficulty over such issues as Buraimi. In the absence of my ambassador, who went on leave a few months after my arrival, I became caught up in negotiations for the constitution of the proposed arbitration tribunal.

Discussions and arguments over this were initially held at the foreign ministry, but then frequently moved to the house of King Abdul Aziz ibn Saud's Syrian adviser, who would sometimes call me round well on in the evening and, during the fasting month of Ramadan, around midnight. Talk was always in Arabic, which with on-the-job practice was coming more easily to me — though looking back now and reflecting on the length of time it takes to become a really fluent Arabic speaker, I cannot help but feel that my knowledge of the language at that time, though adequate for practical purposes, must have been fairly basic.

In April 1953 Ibn Saud had personally agreed with my ambassador to the setting up of the Buraimi arbitration tribunal. Implementation of this was left to his advisers and the foreign ministry, under the general supervision of his son Feisal, then viceroy of the Hejaz, the western area of the country covering the provinces along the littoral of the Red Sea and the Gulf of Aqaba. But it seemed to me appropriate that, as chargé d'affaires for some months, I should pay my respects to the king in Riyadh, his capital in the desert. In those days (when all foreign embassies were in Jedda) foreigners, including diplomats, were allowed there by invitation only; this was duly arranged for me. I flew up in a Saudi airline Convair of the Saudi airline managed by Trans World Airlines and crewed by American personnel.

The airline was regarded as the king's and not as a national corporation; at that time Saudi Arabia was not a member of the International Civil Aviation Organization and the airline was not in the International Air Transport Association. Fare-paying passengers were therefore carried subject to the requirements of the royal family and it was not unusual for a flight between Jedda and the Persian Gulf coast, in either direction, to be emptied of passengers at Riyadh to allow women of the court to be carried. Royal limousines were transported in Bristol Freighters with British crews, some of whom on occasion found themselves nodding over the controls until they discovered that the driver of a car on board had started it up so that he could turn on the heater — a more dangerous variant of attempts by bedouin in passenger planes to light a charcoal brazier in the aisle to make coffee.

It was not until some years after the death of Ibn Saud at the end of 1953 that a start was made on gradually building up Riyadh into the metropolis it is today. When I saw it that year for the first time it was still only a desert township whose history was marked by two buildings. One was the prison fortress, the Mismak, entered, when its main gate was shut for defence, through a side postern so small that a man would have to crawl through it, thus presenting his head first to a swordsman on guard who could take it off if the visitor were not welcome. It was through this that a company of Ibn Saud's men had braved their way in 1902 to open the main gate and let him in with the armed forces that overcame the fortress and drove out the Rashidi tribe defenders — the first step towards establishing the Saudi dynasty. The other building was Ibn Saud's square palace, the Murabba, marked by a tower in one corner which carried a clock presented to him by Winston Churchill during the Second World War.

When I met the king there in my Arab robes supplied by the court, which were obligatory for such occasions, he was confined to a wheelchair, very infirm, with only a few months to live. But he was sound in mind and spoke with regret about the deterioration of Anglo-Saudi relations over Buraimi (which, however, we did not discuss in detail). At the same time he still showed admiration for Britain, at one point gesturing wide to the north and saying that the development there should have been Britain's. This was a reference to his grant of an oil exploration licence in 1923 to Major Frank Holmes, a New Zealander operating out of London. For lack of continuing financial support there Holmes had had to let the licence lapse four years later, so leaving the way open for American companies who went on to consolidate their monopoly in the Saudi Arabian oil industry. I came away with admiration for Ibn Saud.

By this time, however, old for his years (he was 73), he was leaving day-to-day affairs of state to his eldest living son Saud, the crown prince, who was being groomed as head of a newly-formed Council of Ministers — though this was largely cosmetic. Saud succeeded to the throne on the death of his father, but it was soon clear that he did not have the latter's powers of authority and leadership. He made no move to put an end to extravagance and waste at court; and the royal family still regarded the country's growing oil revenue as its own. Breeding corruption, it was a bandwagon on which eager foreigners and Saudis alike were jumping.

One of these was Aristotle Onassis, whom I met when he sailed into Jedda one day in 1954 with his wife Christina in their luxurious steam yacht named after her. It was a time when the market for lease of his oil tankers was depressed. Reportedly by bribery he had secured Saudi agreement to the setting up of what was to be called the Saudi Arabian Tanker Company, which comprised vessels of his fleet. When he told me that the agreement gave him preference in the shipping of oil from the country, I warned him that ARAMCO (the Arabian-American Oil Company), which under its general concession had its own shipping rights, was sure to contest this strongly. He retorted arrogantly that he had the king behind him and he was not afraid of ARAMCO. I told Onassis I doubted if the company would yield to pressure on it to use tankers it did not want; but no argument could convince him. In the event, the matter went to arbitration in

Geneva; ARAMCO won; and Onassis never did operate in Saudi Arabia. Some years later, by chance, I met him (by now with Maria Callas) in Monte Carlo, where he had his head office; he had the grace to admit that I had been right in Jedda and he had been wrong.

My first stint as chargé d'affaires (soon after I arrived in Jedda and marked afterwards by a commendation from the permanent under-secretary at the Foreign Office) had given me a foretaste of the difficulties that were to lie ahead. The core of the problem was always Buraimi. On two further occasions I found myself in charge of the embassy for periods of months when the Saudi government, in protest at London's attitude to that problem, refused to accept an ambassador to replace an outgoing one. At one point there were indications that the Saudis might go so far as to break diplomatic relations. This caused me to marshal all hands in the embassy (wives included); they were formed into teams and sat up all night destroying sensitive papers and handling the flood of coded messages to and from London. Those were the days before embassies had paper shredders and cipher machines.

It was a time of tension exacerbated by the growth of Nasser's influence. In 1954 he became prime minister of Egypt (president two years later) and was soon well on the way to establishing himself as a dominant figure in the Arab world and as a leader of the new Third World. At the first conference of non-aligned nations at Bandung in Indonesia in April 1955 he was given equal status with Tito, Nehru, Sukarno and Chou En-lai. He rejected a Western proposal to include Egypt in a Middle East defence agreement (the Baghdad Pact) and castigated Arab countries that showed any sign of cooperation with the West. Saudi Arabia became one of his paymasters.

Nasser's championing of the Arab cause was enhanced by his personal integrity and simple lifestyle, in sharp contrast to the corruption and extravagance that surrounded traditional con-servative Arab rulers. The Saudi court was fearful of the adulation of him by the hundreds of thousands (which would grow to around a million) Palestinian, Egyptian and other non-Saudi Arabs working in the country. But when, amid the plaudits of the Arab world, Nasser took over the Suez Canal in 1956, Saud had no

41

option but to continue to subsidize him. Anti-British propaganda from *The Voice of the Arabs* radio station in Cairo and the continuing Saudi hostility to Britain over Buraimi combined to create a crisis that meant repeated postponement of home leave for me and my wife and the younger of our two children, who was not yet at boarding school in England, as the elder was. And Jedda was not a comfortable place to live in: apart from a cooler season in the winter for a few months, the climate during the rest of the year and from April to October in particular can become unpleasant in the extreme, with high humidity and temperatures reaching 100 for months on end. The air-conditioning in the embassy was rudimentary and often not working because of breakdowns in the local electricity supply. And there was only the occasional — and illicit — bottle of liquor to relieve the situation.

The Koran explicitly forbids alcohol to Muslims, and in the first years of the new Kingdom of Saudi Arabia, which had embraced the extreme conservative-puritanism of the Wahhabi sect, it was forbidden to non-Muslims as well, including diplomats. But in the 1930s Ibn Saud relaxed the ban in their favour in view of the growing number of foreigners coming into the country to man the infant oil industry. Inevitably this provided a loophole for locals to get a drink from obliging foreigners. Among the latter, unfortunately, was a junior locally-engaged (i.e. not career) member of the British embassy consular staff. He was a British mechanic who had come out to Jedda at the end of the 1920s to set up and operate a small sea-water desalination plant; he could turn his hand to anything from clocks to cars, which brought him to the notice of senior Saudis when they needed something attended to. As a result, he and his wife were allowed to settle in Jedda, where they picked up Arabic and became well known, she among senior Saudi women never seen in public. The embassy believed that the couple's local knowledge and contacts could be useful; so in 1934 the Foreign Office agreed to give him a local consular appointment. Meantime his wife had found work in a British company's office in the town.

In the years that followed, their circle of Saudi acquaintances grew wider and included some young members of the royal family. One of these in particular acquired a taste for a drink with the

Ousmans. However, at an embassy party towards the end of 1951, a dispute arose between them in which the young man's Arab pride was offended and he stalked out in anger. Then two days later on a Friday, the weekly holiday, when most of the staff were out swimming, the young man returned to the embassy staff apartment block. Ousman's wife sensed danger and tried to stall him while her husband rushed to get out through the ground-floor bathroom window at the back; but the young man ran round and shot and killed him as he tried to escape.

On being informed in Riyadh, Ibn Saud ordered his son Feisal, viceroy of the Hejaz, to capture the murderer and slay him on the steps of the British embassy. A posse caught him not far out of Jedda. Wisely the embassy's chargé d'affaires persuaded Feisal not to comply with the king's order because it would be bad for the British image, but to send him to Riyadh for judgement there. This was done and the king consigned him to a dungeon and sent the widow a cheque for £20,000 blood money as the prescribed alternative to execution.

Two years later, on the death of Ibn Saud, the customary amnesty by his successor was to include the murderer. But before releasing him King Saud sent an emissary to me, now chargé d'affaires, to obtain the agreement of the British as the aggrieved party. Since I suspected that he would be released whether or not we agreed, I did agree, confident that the Foreign Office would endorse my decision — which it did. But when the emissary then handed me a further cheque for the widow I declined it, pointing out that the first one had satisfied the requirement for blood money and that in any case she had returned to her home country soon after the murder.

As a direct consequence of this incident, Ibn Saud had come to realize the extent to which foreigners' freedom to import alcohol was corrupting his own people, whereupon in 1952 he reimposed the earlier complete ban. This has never been formally repealed; but with the passage of years an official blind eye is turned to the devices used by the oil companies and the diplomatic corps to get round the ban, provided there is no publicity.

* * *

During my time in Jedda I met once or twice St John Philby, the Arabian explorer and writer who, when chief British representative in Transjordan in 1924, resigned from the Indian Political Service in protest against British government policy in the Middle East. He was outspoken in his conviction that the Arabs had the right to run their own affairs, and he condemned what he regarded as the British imperialism that denied them this. He opposed the policies of Britain and France that gave them control of Lebanon, Syria and Iraq after the First World War. His opposition was the greater because these policies were based on support for the Hashemite dynasty then headed by Hussein, the Sherif of Mecca, while Philby championed Hussein's rival, Ibn Saud. In the event, of course, the latter drove Hussein out of Arabia and the British government came to terms with the Saudi dynasty. Philby's judgement had been vindicated and he henceforth enjoyed the patronage and favour of Ibn Saud as king of Saudi Arabia. This served Philby well, not only as resident representative there of Mitchell Cotts, a leading British trading company, but also in his many epic journeys of exploration in the country. His discoveries, his mapping, his recording of antiquities and inscriptions put him in the forefront of a long line of famous explorers. And his association with Saudi Arabia and the king led him to embrace Islam and set up a family in the country, in parallel with his family in England.

When I first met him on one of his visits to Jedda from Riyadh, the capital, I found him still bitterly critical of the policies of the government in London. (While there in 1940 he had been imprisoned for six months for activities regarded, with some exaggeration at a time of tension in Britain, as prejudicial to the safety of the state.) But inside himself he remained British: the tradition of Westminster, Cambridge and the Indian Civil Service could not easily be shrugged off, whatever his political views.

One sweltering afternoon, just down from Riyadh, he came to my apartment, flung off the Arab robes he habitually wore, and asked me to renew his British passport. Notwithstanding his intolerance of his own government, he had no intention, he said, of arriving without documents if he ever had to return to England for good in a hurry. When some years later his son Kim showed his true colours and defected to the Soviet Union I often wondered if his attitude to his own country had not been influenced by his father's.

I enjoyed my occasional talks with Philby senior, by then reaching 70 years of age. Highly intelligent and always to the point, he could discuss knowledgeably history and literature, politics and economics, as well as Arabia in all its aspects. In politics he tended to be dogmatic and disinclined to listen to any defence I might make of British policy in the Middle East. He would cite his support of Ibn Saud 30 years before, in contrast to the British government's eventually proved wrong-headed support for Sherif Hussein, as an example of his superior judgement in Arab affairs. I had the impression that he always thought himself right and others wrong. But he was entirely civil towards me and I did not experience anything of the bad temper others had told me he was capable of.

It was to his credit (and ultimate undoing) that he was not above criticism of the Saudis as well as his own people. The year before I arrived in the country his book (*Arabian Jubilee*) commemorating Ibn Saud's capture of Riyadh in 1902 and eventual founding of his dynasty was published in London. In it Philby hinted at the personal extravagance, funded by growing oil revenue, which he saw creeping into the king's family. It was the first in a series of criticisms. In 1955, while I was in office, his history of Saudi Arabia appeared with now outspoken strictures: again on extravagance and on the inefficient running of the country. Official Saudi reaction was not slow in coming.

Early that year Philby gave a number of lectures on Arabia to Saudi and American officials of the Arabian-American Oil Company (ARAMCO) in which he spoke of the deterioration of traditional Saudi values in an increasingly venal and extravagant court environment. Without the protection of Ibn Saud, who had died towards the end of 1953, he was now vulnerable; and early in March 1955 a delegation of senior advisers at the royal court conveyed to him King Saud's displeasure at his criticisms and ordered him to leave the country — which he did in April, followed later in the year by his Arab family. He left Riyadh overland by the northern desert route without calling at the embassy — as I had been expecting him to do — but I never discovered whether that was his own decision or one forced on him by the Saudis.

I then learned that he had taken up residence in Beirut. From there he had written articles for the *Sunday Times* which brought him further Saudi opprobrium, including — and I could hardly believe it when I heard it — the accusation that he was an imperialist and a broker of Zionism. By the middle of 1956 these attacks on him had diminished and he was allowed to pay a short visit to Riyadh to try to wind up some business affairs; but he got nowhere and returned to Beirut. Shortly after this his son Kim arrived there as correspondent for the *Observer* — something I was amazed to hear, since although he had in 1951 been acquitted of implication in the Burgess–Maclean spy affair (an acquittal that of course eventually turned out to have been a misjudgement) he had had to resign from the Foreign Office; and in 1955 a question in Parliament had again raised speculation about his role in the affair. I never saw Philby senior again after he moved to Beirut, where, after a further two years in Saudi Arabia, he died and was buried in 1960. On his grave his son had the inscription put: THE GREATEST ARABIAN EXPLORER. Three years later Kim Philby defected to the Soviet Union.

* * *

Early in my years in Jedda I came up against the problem of what to do about presents given by Arab rulers to a wide range of people, including foreign diplomats, on certain occasions. It was something that was to concern me at a number of posts during my career in the Middle East. But as long ago as 1930 it had been the subject of correspondence between the Foreign Office and the distinguished first British minister to the new Kingdom of Saudi Arabia following Britain's recognition of it in 1927 (before which there had been only a consular post in that part of the country then controlled by Ibn Saud). The minister was aware that British diplomats were prohibited from accepting presents or decorations from foreign rulers, and he had told the Saudi foreign minister so. But the latter had made it clear that giving presents was an Arab custom from which he would not even try to dissuade Ibn Saud.

From the tone of that conversation the minister came to the conclusion, and told the Foreign Office, that to refuse the king's presents would give offence by belittling the custom and implying that the minister regarded them as an attempt to influence his judgement on some issue in favour of Saudi Arabia. It was an argument accepted by the Foreign Office, which then issued a circular to all posts giving discretion to recommend acceptance of presents in cases where refusal might prejudice relations. It was on this basis that my wife and I came away from Jedda in the summer of 1956 with the presents that had been given to us.

7

Promoted Counsellor–Aden Protectorate–Socotra–Oman

I had served there for over three and a half years of frequent difficulty, but had finally managed to secure Saudi acceptance of a new ambassador (who had, however, to leave only a few months later when Riyadh broke diplomatic relations with London in November 1956 in protest at the Suez affair, which were not resumed until January 1963). Being a Jew had not affected my successful relations with the Saudi authorities, to whom I was simply a British diplomat. In the upper echelons my background was not known, but it was to a number of officials lower down, possibly through mention of it — not with malice — by an apostate American Jew who was *persona grata* in the country and whom I came to know on his business visits to it. It was only some years later that my Jewishness became material to my career on an issue involving Saudi Arabia, which is described in a later chapter.

Meantime, in 1956 I came out of one desert into another. The Colonial Office had asked the Foreign Office to second it a diplomatic officer to run the Aden protectorate. On affairs there this officer would stand in the same relation to the governor of Aden as the chief secretary (a colonial service officer) stood to him on Aden colony affairs. The Foreign Office proposed to appoint me to the post but, since I was not obliged to move outside the diplomatic service, it asked me first whether I would accept it. I was attracted by the prospect of another job in Arabia and after my years in Jedda my Arabic was much more fluent. An added attraction was that I would be promoted to counsellor — at 39, a further rung on the ladder. And I was assured I could return to the diplomatic service in the notional seniority I would have attained in it by the end of the secondment to Aden. So I accepted the appointment and arrived there at the end of 1956, just after the Suez affair.

This event had aroused the hostility of Arab townspeople in Aden colony, who chafed under British rule with encouragement from Nasser and the Arab League. But with one or two exceptions the rulers of the various small states that made up the protectorate did not come under that influence. They were autonomous, protected and subsidized by Britain by treaty, often preoccupied with disputes among themselves and some of them with threats from the Yemen, which had long claimed Aden. Our relations with the protectorate states were maintained by a number of able British political officers under one of two resident advisers — one in Aden, responsible for the western half of the protectorate, and one at Mukalla in the eastern half (the Hadramaut), both answerable to me. The whole area, fronted by the Gulf of Aden, extended from the Red Sea to the sultanate of Muscat & Oman and was bounded in the north by the frontier with the Yemen and an indeterminate border with Saudi Arabia.

* * *

Until just before the Second World War the Aden colony and protectorate were controlled by the government in Delhi as an area of importance to the security of India. Aden itself then became a colony under the jurisdiction of London, while the protectorate, although ultimately also controlled from there, was ruled by the tribal leaders of the various states which comprised it. There was frequent intertribal fighting particularly in the east (the Hadramaut), which, over 300 miles from Aden and not easily accessible at that time, had tended to be neglected by the government there. It was left to Harold Ingrams, an outstanding officer in the colonial service, prewar, to pacify the eastern protectorate by negotiation of a series of treaties with the tribal rulers. These, in return for British protection, arms and money, undertook to accept only British advice on the development of their states, except insofar as this concerned matters involving Islamic custom. By the end of the war these advisory treaties had been extended to the western protectorate — though they did not put an end completely to internecine fighting.

Until then there were very few British officials who had any idea of conditions in either part of the protectorate — the Hadramaut in particular, start of the ancient route for transport of the locally grown frankincense and myrrh overland for the funeral mounds of Rome. Even by the time I arrived in 1956 there had been few travellers there from outside — Freya Stark only 20 years before. The journey along the floor of the two-mile wide 1000-feet deep gorge (the *Wadi*) that runs the length of the Hadramaut 100 miles inland from the southern coast of Arabia was spectacular: the ancient capital Shabwa, and Shibam and Tarim with their narrow eight-storey buildings of baked brown mud outlined in white. Then the descent to the Gulf of Aden over layers of desolate flat tableland down to the coastal belt and the capital of the eastern protectorate, Mukalla, seat of the senior sultan and the British resident adviser. This was a small whitewashed town sitting round a picturesque fishing harbour, a place of unsophisticated charm which I found the most attractive spot in the whole protectorate.

The advisers, and the political officers under them, in both the western and eastern protectorates had a deep knowledge of the area and the tribes, which they made available for my discussions with the governor on the management of the protectorate as a whole. It was my job to take a wider view of affairs than the men in the field: a view that covered the state of relations with the Yemen, Saudi Arabia and Muscat & Oman; the international implications, especially in the Middle East, for British policy in both colony and protectorate; the compilation of Intelligence assessments; and the use, when necessary for political reasons, of the British army units and RAF squadrons stationed in the area. It was because all these activities lay outside the general run of colonial administration that the Foreign Office had been asked to provide someone to manage them.

The governor warned me of possible resentment at this outside appointment among one or two of the colonial staff who perhaps felt they might have been promoted to it. But I sensed very little of this and for the most part enjoyed full cooperation — although on one occasion of disagreement I suffered the caustic remark by one official that I might be experienced in the politics of the Arab world but knew very little about the tribes of Aden. I could only tell my interlocutor that I was not expected to know a lot: it was his job to, and to brief me so that I could assess a given situation at long term, as distinct from his tactical view of it.

Occasional exchanges of this kind arose out of a situation that was very soon clear to me. The political officers, following in the tradition of British Arabists since the nineteenth century, had a romantic affinity with the bedouin tribes of the protectorate and felt it was with them that Britain's best interests lay, since the main threat to the protectorate came from the Yemen and Saudi Arabia — a threat which could be met only with the loyalty and help of the rulers of the protectorate states.

The political officers by and large distrusted the town Arabs in the colony, aroused as they were against the British by local politicians and trade unionists and by radio propaganda from Cairo. Some of the officers had the idea that leading friendly tribal rulers might one day replace British administration in the colony and join it to the protectorate. Meantime, to keep them sweet and genuinely to help them defend themselves, rulers were given arms and money regularly by the British government.

I could see the value of this in strengthening border states against aggression by the Yemen, the state forces being under-pinned by British troops stationed in the protectorate. To that end I agreed that the rulers should be left in no doubt about the resoluteness of Britain to continue to support them. But at the same time it seemed to me that, with an eye to our inevitable eventual withdrawal from the area in the general move towards decolonization, we should begin now to cultivate those Arabs in the colony whom we could identify as being in fact less extreme than they appeared to be in a pan-Arab context and who might therefore cooperate with us in planning for the future.

The colonial administration, however, could not see things that way. Local Arabs who were considered to be openly supporting the Arab League, Nasser's creature, were imprisoned or exiled, including some of the more sophisticated and politically moderate Arabs with whom dialogue might have been possible. But even these could not deny their Arab loyalties. The Suez affair at the end of 1956, just as I arrived in Aden, had made Nasser champion of the Arab world and it could hardly be expected that Arabs still under the rule or influence of Britain, chief perpetrator of the affair, would not come out in support of him. In Aden colony there was an upsurge of nationalist agitation, while the western protectorate came under increased attack from the Yemen.

In early 1958, when Nasser was at the peak of his power, he formed the United Arab Republic with Syria. In the middle of that year the young King Feisal of Iraq and his pro-British prime minister were assassinated and a republic was set up which established close links with Egypt. Feisal's cousin Hussein, the king of Jordan who had initiated a federal union with Iraq, now felt threatened and had to seek the protection of British troops — and this barely two years after he had bowed to internal opposition and dismissed his British military adviser, General John Glubb, who nearly 25 years before had built up the Arab Legion, later to become Jordan's army, and had commanded it since then. In this atmosphere in the Arab world several leading tribal rulers in the Aden protectorate supported British proposals for a federation of all the states in that area. This was welcomed by us as a step towards the security of the Aden base; and the possibility was conceived of eventually also incorporating the colony in any such union.

The outcome was that in spring 1959 a number of western protectorate rulers joined together in a South Arabian Federation. This development incited the Yemen to further attacks — some of them severe enough to tie down considerable British forces along the frontier. This growing danger encouraged more rulers to bring their states into the federation and, by 1962 (I had gone by then), this would comprise 12 in the west, though only one of the four in the eastern protectorate. Following this, at the beginning of 1963 the colony of Aden reluctantly became part of the federation. This step, however, did nothing to stop the slide of Aden into terrorist violence, which was to end four years later in the collapse of the federation, an ignominious British withdrawal and the abandonment of the protectorate rulers — in some cases to a sad fate.

The origins of this debacle had taken root in the 1950s, before and during my service as Aden protectorate secretary. Demands for autonomy had begun to be heard — but at two levels. The prosperous middle-class Arab commercial community, moderate in political ambition, had formed the Aden Association in 1950; and in 1952 the Sultan of Lahej, the protectorate state adjoining the colony, a ruler of stronger ambition, led a group of more actively political notables in founding the South Arabian League. Then in 1956 young nationalists fired by Nasser's success formed the Aden Trades Union Congress, a political front that brought thousands of industrial workers — many of them Yemenis and Palestinians — into the nationalist ranks.

Predictably the colonial government supported the Aden Association and established a legislative council dominated by its members. Almost from the start the government was hostile to the South Arabian League, and eventually exiled the sultan — an action which in my opinion deprived the government of a figure who, while not hiding his support for Nasser, was friendly in his dealings with the British and could have been a moderating influence on the nationalists. But the Colonial Office seemed to be fixated by its own preference for the rulers of the protectorate states and the merchants of the colony. It banned the TUC in 1960, but failed to appreciate its underlying strength until, two years later, it emerged as the People's Socialist Party. With at the same time the military coup in the Yemen, which overthrew the Imam and established a republic, nationalist agitation in Aden began to grow stronger.

The first manifestation of this was the foundation in 1963 of the marxist National Liberation Front (NLF), which epitomized the Arab sentiment of the times: opposition to imperialism, capitalism, feudalism. There then followed in 1966 the Federation for the Liberation of South Yemen (FLOSY), a union of the NLF and the trade unionists. By now the middle-class merchants had faded into the background. The left-wing extremists were coming to the fore.

It is highly probable that they were encouraged by the vacillation of the government in London. Early in 1952 it was announced that Britain would fulfil its overseas commitments from three bases — the United Kingdom, Aden and Singapore. In

53

1964 the new Labour government confirmed that the Aden base would be retained; then, less than two years later, it announced that Aden was to be given independence by 1968. That would mark the end of any British commitment to the Middle East. These conflicting announcements were the signal for intensification of the local struggle to succeed British rule in Aden.

So far as the government there still had hopes of influencing the situation, its aim was to see the South Arabian Federation installed. Nasser and the Arab League favoured the trade unionists by supporting FLOSY. But meantime the NLF radicals (in 1965 declared a terrorist organization) had strengthened their hold in the protectorate to the point where they broke away from FLOSY and went all out for sole control of Aden. By 1967 (when I followed the sorry events from thousands of miles to the east, as ambassador to Indonesia), the South Arabian Federation was in a state of collapse, its armed forces refusing to suppress the nationalists. The Colonial Office, now realizing that it had no moderates to turn to, lifted the ban on the NLF and tried to negotiate with it. But its answer was that it would not lay down arms so long as the British were still in place.

It continued its advance through the states of the protectorate, its fighters emerging from the mountains as the British army withdrew into the colony. There the NLF turned its attention to FLOSY, which it attacked and gradually overpowered. Leaving the two groups to fight it out in the centre of Aden, the British forces had no alternative but to withdraw step by step. Each unit covered the one ahead of it until they reached the airport and embarked for home at the end of November 1967, when, having perforce had to recognize the NLF as successor, Britain transferred power to it, and the People's Republic of South Yemen came into existence after nearly 130 years of British rule. It was not long before the Soviet Union was using the naval base facilities in the region which Britain had enjoyed exclusively throughout that time.

* * *

One of these bases was the island of Socotra. Although lying just off the Horn of Africa, Socotra was part of the eastern Aden protectorate state on the mainland opposite, across the Gulf of Aden. The ruler was a defiant individual, barely amenable to the jurisdiction of the governor of Aden; and to evade this he tended not to live in the mainland township, his seat in the state, but on Socotra. There was no radio communication with Aden and the former wartime RAF landing strip was unusable for much of the year, since it did not have navigation equipment to deal with the frequent local storms. On one occasion, for some shortcoming in the ruler's administration of his state, the governor wanted the riot act read to him and, to do this, I travelled to the island in a Royal Navy frigate that was exercising in the area. With heavy seas making it impossible for the vessel to sail inshore, I was taken off in a pinnace manned by marines; but even this could not go right up to the shore, so I was carried to dry land on the back of a brawny sergeant who waded in. There were not many visitors to Socotra in those days and there can be few who arrived in as undignified a manner as I did.

By this time the sight of the frigate and a party coming off had brought the ruler and his armed followers to the beach to see who they were. Recovering my dignity as far as I could in the short time, I introduced myself as the governor's representative. The ruler, though hardly affable, was polite, and led me in for coffee, after which I raised the matter I had been sent to discuss — which, given his local Arabic dialect, was not easy. However, I managed to convey the governor's displeasure, and was assured by the ruler that he would go across to his state on the mainland as soon as the weather allowed it, and spend more time there. A few hours later, after an escorted tour of the island, I returned to the frigate — the tide now being far enough in for me not to have to be carried.

As the pinnace pulled away and the armed men on the beach grew smaller to view I reflected how easy it would be for the followers of any of the rulers in the protectorate to kill a visiting British official for a handful of Maria Theresa dollars from the Yemen. It was the custom for a visitor to be honoured by having him approach the ruler through two lines of his armed followers who would raise their rifles and fire a salute in one combined volley. It was while running this gauntlet on frequent occasions that I sometimes wondered anxiously whether one of the rifles might not just be lowered 30 degrees.

The real trouble from the Yemen came in the form of attacks across the frontier on the contiguous states of the western Aden protectorate, for it was the unrealistic ambition of the ruler of that country to possess these and all the other states to the south, down to and including Aden colony. The Yemeni attacks were sometimes aided by subversion of some rebellious protectorate tribes; but by and large the attacks were contained by the rulers' armed followers with the help of British troops. In these skirmishes it was often necessary to use the RAF in support, the most frequent role of fighter aircraft being precision attacks on hostile tribesmen's houses and the headquarters of their leaders.

In the eastern protectorate it was the undefined northern border with Saudi Arabia, and the eastern border with Oman, that created trouble for the government in Aden. Incursions from the north were not by armed Arabs but by the Arabian-American Oil Company (ARAMCO) operating its concessions in Saudi Arabia. Geologists and seismic survey parties would from time to time penetrate south into areas that, although not demarcated, we regarded as Aden protectorate territory. Since the company did a great deal of mapping for Saudi Arabia it was unlikely that these parties were unaware of the position and status of such areas. We could only assume that the company was there on instructions from the Saudi government to probe for reactions from Aden.

One incident, in particular, required more than simply the usual diplomatic protest to the Saudi authorities by the British embassy in Jedda at our request. This time the armed bedouin force at the disposal of the British adviser in the Hadramaut arrested all the members, American as well as Saudi, of a survey party from ARAMCO that had crossed the border, together with its heavy equipment. There followed an exchange of acrimonious messages between Aden and the Saudi authorities. But I was able to get into direct radio contact with the company's American representative in Jedda, a good friend from my years there, and to agree that the party should be released and flown to Aden then on up to Jedda — but without its equipment. ARAMCO was then invited by me to apply to Aden for permission to send a recovery team in to take the equipment back, but they declined this — presumably because the Saudis feared that to accept would imply that they had no authority in the area. So the equipment was left to rot in the sand. The episode did nothing for Anglo-Saudi relations, already bad enough over the Buraimi dispute; but it did put an end to the oil company's incursions.

* * *

Less serious in its effects, but more intractable, was a dispute about the border between Oman and the Mahra sultanate, the easternmost state in the Hadramaut. Britain acted for both parties: the state was part of the Aden protectorate; Oman was independent but in treaty relations that gave Britain control of its foreign and defence affairs — a role invoked by the sultan in 1960 in the hope of resolving his border dispute with his Hadramaut neighbour. As protectorate secretary I was detailed to handle the problem, which involved delicate balancing of the interests of both parties, each of whom looked to Britain for a decision in its favour. Having heard the protectorate ruler's case I went to Oman and lived for a week with the sultan in his palace at Salalah in the south of the country, a cool spot which he preferred to the humid heat of Muscat 1000 miles to the north. But I knew after my first meeting with him that I could have little hope for my mission: his views were diametrically opposed to his neighbour's and any British attempt to impose a solution would have alienated one party or the other to the detriment of British influence in the area as a whole. My succeeding days in Salalah, and an escorted visit to the disputed border, only confirmed my first impression; and I had to return to Aden empty-handed except for a handsome Arabic dictionary given to me by the sultan, leather-bound, with his arms tooled on it in gold leaf. The governor himself had had little hope of a solution.

8

Iran–OPEC–Khomeini
Exiled–Bahrain

B y this time my secondment to the colonial service had gone
on for over three and a half years and the Foreign Office
wanted me back, as a Persian speaker, to head the economic
and commercial department of the embassy in Tehran from
October 1960. I decided to drive out there from London alone,
leaving my wife to follow by air, to spare her what I knew would
be a hard drive on mostly unsurfaced roads. I chose the route
through Germany and Austria into Yugoslavia and Bulgaria, then
across Turkey into Iran, on atrocious roads in these last two: hundreds of miles of bone-shaking corrugated gravel. My car was not
new and I had been imprudent enough to set off with its original
tyres, with the result that I was dogged by a series of punctures,
once or twice on a lonely stretch of road where, by now with the
spare wheel also unserviceable, I had to do inner-tube repairs
myself. Generally, however, punctures being the order of the day
on such roads, it was possible to come upon a tyre repairer in a
small roadside hut marked by a tyre hanging up outside.

One evening, approaching Erzincan in Anatolia, I was stopped
by a Turkish military patrol and instructed by sign language (I
knew no Turkish in those days) to follow them to a hotel in the
town, where I found a number of other foreigners who had been
similarly diverted. It was not until the arrival of a young English-
speaking officer that we learned that martial law was in force,
with night curfew, and that we would all be confined to the hotel

overnight. We were treated politely and considerately, and allowed on our way next morning.

It was only later that I learned the background to this episode. The Turkish army, guardians of the principles on which Kemal Atatürk founded the new secular republic in 1923, had in May 1960 ousted the government, accusing it of deviation from these principles by repressing the opposition, assuming dictatorial powers, and — most serious of all in the eyes of the generals — appealing to the Islamic tendencies of the large rural population in order to win its support. The prime minister, Adnan Menderes, was held personally responsible for these policies, and, with two of his ministers, was tried, convicted and hanged in 1961.

I arrived at the embassy in Tehran in October 1960, exactly 13 years after I had entered the diplomatic service as vice-consul at Shiraz in the south; and my wife and I were delighted to be back in the country. The Persian I had learned so thoroughly there and in Afghanistan was still with me and was to become better. But the job of economic and commercial counsellor was quite new to me and I had had only a couple of weeks' briefing at the Foreign Office and the Board of Trade before coming out; it was very much a case of on-the-job training, but this turned out to be not too difficult. Outside critics sometimes derided the appointment of diplomats to such posts without thorough knowledge of economic and commercial theory and practice. But I found that once I had learned the principles and the jargon I was soon at home in the practical field and able to contribute to the embassy's evaluation of the Iranian economy. This, and an understanding of the political situation in the country, combined to form the background essential to my briefing of the many resident and visiting representatives of British companies who called at the embassy for advice on the general question of doing business in Iran or on particular problems they had encountered.

With resident representatives I held regular meetings to put them in the broad politico-economic picture. This kind of exchange had not always been the custom in embassies. Up to the Second World War diplomats had tended to see their role solely in political diplomacy and the social graces that went with it: trade was, if not a dirty, generally a derogatory, word to them. It took the hard economic realities of the postwar years to give commercial work a real place in an embassy. Today it accounts for a considerable portion of the cost of any major trading nation's diplomatic service. It is now fashionable for senior British diplomats to have been employed in it at some time in their service; and this has become almost a requisite for eventual promotion to ambassador. But the function of an embassy in this field cannot be a substitute for the work of the businessman himself; it is essentially only a contribution to it, designed to guide him in areas where he has no access himself

I found that this fact was not always appreciated by business visitors. On the one hand there were those who saw the embassy as a cost-free substitute for their own home office and expected it to do the visitors' own legwork — and entertain them on duty-free whisky besides, fondly believing that ambassadors did not have to pay for this. On the other hand there those who took a delight in putting it about that they never went near an embassy because it was useless. But for the businessman who maintained friendly contact with it, its value to him could be summed up in one word: background. No matter how detailed the visitor's brief or knowledge of the country, only the embassy has access to the full and up-to-date political and economic picture, which is the essential backdrop to the local business scene. And this is something the wise visiting businessman needs if he is to have a full understanding of the market.

He must know if an adverse political situation is likely to develop, or if the economy is deteriorating; without this knowledge his company's investment could be at risk. Moreover, his own government's attitude to commercial relations with the country he is operating in is shaped by the embassy's reports. Export credit policy, support for an international loan, International Monetary Fund policy; these and more are determined to a great extent in consultation between London and the embassy. And in Iran in the 1960s this was more crucial than ever at a time of rapidly increasing oil production.

Until 1951 the oil industry had been run entirely by the British concessionaire (forerunner of the present BP); in that year, following disputes over royalties and dividends, and widespread demonstrations against the company, it was nationalized and came to a halt — a situation that led to a break in diplomatic relations between Britain and Iran towards the end of 1952. It was not until 1953, after the fall of the prime minister (Mossadegh) who had instigated the nationalization, that agreement was reached to run the industry by a consortium of major international oil companies (including BP) and a new national oil company; and at the end of that year diplomatic relations were restored.

* * *

But when I arrived in the country in 1960 I found it at the forefront of growing discontent among Middle East and other oil-producing countries over the terms under which their foreign, largely British and American, concessionaires were operating. The Shah led the support for an initiative by Venezuela in 1960, which resulted in the formation by the major producers of an Organization of Petroleum Exporting Countries (OPEC), which sought to check overdevelopment by the oil companies and thus maintain steady prices. This was only a beginning; it was soon clear that member governments intended to use the organization to further their demands for closer cooperation to their own advantage on price, commission, royalties and output, while at the same time looking towards even wider nationalization. The development seemed to me to pose a long-term threat to British oil companies.

London on the other hand seemed to take it lightly. It was not believed there that such a group of countries could subordinate their different national interests to a common policy; even if they did, they were not thought have the expertise to run such an organization; so it was held to be only a matter of time before OPEC broke up. To strengthen my argument with London against this misperception I discussed the development in detail with one of the Shah's oil advisers, a top man in the National Iranian Oil Company who had been educated partly in Britain and with whom I had quickly become friendly. He was emphatic that OPEC was here to stay and would grow stronger; he begged me to try to get the British government to face up to that fact and cooperate with it so as to earn its goodwill towards British oil companies.

I was under no illusion that such cooperation would automatically benefit these; but, equally, to refuse to cooperate would deprive them of any leverage they might aspire to. Predictably, as the power of OPEC governments increased during the 1960s, so did their demands on the companies. These demands reached the point where in the Arab–Israeli wars of 1967 and 1975 there were threats (and partial implementation) of stoppage of oil exports as a political weapon against Western countries actually or tacitly supporting Israel. By now the British and other Western governments had come to accept the reality of OPEC; and this enabled them and their oil companies to treat the organization seriously and discuss with it ways and means of controlling the dangers to them inherent in its aggressive policies. These were to lead to spiralling prices for crude oil, which put a severe strain on the world economy but which eventually redounded to the disadvantage of OPEC members themselves. It was a subject that was to take up considerable time in my first couple of years in Tehran.

At the end of that period I was switched from the economic/commercial desk to replace the outgoing political counsellor and deputy to the ambassador. It was a time when the Shah perceived the need to avert growing discontent in the country. This had been brought on largely by widespread poverty, which contrasted starkly with the wealth at the upper end of the social scale and the opulence of the monarchy itself. In an attempt to counter this he initiated a plan for social and economic reforms — his so-called White Revolution. This included the break-up of large estates and the transfer of the major part of them to the peasant tenants. Predictably there was opposition to this from the big landowners; but even more from religious leaders because of the inclusion of religious-endowment lands in the scheme. In the middle of 1963 these leaders invoked the support of their traditional allies, the conservative bazaar merchants, to fan the opposition into street riots in the main cities, which resulted in many deaths among civilians and the security forces.

In Tehran the first sounds of firing in the bazaar not far south of the embassy came to us during a morning staff meeting with the ambassador, who sent the military attaché to investigate. The latter reported serious rioting — which soon after prompted the

Shah to declare that there had been a plot to overthrow the regime. In addition to those arrested at the site of the riots there was a wide roundup of suspected ringleaders behind the scenes. Chief among these was Ruhalla Khomeini, a senior ayatollah (Token of God) who saw the power of the clergy threatened not only by the break-up of their lands but also by modernization, industrialization and the introduction of Western innovations such as bars and nightclubs — all contrary to the tenets of Islam. His hatred of the Shah for this was compounded by the memory of the alleged murder of his father (when Khomeini himself was only a child) on the orders of a local landlord.

* * *

The Shah realized that to punish physically such a leading figure as this could arouse nationwide hostility to the regime; he therefore limited himself to arresting him in 1963 and exiling him the following year. The ayatollah went first to Turkey, where though politely received and sheltered he was not welcome as a long-term resident. Early in 1965 he went on to Iraq, and in Najaf (south of Baghdad), holy city of the Shiite sect of Islam, which is dominant in Iran, he settled down for a stay that was to last 14 years. In 1979 he was to have his revenge on the Shah — a historic occasion which I witnessed when living in Tehran again at that time.

As the ambassador's deputy in the early 1960s I saw something of the Shah on official occasions, at his private receptions, at formal talks. He came to know me — well enough to allege once to the ambassador that I had had a hand in encouraging opposition to a move to have the National Assembly grant jurisdictional immunity to American armed forces advisers in Iran. And he went on to say that he was thinking of having me declared *persona non grata*. Happily the ambassador — by then Sir Denis Wright, who had close relations with him — was able to convince him that, whatever had been reported, there was no truth in it. The Shah was not infrequently misinformed by the people around him, often speaking in their own interests.

He had long since become chief executive, as well as head of state. His suppression of the 1963 riots, social reform, growing oil revenue, much of it applied to economic and military development, all combined to give him a self-confidence which often seemed like arrogance. Under his rule the country asserted itself as a power of growing importance in the region and, as such, was wooed by a constant stream of Western political and business leaders hoping to cash in on what they saw as a bonanza — but shutting their eyes to the realities of a system of government that depended to a great extent on the ruthlessness of SAVAK, the secret police, described as the Security and Intelligence Organization.

Iran played a leading role in CENTO, the Central Treaty Organization, a military and economic coordination and planning body whose other members were Pakistan, Turkey, Britain and the United States. The Shah remained basically pro-Western with special relations with the United States, particularly on defence, though he made it clear that he was not dependent on that country or any other. The defence build-up, believed by many inside and outside the country to be excessive, was ostensibly to protect Iranian oil installations and to strengthen Iran's position in the Persian Gulf. For the Shah saw himself becoming the major power there on the eventual withdrawal of British forces. This was expected to follow the assumption of full independence in the next few years by the small Arab sheikhdoms on the southern littoral under British protection, the first having been Kuwait in 1961.

In this process, however, there were initial difficulties over Bahrain because of the Shah's continuing claim to the island on the strength of Persia's intermittent rule over it in the seventeenth and eighteenth centuries. It was officially described in Tehran as the country's fourteenth province and two empty seats were kept in the National Assembly for notional deputies from the island. This situation was to last until 1970, when a public opinion poll in Bahrain, supervised by the UN secretary-general, showed a decisive majority in favour of independence and not incorporation into Iran — a finding the Shah finally accepted. But in 1964 his campaign over the island was still in full swing, which put my ambassador in a dilemma. Towards the end of that year — when I had been in Tehran for four years — the Foreign Office decided to transfer me to Bahrain. I was to be deputy to the political resident in the Persian Gulf, who would remain there until all the protected states were independent. He was Sir William Luce: I had been protectorate secretary in Aden when he was governor there and he now asked for me to serve him again.

Rightly, the ambassador thought it would be imprudent for me, known to the Shah as I was, simply to leave Iran quietly and let him only later discover that I had been moved to Bahrain. Accordingly, Sir Denis took me with him on one of his periodic visits to the palace on official business, in the course of which we broke the news of my move to the Shah. He was of course well aware of the role of the political resident and perhaps reflected that the latter might be a useful ally in the changes that would lie ahead in the Gulf. At any rate, after a short silence, he put out his hand to wish me goodbye, adding quite seriously (in Persian) that he trusted that in Bahrain I would look after the interests of Iran's fourteenth province!

There were no communications between Iran and Bahrain in 1964, so I drove from Tehran to Kuwait with my wife, put ourselves and the car on a coaster for the rest of the journey and arrived in Bahrain just before Christmas 1964. The Political Residency I now joined had been there only since 1946, when it had moved across the Gulf from the small Persian port of Bushire. It was as vice-consul there in 1948 that I had negotiated with the local authorities the outstanding questions relating to disposal of the Residency property to them. Bushire had been the headquarters for British interests in the Persian Gulf since 1763, when what was then called simply the British Residency had been established by the East India Company. Before that, since 1623, except for a short period in Basra, the company had had its base in Bandar Abbas, also on the south coast of Persia.

The modern existence of the Political Residency was related to Britain's continuing responsibility for the defence and foreign affairs of the string of small Arab sheikhdoms from Kuwait to the borders of Oman by virtue of a series of protectorate agreements with these in the nineteenth century. It was related also to Britain's special treaty relations with the independent sultanate of Muscat & Oman. These provided for a British consul-general at Muscat; but relations with the sheikhdoms were managed by British political agents. In some sheikhdoms the British presence also monitored key aspects of internal affairs, such as justice and finance, extending in one instance to endorsement of a decision by local tribal leaders to depose their ruler, whom they judged to be incorrigibly heedless of the welfare of the sheikhdom.

But already in 1961 Kuwait had negotiated with Britain and obtained full independence — threatened shortly afterwards by an invasion from Iraq (repelled by British troops at Kuwait's request), which claimed Kuwait as Iraqi territory on the grounds that it had once been part of the Ottoman province of Basra. In the next ten years, negotiations between Britain and the other protected states in the Gulf were to lead to the independence of them all — seven of the smallest being federated at the end of 1971 as the United Arab Emirates.

The preparations for these negotiations were handled mainly by the political resident himself. As his deputy I had to visit individual rulers up and down the Gulf (flying in small RAF planes) to discuss local affairs with them and the British political agents in the area — discussions which sometimes entailed a confrontation with a recalcitrant ruler. And there were occasions when a ruler's authority was challenged by rebellious elements among his own people and he had to call on British armed forces for help. There was one such serious occurrence in Bahrain in 1965 when student- instigated riots were exploited by other anti-government elements. The causeway to the airport was in their hands for some hours and the Duke of Edinburgh, who was on a visit, had to be ferried from the Residency to his plane by helicopter.

9

Ambassador to Indonesia–The Fall of Sukarno

My tour of duty in Bahrain was unexpectedly shorter than the average length of postings throughout my career: but there was a welcome reason for it. The political resident had been called to London for consultations late in 1965 and he had come back with two pieces of information. The first was that in preparation for the envisaged withdrawal of Britain from Aden in 1968 (precipitated a year sooner by violent riots there) following the establishment (in the event, short-lived) of a South Arabian Federation, there were to be negotiations with the ruler of Bahrain for the transfer of British Middle East Command Headquarters from Aden to his island. The second: that I was to be promoted and appointed ambassador to Indonesia. I was now 48; it was 30 years since I had first dreamed, without much hope at that time, of reaching this height; and having done so now against all odds I was confident that I could go even higher. Indonesia was an unexpected post after the succession of Middle Eastern countries I had served in; but in common with these it was Muslim. Also in common with these was an unstable internal situation which touched on British interests.

At the beginning of April 1966 my wife and I left Bahrain for London — but separately. I had decided to drive to London in the Mini I had just bought, while my wife flew there. I put myself and the car on a barge across to Saudi Arabia, then drove up the long oil pipeline (Tapline) maintenance road to Jordan and on through

Syria to Turkey. Across Turkey, down through Greece, and along the Gulf of Corinth to Patras for the car ferry to Brindisi in southern Italy; and from there drove to London, where I arrived just over two weeks after setting out. It had been an enjoyable journey, the kind I liked.

Having kitted ourselves out for our first ambassadorial post, been briefed at the Foreign Office and received in audience by the Queen ('kissing hands'), I loaded a new car (having put the Mini in storage), mostly with clothes, and set out with my wife in the middle of May for Brindisi and the ship for Indonesia, a stop on its way to Australia. Barely 24 hours later, disaster struck. I had left the car outside the hotel in Paris where we were staying overnight, fully locked, but with all our suitcases in it, which foolishly I thought would be safe because the whole load was covered up. In the morning I came out into the sunshine to find the car forced open and completely empty. As the awful reality of it bore down on me I was appalled. I would get a police report straight away, but it could take weeks for the insurance company to consider a claim; and meantime there was a ship to catch. A call to my helpful bank manager in London solved that immediate problem; money reached me that day. Replacing clothes for myself was not difficult. But I was sorry for my wife, who had spent days in London choosing outfits that were elegant but not too expensive. French friends warned us about the high prices in Paris, so we set off at once for Italy and, on the way to Brindisi, stopped off in Florence for a few days. There she bought what she needed — while still regretting her loss.

We then duly arrived in Brindisi to put ourselves and car aboard the gleaming white Lloyd Triestino liner. We considered ourselves lucky to be able to travel out by sea — and were never able to do so again, since the Foreign Office was by now beginning to send staff everywhere by air. Apart from a heavy monsoon storm down the west coast of India that laid my wife low for several days, it was an enjoyable relaxing voyage to Jakarta that took three weeks from Brindisi; and we even won the captain's impromptu fancy-dress competition.

The heat and humidity of Jakarta struck us as we sailed into its port nearby, where we were welcomed by foreign ministry officials and the chargé d'affaires of the embassy — like myself, a Scotsman. And I was succeeding another Scotsman, the doughty Sir Andrew Gilchrist, who had borne over three years of bitter, often hostile, Indonesian relations, the nadir being the destruction of the embassy in 1963 by anti-British mobs encouraged by Sukarno's government. It was not until early in 1966 that relations began to improve, whereupon Gilchrist, when on leaving Jakarta he was asked by a journalist whether he had anything to say, replied with sharp wit that he was leaving just in time to avoid being declared *persona grata*. This was too subtle for at least one newspaper in Singapore, which reported that he had been declared *persona non grata*.

I arrived in Indonesia in the middle of 1966 at a time of epic change. Until then one name had been paramount in the country and a symbol of it abroad: Sukarno. This was not to be for much longer.

As far back as 1927 Achmed Sukarno had emerged as the young Javanese champion of opposition to Dutch rule and founded the leftward-leaning Indonesian Nationalist Party. He had assumed and retained the role of leader of the people in the years ahead, much of the time in prison or in exile. Then in 1945, in the house which was the headquarters of the naval commander of the Japanese occupation force (to whom he was adviser) and was later to be the residence of British ambassadors, he announced himself president of an Indonesia which he had declared independent — but which was not to be recognized as such by the Dutch colonial power until the end of 1949.

Forceful and flamboyant, utterly sure of himself, a commanding presence, he exuded a charisma that shone through his histrionic and articulate oratory. He could hold thousands of his people spellbound for two hours on end with attacks on colonialism and imperialism and with exaltation of Indonesia and its role as one of the leaders of the Third World. His popularity and personality had enabled him to bring the people to awareness of their nationhood. Indonesia was no longer simply a 3000-mile chain of over 13,000 islands, large and small, peopled by a variety of mainly Muslim races speaking their own tongues. Sukarno had harmonized the discrete elements in the country and imposed a single language (based on Malay) — Bahasa Indonesia, literally, Language of Indonesia. This, and his authoritarian rule by decree as virtual dictator behind the screen of a National Front and a People's Consultative Congress, which he had set up after dissolving parliament in 1960, were decisive factors in the consolidation of the nation.

But his ambition did not end there. He saw himself as a champion of the Third World, and he boosted national self-respect when in 1955 he hosted in Bandung (some 100 miles southeast of Jakarta) the first conference of non-aligned countries, the outcome of discussions between himself, Nehru, Tito and Chou En-lai. By now he was imposing his own personality and will on all aspects of Indonesian politics and economy, and was enjoying a lifestyle that included two palaces, four wives (a Muslim prerogative) and a collection of paintings and *objets d'art*. The extent of these could be seen in five tomes, each weighing ten pounds, specially commissioned and printed in limited edition in Japan, of coloured reproductions of paintings and statues, presented by him to Robert Maxwell, who gave them to me because they were too heavy to take to England with him on the plane.

In his Third World role Sukarno's many public speeches invariably included an outburst against Britain and the United States and showed up his leftist sympathies. In this he was supported by Moscow and Peking as well as the Communist Party of Indonesia, which, with three million members, was the third biggest of its kind in the world. By the early 1960s his crypto-communist authoritarianism — which he brazenly called 'Guided Democracy' — was arousing suspicion and resentment in the army. In an effort to redress this situation he had embarked in 1963 on a grandiose diplomatic and military confrontation with Malaysia (the federation of Malaya and Singapore), facing Malaysian and British, Australian and New Zealand troops: *konfrontasi*, he called it — not war.

Britain had granted independence to Malaya and included the small states of Sabah and Sarawak in it. Sukarno claimed that these (formerly British North Borneo) should be included instead in the greater (formerly Dutch) part of Borneo inherited by Indonesia on independence and that the whole island should be regarded as Indonesian. *Konfrontasi* went on for three years in an attempt to secure this aim by force of arms — but never succeeded. Also in 1963 he took his offensive further by having mobs sack the British embassy in the centre of Jakarta and completely gut it. When at the beginning of 1965 the United Nations condemned Indonesia for all this aggression Sukarno took the country out of the United Nations and declared himself President-for-Life.

There ensued a period of political instability, and in his preoccupation with this he ignored the acute deterioration of the economy — runaway inflation and mounting national debt. It was a situation that gave heart to the Communist Party, supported by the Chinese embassy and encouraged by Sukarno's move to the left. In his often violent oratory he expounded his aim of setting up a government he called NASAKOM — an acronym for nationalism/religion/communism. He seemed unstoppable — a situation of growing concern to the generals and moderate Muslim groups. Then, on the first day of October 1965, occurred an event, devastating in its bloodiness, which brought things to a head and led eventually to his downfall.

* * *

Early that morning elements of the presidential guard sought out and assassinated six top generals (including the chief of staff) known to be opposed to the country's drift to the left. They were brutally mutilated and thrown down a well. It was believed afterwards that the soldiers who carried out the massacre were simply communist pawns, that the Chinese embassy had been involved in the affair, and that Sukarno, if he had not actually initiated it, was privy to it and encouraged it. It was an episode that might well have achieved the result desired by the communists had not a lesser anti-communist general, Raden Suharto, head of Strategic Command, been outside the murdered group and been decisive enough to take over the army immediately. He at once initiated a countrywide campaign to root out the communists, and gathered popular support for this.

There was widespread retaliation against them, including the sacking of the Chinese embassy. Exactly how many were killed, often brutally, by troops and civilians (many settling old scores) will probably never be known. Estimates range from tens to many hundreds of thousands. It was a blood bath that the army command, furiously determined to avenge its murdered comrades and the people as a whole, and aghast at the widely-distributed photographs of the remains of the generals, did nothing to stop. The Communist Party, though not yet completely eliminated, was crushed; and that done the generals now turned their attention to Sukarno.

When I took up my appointment in Jakarta in the middle of 1966 the echoes of these events were still resounding. I found the political situation confusing; it was difficult to know which ministers and officials to contact — or, indeed, which of them was ready to meet the British ambassador. In gradually finding my way around I was greatly helped by the two ambassadors who became my closest colleagues throughout my time in Indonesia: the American, Marshall Green, intelligent and witty, arguably the State Department's leading authority on East Asia and the Pacific; and the Australian, Max Loveday, who, despite his country having troops fighting in the Indonesian confrontation in Borneo, had capitalized on Indonesia's desire not to antagonize Australia, its nearest neighbour, and had by his personal effort maintained good relations locally, acting several times as intermediary for me.

Now, with Sukarno weakened, the prospects for Anglo-Indonesian relations were better; and my task was to improve them further. Executive power had been transferred from Sukarno, under duress, to Suharto, whose so-called 'New Order' would gradually reverse the country's trend to the left. Sukarno, however, remained president, still with considerable influence over the people and still regaling them with long, often impassioned speeches. But the real power was beginning to lie with the army under Suharto. Sukarno could, for example, do nothing to prevent the arrest and trial (ending in the death sentence, later commuted) of Subandrio, his crony and scheming pro-communist foreign minister and erstwhile putative successor, on a charge of involvement in the assassinations of the six generals.

To replace Subandrio, Suharto had appointed Adam Malik, who, with the cooperation of the army, brought the armed confrontation in Borneo to an end and had Indonesia readmitted to the United Nations a couple of months after I arrived. A Sumatran consistently opposed to Sukarno's leftist policies (a term as ambassador to the Soviet Union had brought the realities of communism home to him), Malik now used his considerable political ability to help Suharto. Besides his achievements on Borneo and the United Nations he was to take a leading role in the formation in 1967 of the Association of Southeast Asian Nations (ASEAN) — with a permanent secretariat in Jakarta, it is not a military organization but is designed to promote diplomatic, economic and cultural cooperation in the region. Established at the time it was, it contributed to the swing against communist tendencies there.

Meantime, besides revising the country's foreign relations, Suharto had begun to look to the economy, in chaos after years of inefficient management under Sukarno. With its return to the United Nations, Indonesia was now again a member of the World Bank and the International Monetary Fund; and, in the latter half of 1966, it was able to agree a short-term moratorium with its Western creditors. This gave Suharto's administration essential breathing space.

Despite the strain the confrontation had imposed, diplomatic relations between Britain and Indonesia were never broken. However, the destruction of our embassy in 1963, which had been a by-product of the hostility, had still not been made good. One of my tasks was to negotiate with the Indonesian government for reconstruction of the embassy at its expense — which was finally achieved only after delays that extended well beyond my period of office. Thus I found myself, with my staff, working in makeshift accommodation in the garden of my residence.

When I presented my credentials to Sukarno at the end of June 1966 he received me warmly. His transition from the hostility of the past few years to personal friendliness to my wife and myself at this ceremony seemed as natural to him in the Javanese idiom as it was suspect to the Western observer. New ambassadors often had to wait two or three weeks to be received by him, but I had to wait only three days. It would have been flattering myself to suppose that this was intended as a gesture of contrition to mark the opening of an era of more friendly Anglo-Indonesian relations.

There may have been an element of that in it; but the more realistic explanation was that, before I arrived, Suharto's new foreign minister Adam Malik had invited Michael (later Lord) Stewart, the British foreign secretary, to stop over in Jakarta for 24 hours in the course of a Far East visit.

Their meetings on 1 and 2 July were essentially between foreign ministers rather than governments, to give the two men an opportunity to get to know each other and build on the improvement in relations. The occasion was more notable for its symbolic value in improving the international image of Indonesia — enhanced by a widely attended press conference at which Stewart appeared forgetfully in carpet slippers — than for its material content.

However, the visit gave my term as ambassador an auspicious start, particularly in my relations with Malik, who became my most frequent and most helpful interlocutor with the new regime. It also served me well later for occasional meetings with Suharto. Like Sukarno, he was a Javanese; but there the similarity ended. I found Suharto quiet, almost impassive, a man of great patience, often enigmatic to the point of mysticism, but at the same time a shrewd realist and a soldier of action. Sukarno — egomaniacal, emotional and flamboyant — was a spellbinding demagogue. It seemed to me that the struggle between these two opposite Javanese was developing with all the delicacy, but at the same time inevitability, of their traditional mystical *wayang* shadow play, the contest between good and evil which cardboard figures act out silhouetted behind a screen. The diplomatic observer could not fail to be impressed by what was in effect the attrition of Sukarno, as inexorable as it was subtle. Suharto never put him on trial or made a martyr of him in any other way. He was content to let him remain for some time president in name, while his popular appeal sank.

But eventually, in March 1967, the Provisional People's Consultative Assembly stripped him of all his powers and appointed Suharto acting president. Sukarno was put under house arrest in his palace at Bogor, 30 miles south of Jakarta. There was widespread speculation abroad — not least in the Foreign Office in London — that now the high command might take drastic action against him, even to the point of execution. My own view, given

74

to London, was that this was not likely. Suharto would have been well aware of Sukarno's still lingering reputation as the architect of Indonesian independence and would not have wanted to humiliate him completely. Besides his power was now broken. And in March 1968 the Assembly confirmed Suharto as president, leaving Sukarno to fade away and die at Bogor in 1970, at the age of 69. Other authoritarian leaders before and after him — one can think of Menderes, Bhutto, the Shah of Iran, Ceauşescu — were given shorter shrift by their successors.

Perhaps because of the difficult circumstances in which my embassy had to operate, it was selected by the Foreign Office in August 1967 for inclusion in a television film commissioned by George (later Lord) Brown, the then foreign secretary, to boost the image of the diplomatic service. A Rediffusion Television team came out. The first half of its film had shown the workings of the Foreign Office itself and the handling of its relations with diplomatic posts abroad. The second half was to show the operations of the Jakarta embassy as one of these posts. There were the usual scenes (some of them set up specially for the occasion) — my own assessment of the political and economic situation and foreign relations, my morning meeting with the senior staff, the processing of an urgent message from the Foreign Office from the moment it came in over the cipher machine until it reached me through the staff, and so on. Then scenes of domestic and social life, including staff wives and children at the embassy swimming pool — their one relief from the stifling heat and humidity — which predictably, when the film was eventually screened on British television, gave the critics an opportunity to disparage what they were pleased to call the gin-and-tonic life of diplomats and their families.

A useful and successful part of my official entertaining was based on film suppers in my residence to which I invited leading members of the Indonesian Establishment — politicians, officials, academics, armed services officers, and the like. Feature films were lent to me by the embassy's armed services attachés who obtained them from Far East Command Headquarters in Singapore for showing to their small staff. Since no passable Western films were shown in Jakarta cinemas, I borrowed them from the attachés.

Our Indonesian guests were delighted to be invited to these film suppers. For our part it gave us an opportunity to get to know them better and have useful out-of-office talks. During the visit of the television team the producer asked to record one such evening, which was on my programme at the time. I agreed and the team covered the arrival of the guests and my introduction to them of the film I was going to show, *Lawrence of Arabia*. The evening went off well, the film greatly appreciated.

In due course the television record of the embassy was screened in Britain and the next day I received a panic message from the Foreign Office for my personal attention. This said that Columbia Pictures in London, agents for the producers of *Lawrence of Arabia*, were demanding to know how I had come by the film, warning that I had breached their copyright by showing it in public and threatening legal proceedings against me and/or the Foreign Office. I explained things to the latter and commented that I did not regard my film suppers as public showings: they were arranged in my residence for guests privately invited.

This did not satisfy the Foreign Office, which meantime had been in touch with Command Headquarters in Singapore — and the latter now added its voice of censure: the films they sent to my attachés were for the sole use of them and their staff. I protested that this amounted to very few people, that these were part of the embassy family, and it was absurd that the embassy as a whole, and invited guests, should not also be able to enjoy these films, given the absence of public entertainment outside. I was told sharply that the copyright arrangements with the British armed forces cinema corporations did not permit this, and I must stop; Columbia was still on the warpath.

Shortly after this I learned from the American ambassador (who had enjoyed the film and to whom I had described the aftermath) that two Columbia representatives from New York happened to have come to Jakarta to look into the possibility of getting some local cinema to screen their films; and it might be useful for me to talk to them. I accordingly invited them round for a drink — two New Yorkers, one Irish, one Jewish — and mellowed them on what they said were their first decent gin-and-tonics since they had arrived. I then described my problem. Being from New York, they knew nothing of the complaint by their London office. I went on to say it seemed to me that *Lawrence of Arabia* was a prestige film that portrayed a historic event in British history and was a credit to those who made it. At this my visitors promised me that in London on their way back to New York they would sort things out and I could rest assured that that would be the end of the matter. They were sure that Sam Spiegel, the American producer, would be only too delighted (would 'bust his buttons', they said) to hear that a British ambassador had used his film to — as I had put it — portray a historic event in British history. And that was indeed the end of the matter. And I continued to show films.

Throughout the three years of confrontation in Borneo, Indonesia severed communications with Singapore. International airline flights using that city were still able to transit Jakarta, but there was no passenger traffic between the two. As an ambassador, however, I was given permission and went across to Singapore from time to time, where I made a point of calling on Lee Kuan Yew, the prime minister, and bringing him up to date on events in Indonesia as observed by Western embassies there.

From the moment I saw Lee I felt at ease with him. He had become prime minister when he was 36, and now approaching 45 was the firmly established leader who had developed a city-state and given its citizens a standard of living unequalled in Southeast Asia. In appearance and manner of talking (in English, his first language, perfected at Cambridge) he gave an immediate impression of vigour, and I reflected that his achievements could only have been attained by determination and hard work. His discussions with me on Indonesia were highly intelligent, and his questions about the situation there searching; it was clear that he was a man who could readily grasp intricacies. But talk between us was not all on serious politics. He would grin and lapse into generalities in an engaging way, and it was not difficult to see him as the charismatic personality who could hold his own with Western leaders and be admired by them. There were moments when his self-confidence, it seemed to me, might border on arrogance — perhaps excusable in someone who had achieved as much as he had.

When a couple of years later Lee was on an official visit to

Tanzania, President Nyerere took me by the hand to introduce me to him as 'our high commissioner'. Lee recognized me at once and remarked teasingly that he reckoned my visits to Singapore had had less to do with briefing him on Indonesia and more to do with getting away from the drabness of Jakarta for a few days and savouring the good life. And I could not entirely disagree with him.

But it was in fact possible to escape the heat and humidity of Jakarta without going abroad. For weekends and short breaks the British embassy had two houses 4000 feet up in the area of tea plantations 50–60 miles south of the capital, past the imposing 10,000-foot Gede volcano, which could be climbed (though I never tried to). A few hours' drive further south to the coast there was a palatial hotel on a magnificent beach popular with the diplomatic corps. But it was a place of Javanese legend: the sea could be dangerous, the abode, it was said, of a siren goddess who at certain times lured men to their death in it (as indeed happened to a Bulgarian ambassador); and the hotel had no room number 13. The traditions of the Javanese pervaded the whole island, whose earlier domination by the Portuguese and Dutch colonizers, however, was still evident.

On one occasion, combining pleasure with representational visits to local authorities, my wife and I made a lengthy round trip in our own car along the northern route via Semarang and Surabaya to the eastern tip of Java for the ferry to Bali, and back along the southern route through Malang and the archetypal Javanese town of Yokyakarta. With only one hotel and comparatively few tourists at that time, Bali was virtually unspoiled, a green and fertile land of volcanoes and artists. The one Hindu island in the Indonesian chain, it had resisted the spread of Islam there in the sixteenth and seventeenth centuries. We also visited Sumatra officially, names like Palembang, Padang and Medan reminding me of the often barbaric activities of the Japanese forces during their Second World War occupation.

During his twilight months I had some informal meetings with Sukarno at the house of his attractive Japanese wife Dewi when she invited me with my wife, one of her bridge partners. Dewi was one of the four wives permitted to him under Islamic law; he had met her some years before when she came to Jakarta ostensibly as secretary to a visiting party of Japanese businessmen. At our informal meetings Sukarno would sometimes be in slippers, tunic top undone; and with his unattractive bald head revealed when he took off his *pitji*, the traditional Indonesian black fez-like cap, it was easy to see why he invariably wore it in public.

I had heard him described as a sawdust Caesar; and certainly when he was relaxed and off guard in Dewi's house it was difficult to see in him the ranting demagogue of the stadium. Without a sycophantic audience his chauvinism evaporated. Yet his personality still shone through. In the course of my several meetings with him I gained the impression that if he had capitalized on the people's earlier veneration of him as their liberator, and applied his talents for their benefit, he could have been an outstanding president, as successful abroad as at home. But his contact with them descended into mere demagogy: his main concern gradually became self-aggrandisement and the advancement of his own political and material interests.

It was to Sukarno that I had presented my credentials in 1966, but when I was transferred from the post just under two years later it was from Suharto that I took my leave. I had bridged a historic period in the development of Indonesia and its relations with Britain — to the extent that shortly before I left I had succeeded in having the Indonesian high command invite the British commander-in-chief in the Far East (later Field Marshal Lord Carver) to come over from Singapore on an official visit, the first such contact since the Indonesian confrontation in Borneo.

10

A Jew as Ambassador Unacceptable in Saudi Arabia –Press Distortions– Escape to Greece

I had been appointed at short notice ambassador to Indonesia, after an unusually brief term as deputy political resident in the Persian Gulf. I hardly expected that pattern to be repeated. But suddenly at the beginning of 1968, when I had been in Jakarta barely 18 months, the Foreign Office after consultation with me announced publicly that the Queen had approved my appointment as ambassador to Saudi Arabia. It was explained to me that the incumbent in Jedda at that time was being moved urgently elsewhere and it had been decided that I was the right man to succeed him: I knew Arabic, essential in Saudi Arabia — had served there before as well as in Aden and the Persian Gulf, so was knowledgeable about the Arabian Peninsula; and I knew Iran well. In the flattering way that it has when appointing an officer to a difficult or unpleasant post, the Foreign Office personnel department all but gives him the impression that he is not only the right man for the job, but the only one who can meet the challenge it represents.

In this instance, following the British withdrawal from Aden in 1967 and the projected disengagement from the Persian Gulf, it was important that Saudi Arabia and Iran, in their ambition to fill the vacuum, should not engage in rivalry that could destabilize the region. I would have to work to establish relations with the Saudis close enough to enable me to encourage them in the right direction and to support them, as the biggest oil producers in the Middle East, in a moderate stand in OPEC. And Britain for its own part had a direct interest in developing cooperation with Saudi Arabia for the supply of defence equipment and technology to it. The appointment had all the makings of a substantial and genuinely challenging job and I looked forward to it.

It would have been naïve of me not to have had some qualms about being a Jew in this post — as I had had on taking up my appointment in Saudi Arabia from 1953 to 1956, albeit in a more junior rank. But that assignment had been completed without difficulty and I had had official contact at the highest levels in the establishment there — though admittedly it was only to a number of officials lower down that my background was known. They had asserted what was later repeated by King Feisal on a visit to the United States in June 1966 that Saudi Arabia was not against the religion of the Jews but against Zionists and the Jews who supported them — an assertion hardly borne out by the refusal of Saudi visas to Jews in general.

My qualms subsided, however, in the reflection that I would be going out to Saudi Arabia simply as British ambassador. My wife busied herself at once with overseeing the packing of our personal possessions in Jakarta and having the crates shipped directly to Jedda. She then flew to London early in March 1968. I stayed behind for a couple of weeks to pay farewell calls, and arrived in London on the 22nd in time for the customary audience of the Queen ('kissing hands'), which had been arranged for the 26th. When I came into the house my wife told me that the Foreign Office had phoned that morning to ask me to get in touch with the personnel department the moment I got back. The urgency of this, when everything was ready for my departure for the new post early in April, worried me. And my sense of foreboding was justified.

It turned out that the *Jewish Chronicle*, the leading weekly of the community in Britain, had reported the secondment of a Jewish scientific officer in the home civil service as scientific attaché at the British embassy in Paris for a period. In commenting on this the paper asked why it was that there were so few Jews in the Foreign Office. At this, someone in Glasgow had written to the editor with good intent and brought me to his notice — whereupon I was written up in the paper not only as the first Jewish career diplomat in Britain to become an ambassador but as the newly appointed envoy to Saudi Arabia.

This appeared on the morning of the day I got back to London from Indonesia and the Foreign Office was concerned about the implications for my appointment to Jedda since the paper was widely read by Arab ambassadors in London and the news would quickly reach King Feisal. As indeed it did — with the result that he at once withdrew his *agrément* (formal acceptance of me) which he had already given. It was an action with no known precedent in diplomatic practice. It is not unknown for a head of state to refuse *agrément* (in which case the proposed appointment would be aborted and not made public) or to declare an ambassador *persona non grata* when he is in the post. But his formal acceptance of an ambassador is only given after he has had an informal approach from the latter's government and has discussed the proposed appointment with his advisers. The *agrément* is thus a head of state's definitive acceptance — which in Britain is an essential prerequisite to the Queen's approval of the appointment and the public announcement of it.

A head of state refusing *agrément* in the first place is not required to give a reason for the refusal — though he can generally be expected to. But the reason for withdrawal of the *agrément* already given in my case was stated quite frankly by Saudi Arabia: a Jew was not acceptable as an ambassador in that country. And the officials who had known me there in a junior capacity in the 1950s to be one were presumably not among those who had advised the king on my appointment now — with the result that he had not known about my background until it was disclosed in the *Jewish Chronicle*.

There was dismay in the Foreign Office; but it was recognized that the king's action was his sovereign right and it could not be protested. Sooner or later it would become public knowledge in Britain, and it was decided that the Foreign Office should eventually put out a statement. But this would be bound to hit the headlines, and it was considered that my wife and I, at least, should be spared the hounding by the press that could be expected. I was therefore given leave to go abroad before the statement was put out. I had sold my car on leaving Indonesia and had not yet acquired a new one; but I had a Mini lying in a garage in London and we packed this and headed for Greece. The Foreign Office's only stipulation was that I should phone in to the ambassador in Athens every week to find out if he had any instructions for me from London. The Foreign Office could not have been more sympathetic and supportive, and made it clear from the start that after things had quietened down there would be another post for me.

Meantime the storm erupted in the British press, with reverberations in a number of other countries, on 10 April (by which time I was touring Greece). This followed a Foreign Office minister's statement in the House of Commons that the Saudi Arabian government had agreed on 17 January to my appointment, but that, following an article in the *Jewish Chronicle* on 22 March drawing attention to my background, the *agrément* was withdrawn. The Foreign Office followed this with a statement regretting the Saudis' decision, while emphasizing that it was entirely within their prerogative; but adding that my Middle East experience, including Saudi Arabia in the 1950s, would have enabled me to make an important contribution to Anglo-Saudi relations. And indeed, besides the importance of these in the context of regional stability once Britain withdrew from the Persian Gulf, they were crucial to the development of major British defence contracts with Saudi Arabia.

The civil service examining body investigates the character and qualifications of a candidate for the diplomatic service without asking about his religion. Once he is admitted, his progress in the service depends only on performance and merit. For the Foreign Office a man's religion is his own affair. Clearly of course mine had been known to it since my appointment to Saudi Arabia in a more junior capacity in 1953. But the press now had a field day speculating on that point. How was it that the Foreign Office did not know; or if it did, was it not extravagantly optimistic to suppose it could get away with the appointment? Though most probably — the speculation went on — it was not thought that there was much to get away with now, since the Foreign Office had long since got away with my earlier appointment to Jedda without local objection.

✻ ✻ ✻

However, the press was not prepared to leave it at that. In what was presumably intended to show up the Saudi king's action as even more unreasonable than it was, some papers described me (one of them in a front-page spread headline) as 'our ex-Jewish envoy'. Some said that only one of my parents was Jewish. Others asserted that, according to friends, I had abandoned the faith in my teens. Who these friends were, I never discovered: it could only be concluded that this was journalistic sensationalism without foundation. The Foreign Office said nothing on the point, and I myself was never consulted by the press. The *Jewish Chronicle* for its part said nothing to suggest that I was not still a practising Jew; on the contrary, it repeated that I was the first Jewish career diplomat in Britain to become an ambassador. The editor, asked by the press why he had published the report, said that it was his paper's job to record news — and here was a particularly interesting item about a Jew being sent to an Arab country.

Commenting on this in a book he wrote years later, a journalist who covered the event alleged that the editor of the *Jewish Chronicle*, when questioned at the time, showed no concern about being instrumental in 'spoiling my career'. But in fact, far from being spoiled, my career progressed very well; the Foreign Office never wavered in its support for me. A rumour went round afterwards that, while supporting me, the Foreign Office had had the stories about my doubtful Jewishness put about without attribution in order to counter criticism that it had been rash in appointing me to the post, and to exonerate itself to some extent from the charge made against it in the press at the time that it could look foolish over the appointment. But I never discovered the source of the rumour, or whether the Foreign Office had in fact been behind it. I very much doubt it.

As for the Saudis, their London embassy said that rejection of me had been the only answer, since (the embassy went on) it was quite clear to the Foreign Office when it nominated me that I was of the Jewish faith, and it must have said so in my file. Clearly this was a statement made to save Saudi face. But the ambassador personally (whom I had known in Saudi Arabia in the 1950s) treated me most civilly. He had already arranged, and sent out invitations for, a dinner in honour of my wife and myself before we were due to go out to Jedda. I now phoned him to say that in all the circumstances he might prefer to cancel this; I would perfectly understand. But he would not hear of it, and further argument by me could not make him change his mind; he was adamant that the dinner should go ahead. I had to admire him.

In one way it was a rather bizarre occasion in that the date was 3 April, five days before I was going on leave to Greece to be away when news of the *agrément* debacle would hit the headlines two days later. So the only people at dinner who knew about it yet, besides my wife and myself and the ambassador and some of his staff, were the head of the Foreign Office and some under-secretaries among the guests. The remainder, including a number of other Arab ambassadors, had no inkling of it. I just hoped that our generous host would tell them before they opened their papers a week later, when I would be in Greece.

Although the whole affair was of course distressing to me personally, in my professional capacity I had a realistic attitude to it and shared the Foreign Office view that it could not be allowed to damage Anglo-Saudi relations in general, however put out we all were. There was therefore no support given to the leading Jewish MP's proposal in the House of Commons (after the affair had been made public) that Britain should break these relations. And indeed one of my colleagues was appointed to the post soon after, instead of me.

On later reflection I consoled myself with the thought that had I in fact gone there, the publicity afterwards would have made things worse not only for relations but for me personally. For notwithstanding their professed distinction between Jews and Zionists, the Saudi rulers were in practice uncompromising in their hostility towards all Jews on the strength of various strictures on them in the Koran: that they plot and blaspheme against the Prophet, are liars and unbelievers, deify Ezra and believe in sorcery; and more.

It was an attitude that the Saudis did not begin to relax — and then only slightly and in their own interest — until the 1970s. American companies as well as a US military training mission operating in the kingdom had always been forbidden to bring in Jewish personnel — a prohibition strongly resented in Washington, but to no avail. But it was a ban eventually lifted *ad hoc* when, in their urgent need of certain US technology, they had to admit companies in which a number of Jews held key positions. And in 1973 King Feisal relented so far as to receive Henry Kissinger, the American secretary of state, for a discussion on the Arab–Israeli dispute (which Kissinger was reported to have found distinctly uncomfortable). I wondered then what the king's attitude would have been to my appointment to Jedda if it had come after that visit.

* * *

I have always been resilient, not allowing myself to yield to adversity; and I went to Greece taking the shock of rejection in my stride. But unknown to me it was leaving its mark on my body, which I could not control as I could my mind. My wife and I were barely a week into our holiday when I was struck by severe shingles, the outbreak tracing the path of the nerves all down one side of my face and neck. By this time we were in the Peloponnese, and we had to drive back to Athens for attention by the embassy doctor, who started a course of injections. The condition got worse before it began to get better, and meantime I was laid up in a hotel in considerable pain, comforted by my attentive wife. It was a couple of weeks before I was well enough — though still bearing scars that were not to heal for a long time — to resume our travels in the south. These were enjoyable weeks but I was anxious to get back to work; and the prospect of this was raised in a message through the ambassador in Athens recalling me to the Foreign Office. When I got there in June 1968 I was instructed to report to George (later Lord) Thomson, the Secretary of State for

A Jew as Ambassador Unacceptable in Saudi Arabia ...

Commonwealth Affairs, whose staff were interchangeable with Foreign Office staff but whose office existed separately until October 1968, when it merged with the Foreign Office to form today's Foreign and Commonwealth Office — for convenience, however, still often referred to simply as the FO.

11

High Commissioner in
Tanzania–Nyerere's Idealism

A t the end of 1965 the Organization for African Unity had passed a resolution calling on all member states to break diplomatic relations with Britain if it did not take steps to bring down the recently illegally declared government of Rhodesia. Not all the members obeyed the call, but leading among those that did was Tanzania, under its charismatic president, Julius Nyerere, always a loyal supporter of African solidarity in opposing whatever he regarded as a threat to it. Towards the middle of 1968, however, albeit still no settlement in Rhodesia, he had made overtures for a resumption of relations with Britain, and London had responded favourably, reopening the high commission in Dar es Salaam. There was now the question of a high commissioner. Some British politicians felt that this should be a political appointment (and there were already a couple of aspirants to it) in view of what was likely to be a sensitive period in the re-established relations. The Labour government of the time in London had to show understanding of Nyerere's ardent socialism while at the same time protecting the interests of British planters and others in Tanzania, which were threatened by it.

But the secretary of state told me he did not share the view that the new high commissioner should be a politician, and he had said so to Harold Wilson, the prime minister. He believed that a professional diplomat of my background and character brought up in Glasgow — Nyerere had been at university in Edinburgh —

should be able to get close enough to him to build up good Anglo-Tanzanian relations again. I was therefore to take on this challenging appointment and in October 1968 I found myself heading the reopened high commission. It was six months since the Saudi Arabia debacle; the Foreign Office had supported me throughout; the trauma was now behind me. All that remained to do was have my crates of heavy baggage, in the port of Jedda since being shipped from Jakarta six months before, reshipped now to Dar es Salaam, where they eventually arrived, much the worse for wear.

* * *

I found Julius Nyerere to be a man of intelligence and integrity, a clear leader among the heads of the recently independent states of Africa. I established a rapport with him that was to last throughout my tour of duty of over four years in Tanzania, notwithstanding occasions when we crossed swords over the adverse effects of some of his policies on British interests and over his perception of some of Britain's policies in regard to Africa and the Middle East. This is not to say that he had singled out Britain: he had a robust attitude to relations with all foreign states. His policies were simply built around his basic concept of Tanzania for the Tanzanians. Staunch Catholic, humanitarian socialist of high ideals, he was 46 to my 51 when I first met him as president. He was friendly and approachable from the start and I felt that here was a man I could do business with, in good times and bad — as turned out to be the case. He had an openness and directness that reflected an integrity based to a great extent on his religious beliefs. He lived simply on a small salary in a small house, and was free of the corruption and self-aggrandisement indulged in by so many African rulers.

It was as leader of its only political party that, at the end of 1961, he secured the peaceful transition of the then Tanganyika (before its union with Zanzibar in 1964 — hence Tan-zan-ia) from British mandate to independent sovereign state, soon a republic. He had had the courage not to feel obliged to copy some other African political leaders who either engaged in violence to secure independence, or, having obtained it by and large peacefully, sought to make heroes of themselves afterwards by claiming to have fought for it. He had announced that his party would wage a determined political battle against colonialism until Tanganyika was free; but it would use no violence, stoop to no dishonesty, be as clean in its methods as in its aims, and these would be publicly declared. For over 40 years his country had been a British mandate, and before that more than 30 years a German protectorate. The legacy of all that era was the entrenchment of foreign (mainly British) enterprise in the commanding heights of the economy and major means of production — a situation that Nyerere was to reverse.

His philosophy of socialism and self-reliance was translated into policy guidelines in his so-called Arusha Declaration, accepted at the party conference in the northern Tanzanian town of that name at the beginning of 1967. This marked a turning point in Tanzanian politics. The ideology of the country was made explicit by it. And the introduction of leadership qualifications and measures for public ownership began a new series of deliberately socialist policy initiatives. The first of these, a few weeks later, led to the nationalization of foreign (mostly British) banks, insurance societies and trading companies — with compensation promised, though often long delayed. The country simply did not have the means to pay quickly, and there was constant dispute. Nyerere had been concerned to nationalize banks above all, to give Tanzania full control over the way money and credits were used, and to ensure that profits were retained in the country for the benefit of its people. It was a policy that hit, among others, tea, coffee and sisal planters, again mainly British.

Before taking up my appointment I had been briefed on this in London and had become aware of the anger of British banks and trading companies at the loss of their profitable business in Tanzania. The Foreign Office took the more rational view that if this was Nyerere's policy there was nothing Britain could do about it except press for compensation — and this would be one of my first tasks. But while I accepted that as the unavoidable official attitude, I could have wished for some sympathy in London for the reasons for his policy. I found little. Westminster seemed to be subservient to the City.

But that did not inhibit me, once I was in Tanzania and had begun to deal with Nyerere and press for compensation, from letting him know that I personally understood his policy. I could not see it in any way wrong for him to want his government to have complete control over what he described as the commanding heights of the economy. After all, British enterprises had had a virtual monopoly, and repatriated considerable profits, throughout the years of the British mandate that had in 1919 followed German colonial rule.

I found it difficult to get this across to the bankers and other businessmen who came out from London to lobby me. For, predictably, as soon as I arrived in Dar es Salaam I began to be approached by them, and by local British planters and traders, all wanting me to put their cases to Nyerere. To these were added later hundreds of British-passport-holding Asians affected by further legislation in the National Assembly. For this abolished investment ownership of houses and other buildings let for profit: to Nyerere this was parasitism. And hundreds of Indians and Pakistanis, descendants of indentured or volunteer workers brought in during British rule and still holding their pre-independence British nationality, had over the years made a handsome living by buying up properties, often in poor shape, and letting them out to African townspeople at high rents. Now they could retain only one property, for their own use. They would be compensated for any others they had owned, which would be made over to a national housing corporation for letting at rents just sufficient to cover maintenance costs.

Some of the British whom I did finally convince that all I could do was continue to press for compensation, went on to do business again on amicable terms, such as joint ventures, with Tanzanian state entities. The chairman of the Standard Bank, one of those nationalized, made a point of coming out for the opening of the Central Bank of Tanzania in 1969 and presenting its governor with a handsome silver desk-set. But I fear there were also those, like Tiny Rowland of Lonrho, who came away from a meeting with me undoubtedly thinking me wet for not — as he put it — standing up to Nyerere.

The latter was particularly sensitive about land-holding, and his policy on this had a severe impact on his own people as well. Unconditional or freehold ownership had led to speculation and exploitation for personal profit and had to be abolished. In its place cooperative villages were established, which involved collective production and equal opportunity, with village families sharing decision-making, costs and benefits. It was a system he named *Ujamaa* (familyhood, communal living), a Swahili word derived from the Arabic in that sense. There was something of the Israeli kibbutz in it. Being a socialist system, however, it ran counter to the African tradition of smallholdings handed down by peasant owners from father to son over generations; these now found themselves required to work largely in the communal fields. They did not take kindly to this change, and overall production suffered instead of improving.

All Nyerere's reforms were achieved by legislation in the National Assembly inspired by him as head of the government and leader of the only political party. He saw no conflict between one-party rule and democracy. He had a paternalistic belief that he knew what was best for his largely unsophisticated people; and when on that basis he instituted the one-party system they accepted it without demur.

He believed that system reflected the African tradition of discussing matters by talking until full agreement was reached. This he regarded as the essence of democracy, in contrast to Western multiparty practice which he saw as meaning that, if their party lost, a high percentage of the population, although they had voted, had no say in the conduct of affairs of state. He did not deride that practice and did not rule out the possibility that his people might one day opt for it: but it could not be forced on them. Nyerere, however, had his doubts about the suitability for Africa of the Anglo-Saxon form of democracy. He saw it as inevitable that the national movement which had united his people and led them to independence from colonial rule should form the government of the new state. A united country could hardly be expected to halt its progress and divide itself into opposing political groups just for the sake of conforming to the parliamentary system of its erstwhile colonial rulers.

Nyerere regarded capitalism as the exploitation of man by man.

But his socialist beliefs did not carry any danger of a slide into communism — a misconception which was held in some government and Conservative Party circles in London and which I had to fight hard to correct. Tanzanian foreign policy was based on non-alignment; each problem had to be viewed and judged on its merits and in the country's best interests, whether this meant an *ad hoc* arrangement with the West or the East.

This was demonstrated strikingly at the beginning of 1964 when a major part of the country's small armed forces mutinied, taking control of government buildings in Dar es Salaam, including the airport and radio station, as well as the grounds of the president's official residence; and arresting their own officers and a number of leading citizens. There was no evidence to suggest that this was instigated from outside or that it was the spearhead of a popular revolt; it seemed to have stemmed from dissatisfaction with service pay and conditions. But some dissident merchants opposed to the president's policies began conspiring with the ringleaders and encouraging further action in what looked like an attempt to cause wider disorder. It was a situation beyond the power of the government to control unless it could disarm the mutineers — for which help was needed urgently.

Nyerere's first instinct was to look to his neighbours Kenya and Uganda for this; but, in a chain reaction, sections of the armed forces there also were in revolt and British troops had been called in to bring the situation under control. Nyerere saw no alternative to asking London to help him as well, and British troops were flown in and quickly disarmed the battalions involved, then stayed on for a short time until law and order and confidence in general were restored. He was grateful for this help, so speedily given. But he felt keenly that the import of troops from a country involved in the Cold War — and in this he made no distinction between East and West — had serious implications in the context of African nationalism and the continent's declared common policy of non-alignment. In explaining these events and his action to a special meeting of the Organization for African Unity shortly afterwards, Nyerere emphasized the need for African states somehow to be able to go to each other's help in any future emergency.

It was this concern for African unity and solidarity that put

93

Tanzania in the forefront of the nations that had broken relations with Britain over Rhodesia in 1965, more in sorrow than anger. Nyerere acknowledged for example that, up to the break, Tanzania received more aid from Britain than from any other country. But he had held to his decision to break, even though it meant that a pending further large interest-free loan was frozen as a result. At the same time he had expressed the hope publicly that Britons working in the public services of Tanzania would stay on; and if this meant that they had financial problems (because of withdrawal of sterling subsidies by London) his government would do its best to help them.

Nyerere had no desire or intention to be anti-West; on the contrary, he was not afraid of keeping the country in the British Commonwealth once it became clear that South Africa was no longer to be a member. Even before independence he gave it to the National Assembly as his opinion that nothing but good could come from Tanzania's request to join an association that really did work. More than any other group of nations at that time, he saw the Commonwealth as binding together in friendship and like-mindedness an astonishing variety of nations great and small, without distinction between them or discrimination among themselves. Stronger than ties and treaties (he declared), less selfish than alliances, less restrictive than other associations, it offered hope in the world for lasting peace and friendship among its peoples.

After independence he declared himself to be one of the staunchest supporters of the Commonwealth, and during the two and a half year break in diplomatic relations with Britain over Rhodesia he did not leave it. But he made it clear that he was also one of the staunchest supporters of African unity, and he gave the National Assembly an assurance that if at any time it appeared that Tanzanian membership of the Commonwealth was not in the best interests of the country's efforts to advance the unity and welfare of the continent, it would pull out. It was a threat that was to become real during my years in Dar es Salaam.

Similarly, he resigned himself to the withdrawal without notice of a five-year air-force training and aid agreement with West Germany because Bonn had protested at Tanzania's recognition of

East Germany. He made it clear that his country was not willing to sacrifice real independence by bowing to demands from that or any other capital. It would continue to enter into agreements and contracts for trade and economic assistance with friendly peoples and nations from all parts of the globe. But it would never compromise its national independence or its policy of non-alignment in international disputes that did not concern it. From no quarter, east or west, would Tanzania yield to direction or neo-colonialism. It was neither capitalist nor communist in philosophy, nor part of either bloc. Tanzania was its own man, part of Africa, and would never allow control over itself to pass by any means to any other country.

Having made his non-alignment clear, Nyerere was particularly concerned to rebut frequent assertions in the West that, through its close relations with China, the country was coming under the domination of Peking, even to the extent of moving towards communism; and that his adoption of a jacket on the lines of Mao Tse-tung's as standard wear for Tanzanian officials was evidence of this. The fact was simply that he saw much to admire in China's fight against its own poverty and backwardness, and was grateful for the aid it gave his country. He derided Western speculation that the Chinese then building a railway from Dar es Salaam to Zambia would remain in Tanzania afterwards as the nucleus of a colonial offshoot of China itself. I assured the Foreign Office that I myself regarded this as completely unfounded speculation — which of course time proved it to be.

The railway was designed to give Zambia an outlet to the sea through Dar es Salaam instead of through South Africa by way of Rhodesia. Nyerere made it known publicly that he had tried to get the West to build it, but the countries approached, including Britain, had declined on the grounds that it was not an economically viable project — which of course he had never claimed it to be. On learning this, China had stepped in with a generous offer that had been accepted. Nyerere did not regard it as any concern of his that the Chinese were competing with the Russians for the favours of African countries. Chinese aid, he was at pains to tell me, was no more putting him in the communist camp than British military help in the 1964 mutiny had put him in the capitalist.

He was relieved at the resumption of relations with Britain and was always available to me without formality if there was a problem I wanted to take up with him personally, whether or not I had discussed it with his foreign minister. One such was of course the nationalization of British enterprises. This had been carried out during the break in relations and the Britons involved had felt that the lack of an official British presence in Dar es Salaam at that time meant that representations could not be made to the Tanzanian government on their behalf, or, if they were, only marginally by the Swiss embassy, which was protecting British interests.

It was of course not open to me to challenge nationalization itself; my representations were aimed at ensuring that timely and adequate compensation was paid to the dispossessed owners. There was no dispute over the principle of this, but I was concerned about the considerable delay in actual payment, delay due to the government's difficulty in agreeing a figure in each case and in finding the necessary money. I was satisfied with Nyerere's assurances on this score, though it was to be a long time before payment got fully under way. But meantime it was not easy for me to get those waiting for compensation to accept that it would eventually come.

Despite this problem, and the ongoing difference of opinion over Britain's policy towards South Africa, Anglo-Tanzanian relations slowly improved. Nyerere seemed ready to let bygones be bygones and I looked forward to being able to put relations on a firm footing. But in the middle of 1970, when I had been in the post less than two years, my efforts suffered a critical setback.

12

Tanzania Threatens to Leave Commonwealth–Obote and Idi Amin

A Conservative government headed by Edward Heath had come to power in Britain just after the middle of June 1970. Very soon afterwards the South African foreign minister, Dr Muller, appeared in London; and it was put about in black Africa that he was there to persuade the new government to reverse its Labour predecessors' policy of not supplying arms to South Africa. When Nyerere suddenly called me in to discuss the current reports I was without instructions or background information from the Foreign Office. But I told him that in point of fact Dr Muller was in England to visit his son in boarding school there and that I would imagine he had simply taken the opportunity to pay courtesy calls on the new government. Nyerere, however, was not convinced, and asked for a categorical denial from London.

Meantime, in the last week of June, the leading local paper quoted the *Guardian* of London as saying that the British government might well cite the Simonstown base agreement, the Russian submarine threat and the need to safeguard the Cape route for British trade as reasons for now considering resuming the sale of arms to South Africa. But these were all spurious reasons (the *Guardian* went on). The fact was that Britain was in it for the money. *The Times* was also said to be against the policy; and it was attacked by the United States.

The denial requested by Nyerere was not immediately forthcoming and when it did come it was from Sir Alec Douglas-Home, the foreign secretary. I cannot recall his exact message, and in view of the cabinet discussions which must have been going on at that time and which culminated later in a fierce parliamentary debate, the cabinet may have simply hedged. But there must have been enough in the message for Nyerere not to reject it out of hand. However, he did insist again that the denial should come from the prime minister himself. I emphasized that Sir Alec's message must certainly have reflected government policy and I trusted that the president would be satisfied with it. But Nyerere persisted in his demand. And he went on in serious measured tones to tell me that failing an assurance from the prime minister he would feel bound to consider withdrawing Tanzania from the Commonwealth.

* * *

This was alarming, since it seemed to me that if he actually took this action his example might be followed by other radical African leaders who regarded him as the most articulate champion of African unity and rights; and if Uganda, Zambia, Nigeria and Ghana pulled out, the Commonwealth could be dangerously weakened. I gave this to London as my opinion and pressed for a personal message from the prime minister. As the weekend approached, with still no reaction to my appeal, Nyerere called me round and told me that he was leaving for his village near Dodoma, over 200 miles upcountry (which some years later was to replace Dar es Salaam as the capital), to work on the land for a while — which he did from time to time to relax and to show solidarity with the people. And he had left instructions with his deputy that, failing the required assurance from Mr Heath, he was to announce in the National Assembly that Tanzania would leave the Commonwealth. I was desperate to avert this disaster, so, still without the reply from London I wanted, on Saturday morning 18 July I told the Foreign Office I was leaving at once for Dodoma to try to persuade Nyerere to hang on a while yet.

Obviously communication with London from a remote Tanzanian village would be a problem. To get round this I arranged with the commissioner of police to have the use of a radiotelephone voice channel under his regional officer's control, and through this I kept in touch with my able deputy in Dar es Salaam who remained on 24-hour standby in the high commission with essential diplomatic radio communication staff. I passed messages to him, reporting my talks with Nyerere, in fractured French (not likely to be understood locally), which were then bowdlerized in the interests of cipher security and transmitted to the Foreign Office. Replies from there were handled similarly in the reverse direction. This worked very well — causing the foreign secretary to tell me afterwards that he was curious about how it had been done.

My African driver was used to taking me hundreds of miles along indifferent roads, and several slow dusty hours brought me to Dodoma. There I freshened up at the railway station hotel, on the outside hardly changed since its pre-1914 days as the Kaiserhof, where the German emperor stayed when visiting his East African colony, but on the inside a picture of faded glory. A guide took me to Nyerere in his village, where I told him of the efforts I was still making to get the assurance he wanted and I tried to persuade him not to take any precipitate action meantime, given that he already had the foreign secretary's word. But he still insisted on having it from the prime minister, and I sent a last despairing message to London through Dar es Salaam, where my sterling deputy Tim Kinnear was on 24-hour communications stand-by. This worked; and next day, Sunday, I was able to convey the desired assurance to Nyerere, who in turn confirmed to me that there would be no walkout of the Commonwealth by Tanzania. With great relief I passed this message on to the foreign secretary and set off back to the capital.

That same evening my wife and I decided to relax at the cinema. Coming out at midnight I was aghast to see on a nearby newsstand the first edition of next day's local newspaper (Monday 20 July) carrying the banner headline declaring 'TANZANIA TO QUIT THE COMMONWEALTH'. The announcement that this covered ran:

> Tanzania has informed the United Kingdom that it will leave the Commonwealth immediately the government announces a decision to resume arms sales to South Africa.

The Tanzanian decision was conveyed to the British government over the weekend. It is not intended as a threat nor as
a last-minute appeal to Britain to change its mind. The
foreign secretary is expected to announce the British
government's decision in the House of Commons later on
the 20th. Unless there is a last-minute change of heart he is
expected to announce that the British government is
opening negotiations with South Africa for the supply of
arms. Tanzania's break with the Commonwealth is expected to be announced after the statement in the House of
Commons and will be effective immediately.

It was an announcement obviously intended to give the man in
the street the impression that the matter was cut and dried, that
Britain was in fact resuming sales. I saw in it (and confirmed next
day) the hand of the South African Indian woman editor of the
newspaper, whom I knew, and knew to be violently anti-British.
She would have known from Nyerere's deputy about the instructions to him to announce in the National Assembly that day that,
failing the required assurance from the British prime minister,
Tanzania would leave the Commonwealth. She almost certainly
also knew of my own urgent visit to Dodoma over the weekend of
18/19 July to try to persuade Nyerere to delay any announcement
until I had heard from Edward Heath himself. But whether she
knew that or not she must have worked on the assumption that I
would not hear anything satisfactory from him, so the announcement in the National Assembly would be going ahead. In
malicious anticipation she then set up the press report before the
Assembly had met.

My first reaction on reading the report was that it would be
devastating: Edward Heath would either write me off as an
incompetent and unreliable envoy or condemn Nyerere as deceitful, or both. I therefore went at once, late though it was, to see the
president's press officer, whom I knew well, and get him to do
something. He at once had all copies of the paper already on the
newsstands rounded up. So the immediate crisis was over (though
copies of the paper still circulated).

But as it turned out, I had been too sensitive about my first reaction — and perhaps too trustful of politicians. For London's stand also turned out to be ambivalent. The government there did not in fact announce in the Commons on 20 July a decision to resume sales, as was provocatively forecast in the Tanzanian press. But, at variance with the prime minister's assurance which I had passed on to Nyerere the day before, the foreign secretary said he was acting to implement the terms of the 1955 Simonstown naval base agreement between Britain and South Africa. The base had been taken over by the latter for defence of the sea route around the Cape of Good Hope. Britain should therefore now consider providing South Africa with 'certain limited categories of arms, so long as these were for maritime defence directly related to the security of the sea routes between the Indian and Atlantic Oceans'.

In no circumstances (Sir Alec Douglas-Home went on to say) would there be sales of arms designed to enforce apartheid. And no final action on the matter would be taken until Britain had consulted the members of the Commonwealths 'to whom the cabinet's decision in principle had been presented'. The Leader of the Opposition challenged the government's assurance that this announcement was only a statement of intention, rather than a final decision. He quoted the South African prime minister, who 'has been reported as having said that the [British] government has intimated privately but officially that they are going to resume sales ... and Vorster intends to hold them to that pledge'. *The Times* warned the government that Tanzania would leave the Commonwealth if arms sales went ahead. The Commons statement stirred vehement reaction in the opposition and among African nations. And on the 22 July there followed a noisy, heated debate in the House, the government being attacked on all sides.

At these developments Nyerere broke his stay at his village upcountry and returned to Dar es Salaam for a hastily arranged meeting with Kaunda of Zambia and Obote of Uganda. However lulled he had been by the prime minister's assurance that I had given him three days before, the subsequent proceedings in the House of Commons had raised doubts in his mind and he decided to discuss the whole question with his two neighbours. Next day, the 23rd, at the end of their meeting, they called me in to tell me of their concern and to repeat the warning I had already received from Nyerere. They had agreed a message of protest to the government in London which they wanted me to convey at once to the prime minister. This I did. And Nyerere went back to his village.

Two weeks later a violent student demonstration in Dar es Salaam was a reminder that the problem had by no means gone away. Some 600 of them marched on the British high commission, whose main offices were up two flights of stairs in a building in the centre of the city. With my staff I blocked off the entrance to the stairs as far as we could (which of course was not enough to stop the mob), then retired to the offices and barricaded ourselves in. But clearly I did not want a siege, so I had a message passed to the students, saying that I would receive a delegation of five of their leaders. They agreed and, face to face with me and in quieter mood, they were by no means unreasonable. As I had of course expected, they were protesting about what they called the British decision to sell arms to South Africa. I was unable to persuade them of the nuances of the problem, so finally accepted a letter from the faculty urging the prime minister to 'reverse his decision'.

The dispute between London and black Africa hung fire for some time, then gradually petered out — though not before there had been further African protests. But it was a relief for me to be able to look forward to a gradual return to normal Anglo-Tanzanian relations. Despite the friction between us from time to time over the effects of Nyerere's policies on British interests in Tanzania, he was well-disposed towards Britain and the Commonwealth; and he had the courage to make no secret of it.

At an official dinner at the end of 1971 to celebrate the tenth anniversary of the country's independence from Britain, seated on his right was Sir Richard Turnbull, the last British governor, whom, with a number of other British colonial officials from that era, Nyerere had invited for the occasion as guests of his government. The dinner was no extravagant banquet of the kind popular in wealthy countries like Iran and Saudi Arabia; it was modest, served at a number of large tables in a local hall. I was also at the president's table, as were the Chinese and Russian ambassadors.

When the meal was over and it was clear that speeches were about to begin, the Chinese had his excellent young interpreter in

Swahili move in and sit behind him. The president rose — and to the general surprise spoke in English, starting off with generous praise of his guest of honour, the former British governor. The Chinese ambassador quickly sent his Swahili interpreter to bring in his place a staff member who knew English. Given the strenuous Chinese and Russian efforts at that time to woo Tanzania away from its traditional links, I felt pleasure at the obvious discomfiture and disappointment of the two ambassadors. I hoped it would make them realize that they were not going to be able to win Tanzania over into their camp, notwithstanding their generous aid to the country and Nyerere's continuing criticism of British policy on South Africa. On this, besides being united on economic policies that often hit British interests, he and his fellow presidents, Obote of Uganda and Kaunda of Zambia, formed a trio of like-minded reformers.

But towards the end of January 1971, while all three were at the Commonwealth Conference in Singapore, Idi Amin the Ugandan commander-in-chief seized control of the capital Kampala, proclaimed himself head of state, dissolved parliament, and formed a ruling defence council with himself as chairman. Returning from Singapore with Nyerere (who broke his journey for a state visit to India), Obote took refuge in Dar es Salaam as the latter's guest. Only six months before, I had met him in the capital at a discussion with Nyerere and Kaunda on British arms for South Africa. Now I was to meet him again.

He was a quiet man; he did not have the presence of either Nyerere or Kaunda, with both of whom he was in close relations. Yet he was clearly anxious to emulate Nyerere, particularly in creating an egalitarian society under one-party rule. But unlike Nyerere, he lacked the political acumen to bring this about without antagonizing certain groups (particularly the army under Idi Amin), a factor that contributed to his overthrow. In 1959 he had bluntly announced his so-called 'common man's charter', explicitly a move to the left; and in this context he planned to expropriate the assets of British and other foreign enterprises in Uganda. It was a policy that could breed widespread corruption and leave the economy of this once prosperous country in ruins.

London, concerned about his planned expropriation of British

103

enterprises, regarded the overthrow of Obote as no bad thing. Anticipating this reaction, Nyerere and Obote invited me to a meeting with them at which they pressed me to advise the Foreign Office to persuade the government not to rush in and recognize Amin as the new head of state. This I did, it being my own view as well. But clearly London thought that anyone would be better than Obote and that we could expect more sympathetic treatment of British interests from this former boxing champion of Uganda and sergeant in the pre-independence British-officered King's African Rifles. So to my disappointment and foreboding, and Nyerere's intense disgust, Britain was among the first to recognize Idi Amin. Five months later he was invited to London to be wined, dined, consulted and negotiated with at the highest level, even as far as lunch with the Queen.

I never met him, but from what Nyerere and Obote had told me about him and from what I subsequently learned in Dar es Salaam I had no reason to doubt the general unfavourable opinion of Amin, which I came to share — an opinion vindicated by subsequent events. He was a big man and his boxer's build and face gave him an air of menace only partially dispelled by lapses into joviality. His moods were said to be unpredictable; and there had apparently been evidence of this during his command of the Ugandan armed forces under Obote, who had made no attempt to integrate the generals into the fabric of the state government.

The British government's invitation to Idi Amin to come to London right at the start of a rule that was to turn into a dictatorship was a fruitless exercise, at times descending to farce, which the government lived to regret. At one meeting in the Foreign Office the banality of the discussion (one of his requests was for thousands of army boots) prompted a leading figure at the table to pass a note to the head of the Foreign Office asking whether 'this nightmare' would ever end. Amin pressed for vast quantities of armaments, including tanks and aircraft. But already by this time the British government's eyes were beginning to open, and he went away with only the promise of a military mission to examine his army's training needs.

On his return to Uganda Amin gave the army powers that amounted to tyranny of the population, thousands of whom were killed. A wave of terror ensued, in the course of which the once buoyant agriculture-based economy collapsed. In 1972 he nationalized British businesses and expelled many British people; he also expelled almost all the country's 30,000 Asians with British nationality after seizing all their properties and assets and dividing these among his followers. Hurling insults at the West, he cultivated the Soviet Union, Libya and the PLO. So much for London's ill-advised hopes of him.

His excesses eventually led to Tanzanian military intervention in Uganda, which removed him and reinstated Obote, at considerable cost to the Tanzanian economy. This was something Nyerere had not bargained for when he restructured his country's economy on socialist lines: his objective was essentially to apply available funds to the welfare of the people and not on military involvements. It was a development that the country could ill afford, for it was becoming clear that Nyerere's policy of broad state intervention in agriculture and industry was removing incentive, creating inefficiency and, for the first time, fostering corruption.

This was compounded by severe drought and the enormous rise in the price of oil. Production kept on falling, inflation grew, shortages increased in every sector until in the late 1970s, after I had left, food and petrol began to be rationed. The government declined standby credit from the International Monetary Fund because it was offered on conditions Nyerere regarded as contrary to the country's socialist principles, conditions that included at various times devaluation, reduction in state intervention, increased interest rates, removal of price controls and a freeze on wages. Instead, Nyerere introduced austerity measures of his own and sought to eliminate economic sabotage and the black market.

He asserted that the problems were not due to socialism and inefficiency but to the effect of worldwide recession on poor countries with no oil. And whether a country was socialist or not, he argued, only affected the distribution of economic difficulties among its citizens — not the difficulties themselves. As the situation deteriorated there were some Tanzanians who considered that it was due largely to the president's inflexible ideology of socialism and self-help. But for this, they said, the country could benefit from less state intervention and a return to some measure of free enterprise, in which case the IMF and other agencies would be ready to help.

That, however, was a minority view. For most of the people Nyerere was still the charismatic leader who knew what was best for them. And in the end what was best was that he relaxed some of his principles regarding land usage to stop the decline in agricultural productivity. It was to be some years — by which time I had retired — before I met him again, in Hong Kong on his way to China, and we discussed this. But notwithstanding the mistakes in his agricultural policy he was a remarkable leader, unique in Africa, whom I admired for his integrity and sincerity.

Having taken leave of him at the end of 1972 on completion of my tour of duty, I was to look back with nostalgia on my stay of nearly four and a half years in Tanzania as an instructive experience that had presented stimulating challenges. And it was a stay in a country of much beauty — from the snows of Kilimanjaro and the wildlife of the Serengeti plains to Lake Victoria and Zanzibar. There the high commission had a house overlooking the sea, where I spent many enjoyable days, with opportunities for discussions with the island's leadership. The buildings and narrow streets of the bazaar reflected the Arab history of Zanzibar dating back to the end of the seventeenth century, after the Imam of Oman in the Persian Gulf had captured it from the Portuguese. The ensuing sultanate, its last 70 years under British protection, had lasted until 1964 when it was united with Tanganyika to form Tanzania. Throughout its history it has grown cloves; and descending from the small plane after the 20-minute flight from Dar es Salaam was like walking into the fragrance of a spice bazaar, cloves lining the sides of roads to dry in the sun, untended, but untouched by any thieving hand.

Sometimes with my wife, I used to call on Sheikh Karume, leader of the island's semi-autonomous Revolution Council, in the former British Residency. A former boatman (assassinated in 1972), ruthless and uncouth, he would take pride in showing us round to see relics of the past still in place, like the grand piano, and the clock presented by Queen Victoria. And he was preserving the old furniture by having had it covered in plastic sheeting — not the most comfortable surface in the summer heat of Zanzibar.

13
Ambassador to Turkey–Role of the Army There

Throughout my career I had made it a practice never to angle for a specific post nor question appointment to one for family or other reasons. If exceptionally I was asked, rather than simply being directed, to accept a post, I accepted. When I was home on leave in 1971 the Foreign Office had brought up the question of my next post — the final one that would take me up to mandatory retirement at 60 in five years' time. I was asked what my preference was, supposing it could be accommodated in personnel department's general planning programme — since any proposed appointment usually had to be considered in the context of consequent moves of other officials in and out of other posts. Having served in Iran over six years in all, knowing the language and leading personalities from the Shah down, and my wife and I both with a liking for the country, I opted for Tehran; but if that was not available I would be happy to serve in Turkey. And in the event that is what it turned out to be, since the incumbent ambassador in Tehran had only recently arrived there. So I was to take up the post in Ankara in February 1973.

If I was at first a little disappointed, the feeling soon passed when I arrived in Turkey. I had driven the length of the country a couple of times in the 1960s on journeys from London to Tehran and back when I was counsellor at the embassy there, so it was not unknown territory. The prospect of now being ambassador in

107

Envoy Extraordinary

Ankara, at a time of problems for Turkey, domestic and external, was exciting. In parallel I would be United Kingdom representative to the Central Treaty Organization (CENTO) headquartered in Ankara. This had developed in 1959 out of earlier Middle East defence arrangements that had broken down leaving Turkey, Iran, Pakistan, Britain and the United States linked in what was essentially a military and economic planning coordination body, but without provision for multilateral military assistance.

To cap it all, my new appointment carried promotion to the second highest grade of ambassador (equivalent to deputy undersecretary) — something that had never entered my mind for a moment as even a remote possibility nearly 40 years before, when it seemed I would never be allowed to get on to even the lowest rung of the diplomatic ladder. It was an appointment that was to cover one of the most interesting and enjoyable periods in my career.

Approaching Turkey by ship from Venice it was not until I had stared from starboard to try and catch the outline of the island of Lesbos (Byron's tale of 'burning Sappho'), passed the next island Tenedos, then Troy on the mainland behind and the mouth of ancient Hellespont ahead that I fully realized what this appointment was to mean to me in terms of old and new. For 30 years in the Punjab, Persia, Afghanistan, Arabia and the Gulf I followed the steps of Alexander the Great. Now I was in the narrows, less than a mile across, where 2300 years before his Asian adventure had begun. A century and a half later, Xerxes the Persian, marching northward on Greece, had also crossed here, on pontoons. Here too Leander was fabled to have swum nightly to Hero until, her guiding light failing, he drowned. And much later, in 1810, Byron and a companion had emulated him — just once. By that time of course the Hellespont had become the Dardanelles, named after a small town nearby commemorating a mythical forbear of the Trojans. And now we were sailing in the strait itself, known to the Turks as the Throat of Çanakkale (the fortress town to the south).

Barely 50 years before, with British troops still in occupation, this had been the scene of what came to be known as the Chanak affair. The enlightened British commander, not sharing the view of his pro-Greek prime minister Lloyd George that Mustafa Kemal (who was bringing his army up from Smyrna in an advance on Constantinople) was a bandit and not the potential founder of a new Turkey, temporized on delivering an ultimatum from London to Kemal. Quiet negotiation between the two generals, soldier to soldier, averted a clash between their opposing forces — a danger even Lloyd George's own party regarded as having been brought on by his intemperate hostility to the Turks. Events in London then led quickly to his resignation while Kemal (soon to be known as Atatürk) went on to establish his own position internationally.

As we sailed through the Dardanelles my memories of Atatürk's 1915 victory over the Allies were evoked by names from history — Gallipoli, Anzac Cove, Suvla Bay, Limestone Hill, Monastery Hill, Anafurta. And so we continued through the Sea of Marmara, past the island of that name once famous for its marble, until the first distant sight of the minarets of Istanbul. We slowed for the pilot to take us into the Bosphorus — the Ox-Ford of Greek legend but to the Turks more graphically the Throat of the Black Sea.

Then, slender and graceful in the distance ahead, growing more defined by the minute, a dramatic steel thread suspended high above the water: the British–German-built Bosphorus Bridge was nearing completion. And I remembered that almost exactly where it stands Xerxes' great predecessor had built *his* bridge, which had carried the Persian armies to defeat at Marathon — Darius 490 BC; Freeman Fox AD 1973. In nearly 2500 years there had been no other bridge across these narrows. But in that time a world of history — Byzantium, Constantinople, Istanbul — that shaped my first impression of Turkey from the sea. We swung into the Golden Horn (to the Turks, this time more prosaic than ourselves, limply the Estuary) and berthed alongside the Galata Bridge, with its milling crowds and hooting cars oblivious of the nearby domes and minarets of Saint Sophia, the Blue Mosque, the Suleymaniye, Topkapı and a dozen others.

Over my first cup of Turkish coffee I cleared customs with the port director and learned that his name was Barbarossa. So, I reflected, that Turkish adventurer had not been forgotten. This was the pirate who, in the service of Sultan Suleiman the Magnificent in the sixteenth century, had led the Ottoman fleet to victory against the Holy Roman Emperor's on the Barbary coast of North Africa and so given the sultan control of the eastern Mediterranean. I knew then that I had arrived.

A newcomer cannot fail to be struck by the lingering history of Turkey. The prehistoric finds by an Englishman at Çatal Höyük go down through the Hittite civilization of the first two millenia BC — not forgetting nine layers of Troy, five of them below Homer's. Then there are the Phrygians (the tomb of Midas at Gordium, of the Gordian knot), the Lydians (their King Croesus defeated by Xerxes at Sardis), Ionian Greeks (Ephesus and Teos, first seen by British archaeologists), even Celtic Galatians (their capital where Ankara now stands). Persian conquest from the sixth to the fourth century BC did not stop the development of Ionian Greek cities and philosophy on the eastern Aegean coast, and Alexander's crossing of the Hellespont in 334 BC and his defeat of the Persians marked the start of a great Hellenistic age on that coast and further inland.

The Greek gave way to the Roman Empire, which unified and ruled over what is today's Turkey — the legacy of both Greeks and Romans being the great classical ruins, which are still to be seen. In its decline an internal power struggle led to the division of the Roman Empire. A western part lasted until it was overrun by barbarians towards the end of the fifth century AD; while an eastern part was set up under the Emperor Constantine who in 330 established his capital at Constantinople, its name changed from Byzantium. This Byzantine Empire was to last for over 1000 years. In it, the impact of Christianity was soon felt: St John's basilica at Ephesus; St Paul of Tarsus preaching his epistles in Ephesus, Galatia and Colossae, and, with Barnabas, establishing the empire's first church at Antioch; then the first seven Councils of the Church, which gradually defined the Catholic faith.

The Seljuks, forebears of today's Turks, appeared on the scene with Islam in the eleventh century; undeterred by the Crusaders they eventually spread their hold until they in turn were succeeded by the Ottomans. With their capture of Constantinople in 1453 the Ottomans then laid the foundations for the wholly Muslim Turkey which, in 1923, Kemal Atatürk brought so dramatically

110

into the twentieth century and what he saw as Civilization — the West, Europe — with its many outward changes (of dress, language, government) that are so familiar today. Not least among these changes was the move of the capital from Constantinople (renamed Istanbul) — symbol of the sultans he had replaced and the country's past — to Ankara on the bracing Anatolian plateau 300 miles inland, Turkey of the Turks. By the time I arrived Ankara's population had grown from fewer than 100,000 inhabitants to well over a million; it was a custom-built administrative and increasingly cultural capital laid out by Austrian and German town planners commissioned by Atatürk.

But it is a place that not all Turks take to. For many of them Asia and Europe meet somewhere along the road and railway between Ankara and Istanbul; and if they are to appear European to the world they want to enjoy the pleasures of Europe — which in Turkey means Istanbul and not Ankara. So I detected early on something of snobbery. Politicians, administrators, technicians, academics and artistes who work in the capital live there because they have to. But many of them, whenever they can, flee to Istanbul to the sophisticated life of big business, the press, café society and cool spacious *fin-de-siècle* summer villas (*yalıs*) on the Bosphorus. And those Turks who live permanently in Istanbul generally come to the capital only when they have to. Neither set, however, finds it a hardship to visit the coasts of the Black Sea, Aegean or Mediterranean for pleasure. But mention more distant parts of the country — particularly in the east, or Anatolia — and they may have barely heard of these, let alone been there. The average urban Turk regards his country as consisting of two capitals, a score of big or medium towns, a number of seaside resorts, dozens of historical sites and very little in between.

I soon found out that there is more to Turkey than that. After talking with Turks, walking their streets and driving their highways it is not long before a foreigner new to the country and recalling its kaleidoscopic past asks himself, 'Where am I? Asia? Or Europe?' It is a fashionable question. But it is soon clear that there is no single definitive answer; it will vary according to the circumstances.

Emotionally, if not intellectually, it may be difficult to regard as

111

European a state, albeit secular, that is wholly Muslim, especially if 97 per cent of it lies in geographical Asia. Fly from London to Istanbul and you are in the Middle East; to Kars near the Russian frontier and you are in Central Asia. But fly from Kars to Istanbul or Izmir and you are in Europe.

Nor do the people themselves help provide the answer; you can see their types from Sicily to Salonika, from Tiflis to Tehran, blond, ginger, dark. The Seljuks invading from Central Asia and the Ottomans who succeeded them were undoubtedly not European. Yet the legacy of Greece and Rome up to the fall of Constantinople, and contact with the West during the Ottoman rise and decline over the next 400 and more years inevitably injected something of Europe. It is this that enabled twentieth-century Turks to respond to Atatürk's call to look to the West as the model for the new 'civilized' Turkey. Since then they have been doing so, and with fair success, if patchy. Western institutions have admitted them — NATO, the OECD, the Council of Europe — and in 1963 Turkey was granted associate status in the European Community, as it then was. In Ankara, at least as often as in Istanbul, one can enjoy very adequate, sometimes outstanding, performances of the classics of the West, as well as indigenous works, by state-maintained opera and ballet companies, orchestras and theatres. It comes naturally to urban Turks, at least, to regard themselves as closer to the West than to the East; and I was soon to find them polite, helpful, direct, reserved at first but opening out on closer acquaintance.

And it did not take long to realize how wide are the misconceptions of Turkey outside the country. One of these is that it is not a democracy; another is that it is ruled by a military government more often than a civilian one. The fact is, however, that democracy does work in Turkey. It is true that from the establishment of the new republic in 1923, following the abolition of the sultanate, until his death in 1938 Atatürk permitted only one political party, the Republican People's Party (RPP) with himself as the authoritarian leader of it. But after continuing this system until 1945, his successor İsmet İnönü, Atatürk's deputy in war and peace, announced his support for a multiparty state and several new parties were established. Finally, in 1950, he agreed to a general

1-2. Maternal grandparents

3-4. Paternal grandparents

5-6. Parents

ABOVE. 7. Sir Denis Wright, ambassador to Tehran, with his deputy, the author (on his left) and senior staff.
BELOW. 8. King Saud and King Hussein of Jordan, Jedda (Saudi Arabia), 1955.

9. The author with a political officer below a building in the Aden Protectorate near the frontier with Yemen.

ABOVE. 10. President Nyerere of Tanzania greeting the authors wife.
BELOW. 11. The author's daughter in Dar-es-Salaam.

ABOVE. 12. The author with Foreign Secretary, Anthony Crosland, at a meeting of CENTO foreign ministers, London, 1976.
BELOW. 13. Presenting Colonel "Johnnie" Johnston, the military attaché of the embassy, to President Sukarno of Indonesia, Jakarta, 1966.

ABOVE. 14. On West Lake, Hangchow (China), 1985.
BELOW. 15. Graduation as Hon.LL.D., Glasgow University, 1977.

election, which was fought freely and fairly and resulted in the defeat of his own party by the Democratic Party (DP), founded in 1946.

This marked the start of a democratic system, albeit put in jeopardy periodically by extremist political violence. It was the army's part in suppressing this that gave rise abroad to the myth about constant military rule. For, to put down violence, the army has on occasion taken over the government for short periods. One such began in 1971 but was over before I took up my post early in 1973. There had been an earlier one in 1960/1 (when I was diverted by an army patrol as I was driving through Turkey on my way to Tehran), and there was to be yet another in 1980. But on all three occasions there were sound reasons for the takeover.

* * *

It was with the support of his army that Atatürk had not only founded the new republic but had created its first administration. In contrast to the degenerate sultanate the Ottoman army was an elite force that by the sixteenth century had expanded the empire to the gates of Vienna. Its tradition assured it of a cadre of officers literate and skilled out of proportion to their numbers. It was on these that Atatürk drew in the first years of the republic, since, under the sultanate, secular education outside the army was neglected in favour of Islamic religious teaching. True, Islam remains the religion of the Turks, but it no longer governs their lives; under the republican constitution it was disestablished and its outward signs abolished.

Atatürk's new Turkey looked firmly westward and he gradually instilled in his people a fierce national pride. In this process the army, and in due course the other armed forces, became completely identified with their leader. But if to start with this seemed to be simply support for him in setting up the state, it grew into something bigger, something that continues up to now. The armed forces came to regard themselves not only as the right hand of Atatürk, but also as the guardians of the constitution and the custodians of his policies and philosophy — Kemalism. After he died they adopted this role with a single-minded devotion that

113

complemented the veneration of his memory by the Turkish people as a whole.

When his one-party authoritarian rule, inherited by his deputy İnönü, gave way in 1950 to a multiparty parliamentary democracy, the armed forces played no part in this and sought no role in government. They saw their task as defending the homeland and preserving Atatürk's principles. So long as the politicians did not jeopardize Kemalism they were left alone to play their politics on the right or left of centre and be entirely democratic about it. As the years wore on, Kemalism in modern times became tantamount to Turkish national unity. And the people accepted that in the last resort this could be guaranteed by the armed forces. It is this that marks the essential difference between occasional military take-overs in Turkey and armed coups elsewhere.

This is not to say that the Turkish armed forces have always acted entirely altruistically. In founding the republic Atatürk's reliance on the army gave it protection and privilege assured by his ruling Republican People's Party (RPP), which saw itself with the army as guardians of the state. The defeat of the RPP by the Democratic Party (DP) in the country's first open election in 1950 gave rise to fears in the army that it would lose its privileged position and that officers openly supporting the RPP would be dismissed, for the DP was making moves to break that party's historical close links with state institutions, including the armed forces. At the same time, as a reward for having supported the DP, the Democrats were loosening some of Atatürk's restraints on Muslim leaders and their institutions.

The army, already resentful at being deprived of the position it had enjoyed under the RPP, now perceived a threat to the constitution and the principles of the secular, progressive Kemalist state. Junior officers in particular, stimulated by the growth in the international standing of the army since the early 1950s when Turkey was admitted to NATO and took part in the Korean war, reacted strongly to that threat. They saw the army as the only institution in Turkey that could stop the DP; and when the party's leader and prime minister Adnan Menderes ignored calls to return to constitutional rule the army ousted him in May 1960 and abolished the party. Some junior officers believed that the army

114

should remain in power indefinitely to restore national unity and impose major political and social reforms in government. This, however, was opposed by the generals and the army went back to barracks after a year, but not before introducing a new constitution and assuring themselves of a direct share in the running of the country. Finally, they tried, convicted and hanged Menderes and his foreign minister.

The RPP returned to power, at first in coalition with the new Justice Party (JP), the successor to the Democrats; but by the mid-1960s the JP had formed a government of its own under its leader Suleyman Demirel, who became prime minister. It was in fact a regime established by the generals and they set themselves up as the guardians of it. Because they saw the armed forces as autonomous and not dependent for their existence on any party but on the integrity of the state, that integrity had to be maintained. They secured improvements in pay and conditions and acquired many material privileges for all ranks and their families. An Army Mutual Assistance Association gave them a stake in business and industry. To preserve all these advantages the generals made internal peace and stability their main aim, and were prepared to impose their will to ensure this. The army continued to uphold the constitution and the principles of Atatürk, but it now had a self-interest also in doing so.

Meantime, throughout the 1960s the two main parties, the conservative RPP and the socialist JP, habitually ran neck and neck in elections and each in turn had to ally with minority parties to obtain a parliamentary majority. Inevitably the leaders of these parties, weak in their own right, gained disproportionate power and were able to indulge their own extreme ideologies: one Islamic, the other national-socialist verging on fascist.

This was not lost on the leaders of the two main parties but they ignored it in their desire to hold on to power when they in turn were in office. The result was that political infighting preoccupied all the parties and the country suffered under the shadow of extremists of left and right preaching their own ideologies and fighting it out on the streets and in the universities. The two main party leaders spoke out against the violence but were incapable of taking effective action. It was cynically believed in some quarters

115

that they might even see political advantage in it as something that each could publicly condemn the other for. But it was probably truer to say simply that the extremists were beyond their control.

As the violence increased in the 1960s, with sporadic attacks on the armed forces themselves and the beginnings of terrorist activity by Kurdish groups in the southeast, the generals began to fear that the officer corps might be infected by the political polarization of the country and that there would be a split between junior and senior officers, as in 1960. The high command therefore forced the resignation of Demirel the prime minister and his government early in 1971 on the grounds that it had failed to wipe out the violence that threatened the country. A series of prime ministers appointed by the military took over, heading governments of conservative politicians and technocrats overseen by military officers. Martial law was imposed in a number of provinces and military courts were set up to deal with the many hundreds arrested. In the latter part of 1973, after I had arrived in the country, these courts were replaced by special security courts; martial law was lifted and the army withdrew.

But left–right violence continued and I witnessed the horrifying results of some of it, particularly among university students. By the time I left office in the middle of 1977 these events had increased, with weak governments still incapable of putting an end to them. If Suleyman Demirel and Bülent Ecevit as leaders of the two main parties had been prepared to go into coalition they might have been able to put an end to the violence, but they could not agree to this. With not only the political, but the economic situation deteriorating — debt, inflation, unemployment, shortages — the generals decided to take action; and in the second half of 1980 the army again intervened in a bloodless coup.

The high command dissolved parliament, abolished political parties and imposed authoritarian rule through a National Security Council, which included appointed ministers who were technocrats with no explicit party affiliation. Army officers were appointed to key positions of control and supervision of ministries, but did not head them. Side by side with this was strict martial law and military action to contain street violence; and as the killings began to decrease the people seemed actually grateful for the military takeover. At the end of 1982 yet another new constitution was promulgated. It was not until 1983, by which time order had been restored (except in the Kurdish areas), that the National Security Council handed back power to an elected parliament (with strong military representation) and selected politicians took over government. Once again the army went back to barracks, with its own honour and privileges and the integrity of the state intact.

In taking deterrent action against violence the generals have always been conscious of the effect of this on the image of Turkey's European vocation, and have not taken their decisions lightly. They would much prefer not to intervene in government. But they had, without success, warned the old politicians and exhorted them to work together and save the nation from irreparable division — a division they perceived as a threat to the armed forces as well. The people, they said, had no patience with those who sang communist marches instead of the national anthem, or who clamoured for a religious state, or wanted a fascist regime. The generals, with an eye on the self-interest of the armed forces as well as the security of the state, felt they had no alternative.

The Turkish armed forces have never been out for power for themselves; they have no political aspirations of their own that they feel they have to assert against existing political government. It is only when the latter loses control and Kemalism is threatened that the military intervenes. When they have done this the people have been with them and have accepted with relief temporary rule by a National Security Council headed by the generals. For there is little doubt that the people have at times had good reason to become disillusioned with their political leaders.

14

The Ankara Residence–Jubilee Year–Knighthood

lthough I was not to learn about it until I had begun to find my way around in the next few weeks, that was the background against which I took up my post in Ankara. Having brought my personal car with me on the ship, I drove the 300 miles there from Istanbul over a road I was to come to know well — and to travel with caution in the face of often reckless driving. Our first sight of the embassy delighted me and my wife. The main building is not just an official residence, but a comfortable family home. The splendid site, higher up than that of any other embassy in town, lies just below what was once Atatürk's residence and remains the presidential palace.

In 1924, the year after the republic was set up, the foreign diplomatic missions in Istanbul were invited to move to Ankara and choose sites there, which the Turkish government would be happy to ensure could be negotiated for. For some time there was no reaction in Istanbul except from the Soviet and Afghan missions. But early in 1925 when a new British ambassador went to Ankara to present his credentials to Atatürk he had to live in two railway carriages in a siding at the main station. It was clear that a permanent residence would be needed for the future. In 1926 the present site was chosen and, prompted by Atatürk, made available for a nominal sum by its owner who had been his aide-de-camp during the war of independence. An existing rudimentary building provided accommodation for a very small skeleton staff and for the ambassador on visits to the capital from Istanbul. It was not until late in 1929 that London agreed to a start on the construction of permanent buildings, the first of these being the Chancery (office block), which also served as a temporary residence for the ambassador.

Today's proper residence was not completed until early in the Second World War, but it was then partitioned temporarily into offices for the many additional civilian and military staff required to handle the growing wartime operations. The ambassador continued to live above the offices; during this period, late in 1943, his Albanian–Turkish valet (later code-named Cicero) got hold of the key to his safe and made copies of secret documents, which he sold to the German embassy down the road. The papers covered political and military matters of first importance, including Foreign Office messages on relations and exchanges of views between London, Washington and Moscow. The German ambassador, Von Papen, sent them to Berlin, but it was some time before the foreign minister, Ribbentrop, could be persuaded that they were genuine. Even so, the Germans made no attempt to apply the valuable information in them to their own strategic planning — largely because of the failure of the political and military establishments in Berlin to agree on how to use it. But to keep Cicero in play the Germans gave him £20,000 in notes, which after the war he discovered were counterfeit.

His Majesty's ambassador of the day finally moved into the Ankara residence towards the end of 1945, having held there in May a victory celebration attended by, among others, the entire Turkish cabinet — for Turkey had joined the Allies in February that year, largely as a result of persuasion by Churchill. And this was the splendid building that was now to be my home for a few years: a spacious residence set in an attractive garden. There, 20 years before, some enthusiastic members of the staff had planted young trees (some from the War Graves Commission in Gallipoli). These had flourished against the gloomy prediction of pundits in the Ministry of Works in London that no trees would grow unless planted and nurtured by experts from the ministry.

Development of the embassy complex in Ankara did not mean abandoning the Houses of Parliament architect Sir James Barry's

Envoy Extraordinary

imposing Italian Renaissance-style building of 1845 in Istanbul, which had housed the embassy until the move to Ankara in 1926. There had been foreign missions in this part of Istanbul since the early centuries of the Ottoman Empire; the British had been there since 1581. On the move to Ankara it was decided that the Istanbul building should be retained to house the office and residence of a consul-general. It later accommodated the British Council as well. And a suite of rooms was set aside for the ambassador to reside and entertain in on his frequent visits to the city, generally for official meetings with local and British businessmen. On one occasion I had to resist pressure by the Ministry of Works in London, at the instigation of the Treasury, to sell the property, a valuable site. Quite apart from my opposition to the loss of British face and parade of British poverty that would be seen locally, the clinching argument was that the site had been made available to us through the sultanate and therefore could not be disposed of without the permission of the present government, which could well be expected to want to take it over itself if we decided to give it up.

* * *

I had arrived in Turkey in its jubilee year — 50 years since the Grand National Assembly, the nationalist parliament created only 18 months before by Mustafa Kemal at the height of his campaign to free Turkey from Greek and other foreign occupation, had proclaimed the country a republic. That was just a year since he had abolished the sultanate and Mehmet VI had, with British help, fled to exile in Italy; barely three months since the Treaty of Lausanne had done away with the capitulations and established a sovereign independent Turkey; somewhat less since Kemal had founded the People's Republican Party that pushed through the proclamation of the republic; and exactly 20 days since he had declared the capital to be Ankara (no longer Angora).

Small wonder that the Grand National Assembly had gone on at once to vote him its first president. By now he was Marshal the Ghazi (Victorious) Mustafa Kemal. By early 1926 he had secured the introduction of a civil code based largely on the Swiss, giving

120

Turkey its first independent judiciary. This marked the legislation of the emancipation of women, who had gradually to discard the veil — as men had to the fez. At the end of 1928 he introduced the reform that was to have the greatest impact both inside and outside the country: the substitution of Roman for Arabic characters in written Turkish. It was a move that marked the beginning of the end of illiteracy in the country, mastery of the complicated Arabic script having been beyond the reach of the country-dwellers who formed the majority of the population. Finally, at the end of 1934 Kemal abolished the Arab system of personal names (A the son of B) in favour of family names on the Western pattern. Families chose their own names, he taking for himself Kemal Atatürk (Father of the Turks).

Three of the main principles of his party were republicanism, nationalism and populism. These have held Turkey together in a way that has enabled it to raise from the ruins of the sprawling Ottoman Empire a compact modern state that has successfully bridged Asia and Europe in pursuit of nationalism without irre-dentism. A state that has assiduously followed Atatürk's precept that it must look to 'Western civilization' — Europe — for its future. And it was essentially his achievement that the jubilee marked. Yet in my years in the post I was sometimes to wonder about the continued homage to him. That he was a remarkable man there is no doubt. He had the charisma, the strength and the purpose to show the way. But it is the generations since then, following that way — and making deviations where necessary — that have brought the country to its place in the twentieth century. It would have been conceivable for the adulation of the man to have diminished over the years without disrespect to his memory. But fear of showing such disrespect is strong among Turks, par-ticularly among politicians looking for popular support. Neglect of the principles of Kemalism can be a convenient taunt of any faction by its rival, observance of them a handy pretext for excesses.

Yet Turkey today is surely the better for these principles, above all in its adherence to one of the most important developments arising out of them, though not a creation of Atatürk himself: parliamentary democracy. If this is not strictly in the style of Westminster it is nonetheless workable. And, given the autocracy of Atatürk and the absolute despotism of the sultans for nearly 500 years before him, it is remarkable that it has come to exist at all. 'HOW HAPPY IS THE MAN WHO SAYS HE IS A TURK.' This is still, on many public buildings, the most often reproduced of Atatürk's many aphorisms exhorting the people of the new republic to a sense of nationhood. And the jubilee, restrained and comparatively unextravagant, brought out the nation's pride in itself.

For myself the high point of the celebrations was the President's opening of the slender suspension bridge across the Bosphorus. British-designed, British–German-built and partly financed by British aid, it is a beautiful structure joining Europe and Asia and, far from spoiling the environment (as was feared by many), it actually embellishes it. For the 100,000 people who walked and danced on it from both sides in the first hour (their vibrations requiring it to be closed until they were cleared off) it was perhaps more of a magnificent viewpoint than a symbol of the country's progress. But to everyone it was a historic occasion; and it seemed quite natural that three sheep should be sacrificed as the president cut the ribbon. Turkey was straining forward into Europe, but still with many a backward glance.

In the official speeches I had wished for more than a meagre reference to the British part in the project, and I ventured to say so to the officiating minister after the ceremony. To this, his bantering reply was that had the bridge fallen down when it was opened there would have been plenty of people only too ready to call it a British bridge: so let its excellence bespeak its origin.

For the rest, the jubilee was celebrated with the standard parades and receptions. There was a VIP cruise on the Bosphorus in the 6000-ton presidential yacht. (Hitler had to withdraw his bid to buy this yacht in 1937 when the Turkey he was then wooing decided to keep it as a floating convalescent home for the ailing Atatürk, who died at the end of the following year.) The State Theatre staged classical Western as well as Turkish ballet, which Dame Ninette de Valois came out from London to direct in celebration of her own 25 years of nurturing the company since, at Atatürk's invitation, she had founded it. If the logistical arrangements for handling the couple of hundred distinguished foreign delegates perhaps lacked Whitehall precision, and the location of individuals did not always coincide with that of their car, aeroplane or baggage, the helpful young foreign ministry escorts were generally able to reduce the occasional shambles to tolerable proportions. Most people agreed that, given the authorities' limited resources and experience, they did their guests rather well.

There was for me a satisfactory by-product of the jubilee. Before coming out to Ankara I had been briefed on the case of a young British teenager jailed in Istanbul after conviction on a drugs charge. He had in fact been used as a courier by his mother, with whom he had arrived in the country in a caravan. In view of the circumstances, and his age, I had made representations to the authorities for his release. And the consul in Istanbul had been visiting him and working energetically on his case. But nothing seemed to be moving. Then suddenly we were informed that a request we had made for him to be included among prisoners to be amnestied on the occasion of the jubilee had been granted. He was released into the custody of the consul, who lost no time in restoring him to his mother and making sure that they both got out of Turkey without delay.

* * *

The month after these celebrations I was back in London for a short time with my wife for what was the high point in my life. In April 1973, shortly after taking up the Ankara appointment, I was informed by the Foreign Secretary that it was proposed to recommend me to the Queen for a knighthood as Knight Commander of the Order of St Michael and St George (KCMG); and would I accept this? I had of course no hesitation in saying yes. When earlier I had presented my credentials to the president of Turkey, the London *Daily Express* gossip columnist (William Hickey) speculated that it would hardly delight the 'title-conscious' Turks to receive a 'plain mister' for the first time, every previous ambassador since William Harborne, appointed by Elizabeth I in 1583, having been a knight. The column, however, did not follow this up when my award was eventually announced in June 1973. In November I was received at Buckingham Palace for investiture.

123

15

Coup in Cyprus–Turkish Intervention–Visit to Israel

Throughout my years in Ankara I frequently found myself, as representative of a NATO country, drawn into ongoing disputes between Turkey and Greece, both of them also members of that organization. The Turkish government was at pains to keep me informed of its attitude on the various issues with a view to gaining the support of London. This was an approach which often put Britain in an invidious position, given our desire to maintain good relations in Athens as well as Ankara. The two countries have remained on speaking terms varying from affable to cool, but their disputes have seemed intractable — a legacy of the historical ill will and mistrust between them. Greeks are taught never to forget the nearly 400 years of Ottoman Turkish rule over them from the middle of the fifteenth century until they won their independence by arms in 1830; or the rout of the Greeks in Turkey by Atatürk in the 1920s when many were massacred in what was then Smyrna (now Izmir).

Against this background it took little to arouse the sensitivities of the two states in the Aegean Sea, with disputes, claims and counter-claims over militarization of offshore islands, delimitation of territorial waters, demarcation of the continental shelf, exploration for oil, sovereignty over air space. In parallel, the mutual antipathy of the Greek and Turkish communities in Cyprus had developed into hostility, the two sides looking to Athens and Ankara respectively for support.

In the sixteenth century the population of Cyprus was largely Greek. Then the Ottoman sultanate, at the height of its imperial power, captured and held it for 300 years. As a result there was an inflow of Turks, who eventually made up something under a fifth of the population. In 1878 the sultanate, now in decline and fearful of aggression by the Russians, handed over administration of the island to the British in return for help against the latter. This gave Britain a base for defence of her vast eastern interests, particularly the route to India. The outbreak of the First World War made this vital, and London annexed the island. After the war Turkey formally recognized this situation, and in 1924 Cyprus was declared a British colony.

Greece, however, consistently opposed this and encouraged the Greek Cypriots to press for *enosis* — union with Greece. This led to riots and terrorism against the British in Cyprus before and after the Second World War. By this time the head of the Orthodox Church there, Archbishop Makarios, had come to prominence as champion of *enosis*. Negotiations opened by him with the British for self-determination came to nothing because of his refusal to accept limited self-government as a first stage. In 1956 Britain exiled him to the Seychelles for a year.

Meantime the Turkish Cypriots, fearing the possibility of union of the island with Greece, were pressing for partition of it between the two communities. This alarmed Makarios, when he came back, into dropping his campaign for union. On the strength of this, independence within the British Commonwealth, with Makarios as president, was conceded to Cyprus by Britain in 1960 at a meeting in Zurich of representatives of Britain, Greece, Turkey and the Greek and Turkish Cypriot communities. Government and administration were to be shared by the latter in the proportion of 70 to 30. Greece and Turkey were given the right to station a small number of metropolitan troops. And it was acknowledged that Britain could retain the two sovereign military bases of Akrotiri and Dhekelia.

A constitution that assumed cooperation between two races so different in ethnic origin, religion and language, and so divided by centuries of mutual opposition, had little chance of success unless they willed it with conscious effort. It was soon evident that the

125

trust needed for this was lacking; and intercommunity rioting broke out. In 1963 President Makarios prepared measures which would have reduced the Turkish community's constitutional share of 30 per cent in government, on the grounds that it comprised less than 20 per cent of the total population. The fierce hostility of the Turks to this brought on violent reaction by the Greek community to the point where it became impossible for the Turks to go on participating at all in government and they were forced to concentrate in enclaves on the island monitored by UN peace-keeping forces.

By this time Makarios had enjoyed leadership of an independent Cyprus for rather more than three years and no longer aspired to union with Greece. His aim now was a unitary state in which the Turks would be simply a second-class minority. As the dominant figure, and with no longer any Turkish presence in parliament in Nicosia, he seemed well set in that direction. But if Makarios had shelved *enosis*, the colonels who had taken over Greece in 1967 had not. Within a few years the junta in Athens, needing a distraction from its domestic problems, saw the possibilities in the popular concept of annexation of Cyprus. And if it was to implement this it had to do so before the archbishop got too big for his boots.

Accordingly, on 15 July 1974, on the instructions of the junta, Nikos Sampson, the leader of the former anti-British Cypriot guerrilla movement (EOKA), figureheaded a coup by which he replaced Makarios, who fled to Britain. The coup, carried out by the commander of the Greek Cypriot National guard with the help of Greek officers sent from Athens, was to be the prelude to the union of Cyprus with Greece. It precipitated the most serious crisis in my years in Ankara. But I was not there at the time. I had driven to Izmir a few days before and taken the car ferry to Venice, from where I was driving to London on leave. I was in Monte Carlo when I heard the news of the coup and immediately phoned the Foreign Office, which instructed me to fly back to Ankara at once. This I did on the 17th, leaving my car with the British consul-general in Nice. When I arrived in Ankara I found that the government had reacted immediately to forestall Greek annexation of Cyprus with its predictable consequences for the Turkish community there and for Turkey's own defence strategy.

Ecevit the prime minister made it known that Turkey would invoke the 1960 Treaty of Guarantee, which assured the independence, integrity and security of Cyprus. This provided for joint action by Britain, Greece and Turkey to implement the guarantee, or by any one or two of them if all three could not agree. Clearly Greece could now be ruled out. Accordingly, Ecevit called me in to tell me that he proposed to ask the British government to join with Turkey in reversing the coup by force and restoring the constitution. I told him that while the government would understand his motive in the context of the treaty I doubted whether it would feel able to meet his request. For one thing, there were thousands of British troops and civilians and their families on the island who would be put in danger. And for another, relations between NATO allies Greece and Turkey were already in a tense state, which could only be exacerbated if Britain as a leading member of NATO now entered the lists.

* * *

While regretting this, Ecevit appreciated it; but he felt nevertheless that he must go by the letter of the treaty and consult with Britain as the only other valid guarantor. He therefore flew to London on 17 July with his foreign minister Turan Güneş to meet Prime Minister Harold Wilson and Foreign Secretary James Callaghan, whom I advised of the visit and of what I had told Ecevit. They said much the same thing to him and he returned to Ankara empty-handed 24 hours later. It was a disappointment for him, but not unexpected; and it left his government legitimately free to fall back on the provision in the treaty for unilateral action by any one guarantor to restore the constitution. The question now was whether, and if so how, Turkey would act.

It was not long before there was an answer to this, when a Turkish naval force sailed south from the southern port of Mersia. In the early hours of 20 July I was instructed by the foreign secretary to raise this with the Turkish foreign minister and ask him what orders had been given to the force. He replied that none had been given. Though it was a reply that was difficult to believe, at two o'clock in the morning he presumably considered it was plausible enough to fend us off, for the time being at any rate. But whether he had been dissembling, or whether orders were not in fact issued until later, things changed within the next few hours. At dawn the force was approaching the north of Cyprus. Troops landed around Kyrenia, the main town on that coast, and quickly secured a narrow bridgehead.

The first reaction to this in Athens came a few hours after the event, when the junta (still in power) announced that it was not willing to accept a British proposal that the three guarantors of the constitution and integrity of Cyprus should meet. The junta then went on to state that it was the intention of Greece to declare war on Turkey if its troops did not pull out. The junta's threat of war was withdrawn later in the day; but on the night of 21/22 July 14 planes carrying Greek commandos were sent to seize Nicosia airport (and the British government protested to the Greek at the violation of the Akrotiri sovereign base air corridor involved). Of these, 12 landed safely and off-loaded 200 troops and unspecified stores, one was destroyed, and one damaged. Seven of the 12 undamaged ones subsequently took off, and there were five still there next morning. Having at first refused, the junta followed the Turks and accepted a cease-fire on the 22nd. Next day it resigned and its puppet fled from Cyprus.

It had already been decided in London that on the 22nd the sizeable British community in the north of Cyprus should be taken off the island. They were advised in a Foreign Office message on the BBC World Service to assemble at a designated time on a beach a few miles along from Kyrenia, to be taken off by two Royal Navy ships. In the middle of the night I was instructed by the foreign secretary to see the Turkish prime minister and, if possible, the chief of the defence staff, inform them of this operation a few hours later, and get their assurance that all Turkish naval, air and land forces in the area would be alerted to it so that there would be no unfortunate mistake over identification of the vessels.

When I went, with a guard from the prime ministry, to Ecevit's apartment in town, the door was opened by his wife, obviously just wakened, who knew me. Gently cutting short my apologies, she said she realized that only an urgent matter of the highest importance could have brought me at that time of night. When she told me that her husband was asleep, having got home from his office only a couple of hours before, I offered to wait a while. But she insisted that he would be upset if he woke up to find that I had been waiting to see him: for he knew that I was as preoccupied over Cyprus as he was. She invited me in and went to rouse him. After a short time Ecevit appeared, wide awake, freshly dressed and spruce; he greeted me affably and assured me there was no need for apologies at so critical a juncture for our two governments. He perfectly understood London's concern over the evacuation of its citizens; and lifted the phone there and then to waken the chief of defence staff and ask him to instruct all Turkish units in the area appropriately. Ecevit got his assurance, which I passed on at once to the Foreign Office, and the evacuation was accomplished without incident.

His ready reception of my approach without notice at such an hour was typical of the man, whom I had always found friendly and cooperative — and an ardent discusser of poetry (which he himself wrote). My relationship with him stood me in good stead, and he invariably discussed problems frankly. In the course of one conversation later he told me there had for some years been a strong body of opinion in and outside his own party that the Turkish government should take some positive action, even to the extent of force, to relieve the wretched situation of the Turkish Cypriots under the heel of Makarios and the Greek community.

He had stood out against this idea and argued for continuing along the avenue of negotiation, long though it might be. Now, however, the danger of Greek annexation of Cyprus, and Turkey's intervention to remove that danger, provided an opportunity to relieve the pressure on the Turkish community there and secure an area where they could live their own lives in peace — albeit at the cost of ongoing failure to establish a *modus vivendi* between the two communities.

On the fall of the military junta in Athens, Karamanlis, the respected elder statesman, formed a democratic government and agreed to attend the meeting of three guarantor powers proposed by Britain but which had been rejected by the junta. On 25 July the foreign ministers of Britain (James Callaghan), Greece and

Turkey met in Geneva, while in the background Kissinger exerted diplomatic pressure on the government in Ankara. Greece was represented by its new foreign minister, Mavros, a liberal-minded democrat. He was anxious to come to some agreement with Turkey and he acknowledged that the position of the Turkish Cypriots should be assured, possibly by a change in the constitution — which was Britain's preference. Some progress was made at the meeting towards stabilizing the cease-fire and planning a UN buffer zone across the island, but the Turkish side in particular showed little desire to compromise and the meeting adjourned without any agreement.

It reconvened on 9 August, this time with the leaders of the Greek and Turkish communities on the island also attending. Personal relations between the two were good, but mutual recrimination between Athens and Ankara, and their fear of appearing to climb down, soured the atmosphere. On the Greek side again there was acceptance in principle of the need to change the Cyprus constitution in a way that would protect the Turks there. But any change would have to be made by the two communities themselves. It was open to Turkey, with the other two guarantors, to contribute to any revision if Cyprus so requested. But Greece was adamant that it was not for Turkey to impose any kind of solution simply by invading then dictating.

The Greek foreign minister and the Greek Cypriot leader were prepared to consider a British proposal for a federal state consisting of two autonomous regions, provided the boundaries of these could be agreed. But Güneş, the Turkish foreign minister, insisted obstinately on an immediate reply to his demand for Greek acceptance that the northern 35 per cent of the island should be put under Turkish Cypriot administration — failing which he would leave Geneva. Which he did in the early hours of 14 July, flouncing out gracelessly — since obviously the Greeks were not going to yield to such an ultimatum. A few hours later the second Turkish offensive in Cyprus began.

Conscious of the narrowness of the Kyrenia bridgehead in the event of a Greek counter-offensive, the Turkish army resumed its advance across the north until, by the time a definitive cease-fire was agreed in the middle of August, it was in control of the 35 per cent it wanted. (A British House of Commons Select Committee of Enquiry in 1975, before which I had to appear in Athens — the Turkish government having refused to let it come to Ankara — put it on record that a second phase of military operations was inevitable because the position reached by the Turkish forces at the time of the first cease-fire, on 22 July, was untenable against attack. One of the members of the committee was Mrs Lena (later Lady) Jeger, Labour MP for Camden, which she told me included many Greek Cypriots.

The new Greek government was all for declaring war on Turkey, but Karamanlis was resigned to the fact that Greece would be no match for it, and the idea of war was abandoned. Britain had already declined to take military action to help the Turks, or to allow the two British sovereign base areas on the island to be used for this purpose. Karamanlis now held that NATO and the Americans were also apathetic towards the Turkish aggression. In protest at this he withdrew the Greek armed forces from the NATO command structure (though not out of the organization as a whole) — a move not reversed until 1981, largely on persuasion by the Turkish generals then governing in Ankara. He also called into question the presence of US defence installations in Greece, and turned down an invitation to Washington to meet President Ford on his installation. Karamanlis declared that his government would make its views known emphatically at the United Nations, and in the European Community as an associate member; and he would do all he could to enlist the help of these bodies in reaching a settlement of the Cyprus dispute. Britain had tried to close the gap between Greeks and Turks, but it was altogether too wide — the legacy of nearly 400 years of Ottoman domination and unbridgeable ethnic and cultural differences.

It had seemed to me, knowing the strength of Ankara's concern to maintain a presence in Cyprus, that the Geneva talks had little chance of success. It said much for James Callaghan the foreign secretary that he nevertheless tried all he could to get something positive out of them. The intrinsic difficulties were probably insurmountable in any case. But by the end of the proceedings the humourless and rigid attitude of Güneş had exasperated the genial and reasonable Callaghan to the limit of tolerance.

Yet this is not to say that the latter lacked sympathy for the Turks at the human level. During the fighting a considerable number of Turkish Cypriot civilians had taken refuge in the British sovereign base at Akrotiri, in the southwest of the island. Athens was pressing for them to be handed over to the Greek Cypriot authorities. I was able to persuade the Foreign Office that this was an obviously undesirable step sure to arouse strong anti-British feeling in Turkey; and I suggested that the foreign secretary might think it worthwhile, in the course of a planned official visit to the Persian Gulf, calling in at Akrotiri to see things for himself. This he did, and immediately decided that the refugees should be flown to Turkey. The praise that was given to me in the Turkish press for having secured this outcome (praise that properly belonged to Callaghan) was a welcome contribution to an improvement in Anglo-Turkish relations, fragile at that time.

During the fighting the Turkish authorities had informed the American ambassador and myself that they had reason to believe that a Greek destroyer was sailing towards Paphos on the west coast of Cyprus, and that we should inform the Greeks of the serious consequences of this. At a meeting in his embassy in the middle of the night the American and I sent messages to our respective ambassador colleagues in Athens and asked them to get the authorities there to clarify the position. The latter replied quickly to the allegation, asserting that there was no truth in it: no Greek warships were moving into Cyprus waters. When we passed this on to the Turks they were not convinced, and they remained so even after the Greeks had again given us a denial.

The affair had a hardly credible aftermath some days later when I received a message from the British ambassador in Tel Aviv. He reported that the authorities there had informed him that an Israeli training ship in international waters off Cyprus had picked up a number of Turkish sailors out of the sea. They had been landed at Haifa and taken to hospital; and the authorities wanted to know what to do with them. I reported this to the prime minister in Ankara and asked him; he undertook to arrange for the sailors to be repatriated. In answer to my obvious question he embarrassedly told me in confidence that Turkish aircraft had sunk one of their own destroyers off the coast of Cyprus. This, he said, had not yet been made public; but at an opportune moment it would be — as indeed it was some weeks later.

I refrained from reminding Ecevit (if indeed he ever knew anything about it from his defence staff) of the exchanges between the American ambassador and myself and our colleagues in Athens over the Turkish allegation during the crisis that a Greek warship was sailing towards Cyprus. I learned later that the Turkish destroyer that was sunk was a second-hand vessel that had just been taken delivery of and was not yet equipped for Turkish air-to-sea recognition procedures. It therefore did not receive the repeated requests for identification sent out by the Turkish aircraft that spotted it; and the latter, getting no reply, took it to be a Greek ship flying the Turkish ensign for deception, and sank it.

At the end of 1974 Makarios returned to Cyprus as president (dying in 1977) and intercommunity talks began soon after. It might have been expected that the Turkish troops would then have been withdrawn. But withdrawal without a settlement could have exposed the Turkish Cypriots to a Greek community even more hostile than before. Meantime a UN peacekeeping force was introduced into a buffer zone that was established between what was now the wholly Turkish northern part of the island, secured by the Turkish army, and the bigger Greek southern part.

Mutual distrust between Greek and Turkish Cypriots, though by no means universal, was the legacy of the wide difference in race, religion and culture — exacerbated by the attitudes of Athens and Ankara, particularly over their rivalry and suspicion in the Aegean. There was in fact no ground for the Greeks to suspect that the Turks were plotting to expand their hold on Cyprus beyond the north–south buffer zone, or for the Turks to fear a renewal of the threat by the Greek government to annex the island.

The two communities in Cyprus, backed by Athens and Ankara respectively, could not agree on a basis for coexistence, despite attempts at negotiation. Some of these were more promising than others, but the Turkish community was feeling more and more the need to establish some sort of constitutional basis for itself in the absence of an overall settlement; and in 1983 it set up what it calls the Turkish Republic of Northern Cyprus. The TRNC has not, however, received international recognition, which is accorded only to what is known simply as Cyprus, in effect the Greek southern part of the island. But the TRNC does have a resident representative in London. As one of the three guarantors of the constitution of the island, Britain had a leading part in the attempts to reach a settlement, and much of my time was taken up with this. But by the time I left there was still no meaningful progress; and, caught between the Turkish and Greek governments, we frequently came under fierce criticism from each for what it saw as our failure to support its case against the other.

The foreign ministry in Ankara made representations to me several times about the British press describing the Turkish action in Cyprus as an invasion. I myself always referred to it in communications to London as an intervention, and pressed the Foreign Office to do the same. For that is precisely what it was: Turkey intervened under the terms of the Zurich treaty to redress the situation caused by the overthrow of Makarios and the threat from Athens — taking the opportunity at the same time to relieve Greek Cypriot pressure on the Turkish Cypriots. Unfortunately Ankara did not make the strength of its case widely enough known internationally and Athens exploited this failure. Greek lobbying in Washington also worked against Turkey, resulting in an American arms embargo against it. This lasted for three years, not only weakening the Turkish armed forces (after the American, the strongest in NATO) but damaging Turkish confidence in the United States. And confidence was further shaken by growing bias against Turkey and support for Greece in the US Congress. In retaliation, Ankara declared its defence cooperation agreement with Washington to be invalid and took control of virtually all American military installations in Turkey, including electronic surveillance stations monitoring Soviet military activity across the Black Sea. It was only after long and acrimonious negotiations that the situation was restored on the basis of a new agreement.

Turkey is on the Council of Europe and is an associate member of the European Union. The European Commission has conceded its right to become a full member, but this does not seem likely to be implemented for years yet. Already during my time in Ankara there was a strong bias in the Commission against Turkey on economic and political grounds. Economically, the country was suffering inflation of around 70 per cent a year and had a lower average annual income than Portugal, the poorest member of the European Union. Politically, the occasional periods of military government (albeit temporary) to end violence on the streets brought on by lack of control by the political parties and the sporadic violations of human rights by law enforcement authorities acting outside the writ of central government raised cries of protest from the human rights lobby among the socialists in the European Parliament.

This situation was exploited by Greece, which in the context of its own relations with Turkey continually blocked any move towards the admission of that country as a full member of the Union. While Turks were resigned to this political fact of life, they at the same time assumed that there was a strong body of opinion in the Union against having a Muslim country as a member. Their bitterness at this was all the greater when they reflected that Christian Europe was anxious enough to add Turkey's military strength to NATO at a critical stage of the Cold War and was ready enough to use it in Korea, but when it came to membership of the European Union, Turkey was apparently not good enough for Europe.

Besides carrying out a wide range of duties in Ankara involving contact with the government, and paying official calls on governors of many provinces, near and distant, my wife and I were hosts to a constant stream of British ministers and officials and other personalities, many on business connected with NATO, CENTO and the European Union, besides Anglo-Turkish relations. And I paid regular visits to Istanbul, commercial and industrial centre of the country, to keep in touch with the leading Turkish men of affairs and the several hundred members of the British business community (bigger than in Ankara). It was useful for the British to hear something from me about the political and economic situation in Turkey, particularly insofar as it might affect commercial relations with Britain; and for me to hear the views and complaints of the community. On these visits my wife and I stayed in the apartment furnished and reserved for the ambassador, and

135

big enough for entertaining, in the magnificent former embassy building there. Elsewhere in the country there was a consulate in Izmir, on the Aegean coast, which I visited for the same purposes as in Istanbul but less often.

In my first three years I also went to Gallipoli in April for the ANZAC remembrance ceremonies, attended by Turkish as well as Allied military delegations. They were moving occasions, held at each of the various war memorials on the peninsula in turn. But I always found the most impressive site to be Atatürk's command post, still preserved, a dugout on high ground from which murderous fire cut down the Australian, New Zealand and British troops pouring across the beach below in a vain attempt to reach the heights. A handful of survivors still came out each year from Australia and New Zealand in an organized party. They were 80 years old and more, some of them very infirm; and it seemed to me in 1975, 60 years on, that it was perhaps time to call a halt to these official annual ceremonies. This was agreed by all parties concerned, though we made it clear that this of course did not rule out unofficial ceremonies in future years organized by ex-servicemen's associations.

In the cold snowbound January of 1977 I had to pay a visit much further afield — to the far eastern province of the country near the border with Iran, historically vulnerable to tremors, which had been hit by a disastrous earthquake. Britain and the United States were major contributors of relief supplies, and the Turkish prime minister invited me and my American colleague to go to the devastated area to inspect the damage and see how our countries' help was being used. A military plane flew us to Van, where we changed to an army helicopter for the frightening flight into the mountains under deep snow where the disaster had struck. It was good to see survivors fairly comfortable in tents with a Greenock manufacturing company's name on them and warmed by oil stoves from the Midlands. British food supplies were also around. There was no doubt that all the material sent out — American as well as British — was accounted for and being put to good use. And it was gratifying to hear words of appreciation from the victims. It made our difficult journey worthwhile.

A few months later, early in May 1977, I had to go to Tehran (and my wife came with me) for the annual meeting of the foreign ministers of CENTO, in the course of which we were all received by the Shah. My mind went back to past meetings with him when I was counsellor at the embassy in the early 1960s; and further back still to the late 1940s when I was consul at Shiraz in the south of the country, my first post in the diplomatic service. Now I was on my last official visit to Persia, where my wife and I had spent happy years. The violent revolution, which less than two years later was to sweep away all we had known of the country, could not have been foreseen.

The CENTO meeting gave me an opportunity to meet Dr David Owen who three months earlier, at the age of 38, had been appointed foreign secretary. My wife and I found him and his American wife, a literary agent, a delightful couple; they were friendly, intelligent and easy to talk to. I regretted that, with retirement only a few weeks away, I was not going to have the pleasure of working under him. In later years I heard stories of how difficult he was at times in his dealings with officials in the Foreign Office. I of course had no way of knowing, and could not vouch for this; I personally have retained that first favourable impression of him.

Shortly before we met, a review of overseas representation by the Central Policy Review Staff (the cabinet think-tank), chaired by Sir Kenneth Berrill, had been published officially. Some of the recommendations it contained seemed to me to be prompted by a desire to strip the diplomatic service of its special status and turn it into just another department of the home civil service. It was for example proposed, as an option, that the diplomatic service should be merged with the home civil service and a so-called foreign service group created in the new body to handle overseas affairs. The review recommended closing up to 55 posts abroad and withdrawing consular services from others. It was proposed that the British Council should be abolished and low priority given to the spread of British arts and culture and the English language. And much more.

Walking with Owen in the delightful Tehran embassy garden I knew so well, I told him I wanted to take advantage of my imminent retirement and allow myself to say frankly that I hoped he would not implement some of the recommendations in the Berrill Report. I conceded that there was room for improvement in the diplomatic service — and indeed the review did contain a great number of sensible recommendations on organization and procedure. But it seemed to me that the radical ideas in it, if put into practice, could only reduce the service to a run-of-the-mill body lacking in the expertise and professional pride that made it the envy of many other countries — not least, from my experience of 30 years, the United States. The foreign secretary heard me out and assured me that he had no intention of accepting the report in its entirety; he would examine it carefully, with special attention to the points I had mentioned. And the following year I was relieved and gratified to see that reflected in the White Paper analysing the report.

* * *

Back in Ankara, the pages of the calendar began to peel off too fast and I had to face the inevitable. In one's early years in the service retirement seems very remote indeed. Yet even in those years it can be foreseen, precise and inexorable — the sixtieth birthday; and I was approaching it. Shortly before, however, I had the unexpected opportunity of a last short break from official duties when I was invited by the captain of a visiting Royal Navy frigate to be his guest aboard on the short voyage to Haifa, where his ship would be on an official visit to the Israeli navy. With Foreign Office approval I accepted. My only previous experience of a naval vessel had been as a bedraggled soldier deck passenger in the evacuation from Dunkirk many years before. But this time I was in an officer's cabin, had the run of the ship and was given an insight into the techniques of navigation and enemy detection. I was full of admiration for the technical expertise of officers and crew.

After watching the exchange of courtesies at Haifa between the two navies I went ashore and hired a car in which I toured Israel widely, including a kibbutz where the daughter of one of my brothers had married and settled with a family some years before.

This was my first visit to the country and I could now see on the ground the development that I had heard so much about. What took me some time to absorb was the fact that although it is a Jewish state it is a secular state. That should not really have been so strange: after all, Turkey is a secular state, albeit a Muslim state. But somehow — emotionally, I suppose — I had expected there to be a stronger feeling of Judaism around me. I realized, however, that that belonged more to the diaspora, was something that bound together the Jewish communities scattered throughout the world and reminded them of their origins; whereas the Jews in Israel are now a nation and do not need the force of the diaspora to hold them together. What did bind them was the need to survive as a nation in the face of Arab hostility all around. But it is a hostility that can only be overcome by negotiation that recognizes and accepts the rights and requirements of both the Israelis and the Palestinians.

16

Retirement–Attributes of Ambassadors–Formulating Foreign Policy

O n my return to Ankara I was not looking forward to retirement; I felt I could have gone on for years yet. But I could console myself. I had been working one way or another, man and boy, in peace or war, for 43 years, since I was 17. My origins and background had stacked the cards against me in my effort to achieve the ambition I had held from an early age, but I had pegged away at it until I overcame the obstacles and got into the diplomatic service. I had looked forward to rising moderately high in this but where I actually ended up exceeded my expectations. I had of course never for a moment aspired to Grade 1, the dozen highest posts in the service: Paris, Rome, Washington, the UN, etc. But I was fourth in seniority in Grade 2, the major posts, which gave me a high final standing in the service as a whole.

In the 30 years it had taken to achieve this I had, quite exceptionally, served only two years in the Foreign Office itself, after which I had served abroad continuously for 25 years. With the exception of Tanzania (though even there there is a Muslim element) I had been moved from post to post in Muslim countries in the Middle East, plus Indonesia. Far from complaining, I had welcomed this as something that gave a pattern to my progress and enabled me to specialize. Nor did my wife complain; she supported me to the full in good times and bad, even though in the early days we might see our children only once a year on holiday from boarding school in Britain.

I could look back on my diplomatic career as more than just a way of earning a living. It was a way of life that had fulfilled all my aspirations and given me complete job satisfaction. Never boring, no two days alike, it was varied and stimulating, often difficult, occasionally hazardous; and not, as sometimes scathingly described by outsiders, a constant round of cocktail parties. To the prejudiced or uninformed, of course, diplomacy and diplomats have long been fair game for criticism. In the past there was the popular image of the ambassador as an 'urbane, glib and deceitful intriguer, so accomplished a liar that he can successfully confuse his rivals by occasionally telling them the truth'. It was a view that down through the years changed only in form, not in spirit — developing into the cynical image of an official more interested in the social round and his own career development than the nitty-gritty of the job.

Today such criticism is behind the times. True, in the past the Foreign Office guarded its exclusiveness by recruiting only from those circles it was then believed could provide the intelligence, erudition, personality — and private wealth — felt to be essential for a diplomat. It was an age when there was a tendency for relations between states to be handled by elegant ambassadors whose connection with their own ruling circles made them equal members in an intimate international coterie that could keep these relations smooth.

* * *

Today's world calls for a new type of diplomat. It is a type that has evolved steadily since the Second World War, with the emergence of dozens of new states and multinational bodies and groupings. The scope of diplomacy has widened enormously, and the ambassador of today is essentially a hard-working pragmatist, of intellectual ability and personal integrity, knowledgeable in many aspects of international affairs beyond merely diplomatic relations. Without these attributes he may fail not only to convince the foreign government of the case presented by his own, but to persuade the latter of the wisdom and accuracy of his advice to it. Although formulating foreign policy is a complex affair in which today more and more foreign ministers, prime ministers and heads of state take a direct hand by consulting with each other in person, this shuttle diplomacy does not, as is often alleged, reduce ambassadors to mere postmen passing communications to and from their governments.

Ministers may be clear about their foreign policy objectives but they cannot come to sensible decisions on these without knowing the politico-economic background of the countries they are dealing with, and the leading personalities in them. It remains the vital role of an ambassador and his staff, with their knowledge of the local scene, to collate that information and make it available to their foreign minister. But this in itself is not enough: it must be accompanied by the ambassador's advice and recommendations on the matter under consideration. His views, which may or may not be accepted, will be taken into account in the formulation of policy. True, the ultimate responsibility for the policy rests with the politicians, not the diplomats; and the latter are not to be blamed if it turns out wrong. But an ambassador shares the responsibility. If his advice turns out to be misleading, the government may fall into error. It is another matter if, for political reasons of its own, the government chooses to ignore advice that is sound.

If a recommendation of mine was queried in London I was generally given an opportunity to comment further before a final decision was taken. But if that was still contrary to any recommendation (as in the question of recognition of Idi Amin in 1971) I had nevertheless to accept it. If an ambassador is faced with a situation about which he feels strongly enough as a matter of conviction and cannot accept the Foreign Office decision, he has no alternative but to resign. This did happen over some major issues like Munich and Suez, but by and large it is a rare occurrence.

As multilateral organizations developed, an ambassador's advice to his government on a subject of common interest to members would generally reflect the views of his colleagues representing those members. On 1 January 1973, a month before I became ambassador at Ankara, Britain was finally admitted to the European Community, as it then was. All the 1957 founder members except Luxembourg had embassies in the capital and I was welcomed into their group. The ambassadors had for some time held regular meetings to exchange views on subjects of Community interest and on matters common to them in relations with Turkey. I was soon able to contribute to these meetings and as time went on found myself often consulted by the current Community presidency ambassador when a joint submission had to be made to the Turkish foreign ministry on some subject, since of all the Community members Britain tended to be the one in most contact with it.

I found that such submissions were not always quickly or smoothly agreed upon in Community capitals and that our current group coordinator (the six-monthly presidency representative) did not always, in my view, lobby his own foreign ministry vigorously enough. It did not take me long to assess the relative professional standards of my colleagues, and among them the French, Belgian and Dutch stood out.

Reciprocally, I would brief the group on meetings I might have had at the Turkish foreign ministry on subjects of bilateral concern that would be of interest to them. On occasion, the Turkish government would make representations to the group as a whole through the group coordinator of the moment. Turkish relations With Greece — on Cyprus and the Aegean — were high on the agenda. Turkey was still (since 1963) only an associate member of the European Community. I cannot recall any formal approach to us about advancement to full membership — although informal approaches were made to members separately from time to time. It was a blow to Turkish pride that in 1981 (by which time I had retired) Greece was admitted as a full member. In 1987 the Ankara government submitted a formal application for full membership — which was accepted by the European Commission but has so far not been implemented.

While I was ambassador most of the Turkish approaches to the local European Community group were made in parallel with bilateral representations to myself in connection with the ongoing disputes between Turkey and Greece, on which Ankara sought to

Envoy Extraordinary

win support for its point of view, particularly from Britain. Initially these mainly concerned the two countries' conflicting claims in, over and under the Aegean Sea: such things as territorial water limits, flight route control and information, oil exploration.

But by the middle of 1974, with the Turkish intervention in Cyprus and the danger of an all-out war between Greece and Turkey, the foreign ministry representations to the Community ambassadors grew in number and severity. As ambassador of the third country specified in the Cyprus independence treaty (with the two potential belligerents) as guarantors of the island's constitution, I was having a hard time at the foreign ministry, and was from time to time with the prime minister, Bülent Ecevit. These discussions, often late at night, had all to be relayed next day to my Community colleagues — a process that involved almost daily meetings of the group.

In such circumstances it is of course all too easy for an ambassador to be biased in favour of the government to which he is accredited. That I avoided this temptation in Ankara was shown by the often acrimonious discussions I had with Turkish officials from time to time and which I reported to the Foreign Office. But the latter for its part, it seemed to me, sometimes overdid its effort to be even-handed to both Greece and Turkey, with the result that justice was done to neither. It took a blatant action by one side or the other to get the Foreign Office to come out with a positive opinion. One such action was the proposal mooted by Greece to extend its territorial waters round its coasts and islands to the point where a Turkish vessel making for its home port of Izmir would have had to seek Greek permission to sail through the narrow channel between the Turkish coast and the offshore Greek island of Samos.

I was concerned at the seeming failure of the government and press in London to show understanding of the Turkish action in Cyprus in July 1974. This was too often labelled an invasion, and I spent much effort (not entirely successful) trying to show that it was in fact an intervention made legally under the provisions of the Cyprus independence treaty of 1960; an intervention to prevent Greece from taking control of the government of the island. In doing this I was not being partisan; I was stating a fact.

144

But it is a fact still often ignored; I had years later to protest to the BBC about a World Service programme on Cyprus that began by describing the July 1974 operation as an invasion designed to rescue the Turkish Cypriots from oppression by their Greek counterparts. The truth was that this rescue was simply a welcome by-product of the operation.

It is in the nature of things today that foreign policy will generally be dictated by party-political considerations as much as by the national interest. There are three main constraints on making foreign policy: it has to take account of domestic policies; it has to be shaped according to external circumstances over which the government may have no control; and it often requires prior consultation with other interested governments. Whether or not there is an expression of public opinion in Britain on a domestic issue, the foreign secretary may have to contend with arguments about it by other cabinet ministers that conflict with his own proposals. A move advocated by him to improve relations with a given country that has until then been at a standoff might be opposed by home departments that are engaged in a dispute with it over airline routes or fishing rights. More topically, the attitude of the British public to closer integration with Europe is a major factor in the government's relations with the European Union and member countries on a variety of matters, particularly where these entail the possibility of some additional financial burden on the people or a change in some aspect of their traditional way of life, such as doorstep milk deliveries or pulling pub beer in pints and not litres — two of the Union's favourite targets for reform.

The Foreign Office has less contact with the people than the domestic departments, which impinge more on their day-to-day lives. Inevitably the public cannot be expected to have a clear view or full understanding of the government's foreign policies. Nor indeed may it have any great interest in them unless they seem to impinge on public rights, or sentiment, or national pride, or sovereignty — as in the cases of European union, the Falklands, the Gulf War and immigration. So far as the general public thinks about it at all, foreign policy is just another item on the agenda of government, like education or the health service, and is handled in the same way as these are.

The Foreign Office is seen as a department of state like any other. But when it comes under public scrutiny in some international crisis, and remains silent, people criticize it as elitist and secretive, and resent not knowing much about its role. They do not appreciate that by its very nature it seeks to avoid publicity and not disclose details of a negotiating process until this has at least reached a stage where there is some concrete proposal in shape. Delicate negotiations are not likely to survive a blow-by-blow account in public of discussions that may involve sensitive concessions. The more crucial and pressing the issue, the more likely the parties to it are to bring into discussion matters touching their national prestige and world image, matters which cannot be revealed to their public at that stage.

Notwithstanding the broadening of the base of the diplomatic service over the past 40 years, the British public still tends to regard it as very much a closed shop. Criticism of it, tinged with envy, is often more emotional than rational and, as such, can spread quickly, particularly at times of national stress and when exploited by news media and politicians to promote their own policies on the issue in question. In my various posts I was always ready to receive visiting press correspondents and brief them within the limits of confidentiality — or even beyond when I knew I could trust them with a non-attributive statement. I felt that, quite apart from their intrinsic value, such meetings were good for the image of the diplomatic service.

Nevertheless, the British press — quality papers among them — too often castigate the Foreign Office for what they regard as its failure in some aspect of foreign policy. It may be alleged that the Foreign Office did not foresee critical events, or, if it did, failed to take action to protect the British interests involved in them. The impression given by the critics is that the diplomats there and in the field are ignorant or incompetent, or both; that they misjudge the significance of events; and that they fail to give due warning of a deteriorating situation. In short, they spend more time on the cocktail round than on business.

Something I recall reading with sadness and anger after I had retired was a leader in *The Times* in April 1984. It blamed the diplomatic service for not taking action against Libya to pre-empt the firing from its embassy in St James's Square in London into a crowd of Libyan opposition protesters, in which one of the shots killed an unfortunate young woman police officer. In tones reminiscent of its century-old nickname, the Thunderer demanded to know why Foreign Office timorousness had allowed the Libyan mission to continue operating when some time ago its true nature was known; whether it was true that the mission had received instructions in cipher from Gaddafi to use force against demonstrators in front of the building; and, if so, what was in that message and was it acted on by the British authorities in time to take precautions against the shooting? And, in effect, why was the Foreign Office as flabby as it was anyway? The Foreign Office, the leader went on, was in many respects a firm within a firm. It had a built-in disposition to avoid a critical appraisal of what lay at the end of a line of diplomacy, regarding diplomacy as an end in itself. It would keep talking with people at all costs, whoever the people were and almost whatever their behaviour. Its role in the making of policy over Libya deserved thorough enquiry.

I found it hard to believe that such questions were genuinely designed to elicit replies for the public good. For one thing, to expect disclosure of anything on the subject of cipher messages — supposing there had been any — was naïve in the extreme. In making its criticisms how could the paper know that information from the British embassy in Libya and from other sources might have been analysed in the Foreign Office? Or whether on the strength of that the government might not have been considering breaking diplomatic relations with Libya at that time and so closing down the embassy? Clearly the whole matter was one for decision by the politicians; but *The Times* chose to ignore that fact and blame the diplomats. In so doing it of course influenced public opinion, which too easily believes what it reads where criticism of the Foreign Office is concerned.

In the last analysis the foreign policy decided upon by the politicians will reflect what the government considers to be in the national interest, at home and abroad, at that time. The decision may be known to be dubious and eventually turn out to have been short-sighted; but if it is believed to be of immediate advantage it will prevail in the cabinet even if dangers are foreseen in it by the foreign secretary and the ambassadors concerned and they argue against it. An example of this was Britain's precipitate recognition of Idi Amin, against my advice, after he overthrew Obote and declared himself life-president of Uganda. Less serious because gradually reversed, but another instance of this failing, was London's disinclination to accept the opinion I gave in 1960, as counsellor at the embassy in Tehran, that the Organization of Petroleum Exporting Countries had come to stay. The initial disparaging British attitude to it was almost certainly a factor that provoked the Shah and other members of it to dig their heels in in subsequent negotiations with the Western oil companies.

In another field I was dismayed at the decisions in London, before and after I retired, to put the sale of arms overseas (euphemistically, defence sales) at the top of the export promotion activities of embassies — a policy pursued vigorously by the then Mrs Thatcher in particular, whom *The Times* described as being 'not too choosy' about the destination of British arms exports, believing that if Britain adopted a moral stance other arms exporters would exploit the gap. Armed forces attachés at the British embassies involved were reinforced by a senior officer whose sole job virtually this was. I could understand the domestic political advantages: each new contract could be broadcast in the British press as saving so many thousands of jobs for so many years quite apart from what it earned. But what I disliked about the policy was the seemingly indiscriminate spread of these exports.

To those of us who knew Iran, for example, it was difficult to see why the Shah needed such enormous purchases of military equipment, and why Britain should have encouraged him. They were bought at a time when the country's rapidly growing oil revenue made it possible. But the money spent on arms could well have been put towards further improvement in the standard of living of the ordinary Persian, particularly in the countryside. True, the Shah did apply much of the oil revenue to that purpose — but there was still a wide gap between the rich and the poor.

In the event, the arms were a godsend to the Khomeini regime in its long war with Iraq in the 1980s. But in the Shah's time it could only be assumed that he had two things in mind: ambition to be the successor to Britain when it eventually pulled out completely from the Persian Gulf, and concern about the possibility of an internal uprising. Added to which there was certainly an element of self-aggrandisement. But be all that as it may, many Iranians believed that the autocratic rule he imposed on them was supported by Britain (and the United States) by their extensive supply of arms to him.

A similar argument could have been made some years later in the case of the Iraqi dictator Saddam Hussein, who was able to buy equipment from Britain which, it later transpired, the relevant government departments in London knew could be put to military use — notwithstanding Iraq's assertion to the contrary. And recently it has been said in London with satisfaction that Saudi Arabia and the smaller states in the Persian Gulf are becoming the most lucrative markets for arms exports.

Looking back, I never did discover whether the report going round Dar es Salaam in the summer of 1970, when I was high commissioner there, about an impending decision by Edward Heath's new Conservative government to sell arms to South Africa, which caused President Nyerere of Tanzania to threaten to take his country out of the Commonwealth, would eventually have been translated into fact, or whether my warning that the possible Africa-wide consequences of this would be against Britain's interests eventually influenced the government against any such decision. What is certain is that the prime minister's eventual denial of it to Nyerere did not come easily. This may have been because, understandably, Mr Heath felt that a denial conveyed through his foreign secretary Sir Alec Douglas-Home should have satisfied the president.

Diplomats, for their part, are expected to show interest in the countries in which they serve; indeed a foreign office will generally avoid posting a man to a place where it is known he would be unsuited. But it is equally undesirable for him to identify himself too closely with any one country. It is often alleged that British diplomats are pro-this or pro-that, allegations directed particularly at the Arabists, the 'old China hands' and the Eurosceptics. It is, however, only to be expected that diplomats should bring their specialist knowledge to bear on the situations they have to assess — as in any profession. And they would not be human if at times

149

preferences and prejudices did not show through. But judged fairly, officials can generally be seen to come up with advice and recommendations they regard as being in the best interests of their own state. It is not for them to modify their views because these do not suit the party in power. That is the job of the politicians. If the diplomat's advice is wrong and ministers act on it, or if it is right and they do not, he is in the front line of public attack. He is the target — even though the wrong one. He is hard put to win. And he is hard put to answer back. It was not until shortly after I retired at the end of May 1977 that I could refute publicly, in the correspondence columns of the *Daily Telegraph*, the allegation in a report by the Select Committee on Overseas Development that the training of diplomatic service officers for commercial posts abroad was 'derisory'.

I cannot recall any businessman who called on me or my commercial staff for local guidance complaining that we were not competent to give it because we had had only four, or six, or two weeks' training (or perhaps none) on commercial work. But I can recall thanks and sometimes compliments from British firms. To whatever commercial training a diplomatic service officer is given he quickly adds on-the-job knowledge and experience that enable him to understand the relevant terms and procedures (what the Select Committee calls 'technical literacy' — some would say jargon) and have intelligent and helpful discussions with local officials and visiting British businessmen.

These businessmen do not expect the commercial officer to have 'marketing qualifications': that is their own stock in trade. What they look for in an embassy or consulate is reliable advice from someone who has enough general understanding of commercial affairs to relate these to the local politico-economic situation (they want to know the background against which they have to operate). They are also looking for someone to guide them through the local bureaucracy and, where necessary, open the right official doors for effective contact. Commercial officers can often go beyond that. Some have been attached to industry, others have economic training, many have specialized in commercial diplomatic work over a long period, often in and around the same area.

Without these men's local market surveys, financial assessments and reports on trading, investment and commodity opportunities, and without the ambassador's well-informed politico-economic reviews and his access to local people at the highest levels, British business could not have the expert guidance on overseas markets available in these reports which are sent back to departments in London.

Wherever the 'administrative rigidity, timidity and slow reaction times' alleged by the Select Committee might have been, it would be only fair to face up frankly to all the factors — not just the official ones — that contribute to poor export performance. Inefficient marketing and follow-up, price increases in the course of a contract, late delivery, currency changes — these and other reasons generally weigh more heavily than any official incompetence.

There must be few ambassadors today so supine as not to do all they can to rectify incompetence the moment they detect it, whether in the embassy itself or in Whitehall. It might be inferred from the Select Committee's report — 'unacceptable throwback to the days of gentlemanly amateurishness' — that today's diplomatic service is a cookie-pushing pin-striped brigade to whom 'business' is a dirty word. By my own career I am among those best qualified personally to refute that. But for me to have pressed that point might have been regarded as bias. I preferred to let the reputation of the diplomatic service with British exporters speak for itself.

It is sometimes argued that an ambassador with political clout at home is of more use than a career diplomat — an argument held by the American government in particular. But the danger is that such a man may believe, mistakenly, that his status will of itself ensure good relations between the two countries. Or he might fail to press on his own government a case presented by the foreign government that he knows to be objectionable to his own — even though it might be in the wider interests of his country. My own achievements as high commissioner in Tanzania vindicated the Foreign Office view that a diplomat with the appropriate background and qualifications could establish a rapport with a doctrinaire socialist executive head of state, and would have negotiating experience lacking in a British political figure who aspired to the appointment.

Foreign affairs have become something of a plaything for the British armchair dilettante looking in on parliament, the press or television. He often thinks he knows better than the professionals: for him, action, not negotiation. He would do well to recall (or, more likely, read for the first time) the definition of diplomacy as propounded in the early part of this century by the eminent British ambassador Sir Ernest Satow (author of what is still a classic on the subject): the application of intelligence and tact to the conduct of relations between governments. The dilettante may have intelligence but too often he lacks tact — to say nothing about knowledge of the government that is being dealt with. The role is best left to the diplomats for whom it was defined.

I was glad to have been one of them; and I would now take that consoling thought with me into retirement. Preparations for this were now in the final stage, the most time-consuming of these being the round of farewell calls on ambassadorial colleagues and leading Turks in the public and private sectors. It was clearly not practicable to go round all of the anything up to 100 heads of embassy, so a judicious selection had to be made in terms of common interests and closeness of relations between governments. A number of ambassadors invited my wife and myself to a farewell meal, as did the foreign minister and the prime minister.

And all the ambassadors in Ankara gathered to present me with the customary farewell gift. When the dean of the corps (who was the papal pro-nuncio) had asked me beforehand what kind of silver salver I would like I ventured to say to him that I had enough of these as presentations in the past, and would like something different this time if possible. The upshot was a carriage clock from Mappin and Webb, which today graces the mantelpiece at home and reminds me of times past — more than would a silver tray stuck in a showcase.

Finally, on the eve of our departure, my wife and I were touched to receive farewell gifts from the assembled staff of our embassy in Ankara and consulate-general in Istanbul. It was a fitting prelude to 1 June 1977, when sadly we climbed into our loaded private car and were pushed ceremonially out of the embassy grounds by the household staff.

152

17
Honorary Degree–Second Career (Taylor Woodrow)

We toured the south of Turkey, then Turkish Cyprus, for a few weeks before driving back to London to our house in Wimbledon. Shortly before leaving Ankara I had been invited by the Senate of the University of Glasgow, my native city, to receive the honorary degree of Doctor of Laws. After the knighthood, this was the second high spot in my career. Had I had the opportunity of going to university it would probably have been to Glasgow. Now, out of the blue, had come this invitation, which compensated somewhat for that gap; and I had no hesitation in accepting. Soon after our return from Turkey my wife and I drove up to Glasgow for the graduation ceremony, at which I was seated beside the Polish composer Witold Lutoslawski, another graduand. I was struck by the amount of detail of my schooldays in the city (much of it forgotten by me) that had been ferreted out by the professor of drama for his sponsorship speech. A dinner dance in the evening at which I met a number of forgotten schoolday colleagues rounded off an unforgettable day.

* * *

But back in London it was not long before I began to ask myself what I was going to do now; whether I could not somehow find a job instead of just settling down to being retired and out of things.

153

The quiet suburban life was not my idea of how to spend whatever years might remain to me. I had been a wanderer abroad too long for that; and above all I had belonged — belonged to the civil service, the army, the diplomatic service. Now I was out in the cold, and I did not like it. Yet it was difficult to know what to do.

Then, while I was wondering how to go about things with any hope at the age of 60, I was unexpectedly approached in August 1977 by the chairman of a major British engineering company who was aware of my knowledge of the business world in Turkey. He invited me to advise them on a problem with a joint venture there, then go out to Ankara with their export sales team for negotiations with the Turkish partners. After briefing and preparatory discussions at the head office in Coventry we paid a short initial visit to the Turkish company and returned to report the outcome and to plan tactics for substantive negotiations. These began a week later in Ankara, after which the Turks were given an outline of our proposals for a settlement and left to consider it while we went on to Tehran for a week to survey market possibilities there. On our return to Ankara we spent ten days with the Turkish company, which discussed our proposals but was unable to reach a settlement. It was left that there would be further discussions at a later date. But for the time being there was nothing more for me to do.

Early the following year I was invited to join a leading commercial corporation in London for a few weeks to study a mound of papers on the subject of a debt of several million pounds owed to it by the government of Iran. I had then to work out some way of making an approach to Tehran on the matter, bearing in mind the Shah's sensitivity on it. I completed the research and made my recommendations, then turned my mind again to the problem of finding a longer-term job.

The value of a retired ambassador in the commercial or academic world is measured variously. In his service abroad he may have been associated with a particular area of importance to a company. If his career kept him mostly in the Foreign Office he will know the workings of the government machine and have useful contacts in it. If his claim to fame is high intellectual ability he can make a useful contribution to a company's strategic planning or to the administration of a university college. Whatever his particular quality, a retired ambassador is generally sought for his wider views beyond the ambit of a company's activities — to say nothing of the title he may bring that looks so good on the company notepaper. He may be responsible for keeping under review the politico-economic situation in which a company's operations in a given area are being carried on, and for using his area knowledge and contacts to expand these.

High-level contacts in Asia and the Middle East in particular can be a decisive factor in a company's impression of the markets there. For local bureaucracy and secretiveness in those parts of the world can often block any routine approach by a company for information about the country's development plans and future contracts. Especially in banking and insurance the personal role of a former ambassador can be even more effectual than in a commercial company. In Asia and the Middle East the approach to foreign dignitaries as potential investors can be highly delicate. There are obvious reasons why they will want to keep their business secret — almost impossible in their own banking circles. What better, then, than to deal with a mature outsider of traditional discretion — perhaps someone known from his diplomatic past — who can make all the arrangements offshore and discuss matters personally as and when required thereafter?

Openings do exist for retired diplomats but they are limited and not always easy to locate. Some of the most eminent ambassadors have no difficulty: they are sought out the moment they retire. Others less eminent take the initiative themselves near the end of their time in office by hinting at their availability to the company chairmen who call on them for local briefing during business trips abroad. Not being in either category I decided on my own tactics.

I drew up a list of about a dozen major British companies with overseas interests and sent the chairman of each a letter (with curriculum vitae enclosed) starting off with an outline of my career and experience in international political and commercial relations and asking whether the company might be able to employ me in some relevant role. Only towards the end did I mention that I was 60 and retired, since I was afraid that the recipient reading this at the beginning might not bother to read further. The companies I wrote to covered a wide range of activities: construction, engineering, electronics, chemicals, export–import trading. I did not know any of the chairmen, but where I could discover their names I addressed them accordingly; otherwise simply by their company title. They all replied, the replies (except in two cases) breaking down depressingly into three categories: we don't carry appointments of a kind that you would be fitted for; we do, but we fill them in-house; thank you for your interest — but don't phone us, we'll phone you.

The two exceptions were both major construction and engineering companies, one British, one the British subsidiary of an American corporation. Both of them wanted to expand their existing operations in the Middle East and thought they could use me in that connection. The American company was the first to invite me to discuss possibilities, and the prospects looked good; but time dragged on while communications passed between London and the head office in the United States. Then during these exchanges I received a phone call from the British company interested, the international arm of the Taylor Woodrow group, inviting me to a discussion next day with the chairman and the director for the Middle East.

The company already had successful construction and engineering operations there, but now wanted to explore the potential market in Iran more vigorously. It was felt that I could serve them in this respect with my knowledge of the country, understanding of the language, familiarity with leading personalities from the Shah down, and the ability my personal status and diplomatic experience would give me to approach these people on behalf of the company. For I would be the company's resident representative in Iran, living in Tehran and keeping my ear close to the ground for news of proposed construction and engineering projects, and approaching principals for information. Then, when the question of a contract arose, I would be knocking at the doors of influential leaders in the Establishment or the private sector to bring Taylor Woodrow to their notice. Having identified a project of possible interest to the company I would then send full details to London for the tender board to decide whether it was one they would want to follow up with a view to bidding. If they did they would send out a technical team to Iran to assess the project.

I was delighted at the prospect (beyond my expectations) of a full-time job of this description abroad, one that would utilize my skills and experience. I offered to break off contact with the American company if Taylor Woodrow would accept me. Within a couple of days it confirmed it would and I signed a contract without negotiation of terms: I was confident that the salary offered by a firm of this repute was appropriate for the job — certainly I myself had no idea of the going rate — and in any case I had a reasonable diplomatic pension. Money was not the object.

The important thing was that I had found regular work again, less than a year after retiring. And I now belonged again — in a company whose thousands of employees were regarded as members of a team under the paternalistic direction of the group chairman and founder Frank (later Lord) Taylor. In 1921 as a boy of 16 he had borrowed £470, added £30 of his own savings and built two semidetached houses in Blackpool, which he sold for £2000. He repeated the process, went on from there and never looked back. To set up a private company while he was still a minor he took his uncle Jack Woodrow into partnership, purely nominal, to give the company its name. Jack died soon after. In 1935 the company went public and gradually expanded into a group of associated companies specializing in construction, engineering and development. It became a profitable enterprise, building motorways, airports, railway stations, power stations, ports and dams, to name only some — not only in Britain but in Africa, the Middle East, Far East, Australia, Canada and the United States.

During the Second World War it played an important part in the construction of the Mulberry Harbours, two huge prefabricated concrete floating harbours that were built in Britain in secret then towed across the Channel to the French coast and anchored there for the Allied invasion in 1944. And in the 1950s the company built at Calder Hall in Cumbria the world's first full-scale nuclear power station.

Frank Taylor ('FT', as he was known throughout the group) never forgot that he had come up the hard way, but he never paraded this. A lifelong teetotaller and nonsmoker, he was the

157

tireless inspiration behind the growth of Taylor Woodrow. He gave an example of hard work and self-discipline to the thousands who worked for the group in management and the field. He regarded these not as mere employees but as part of a vast family who were always described as team-members. It was a philosophy reflected in the group logo of four men pulling together on a rope — teamwork. Having first been knighted then later raised to the peerage, he lived to be 90, dying in 1995.

I was now introduced to Frank Taylor himself as the latest recruit to management; next day the board lunched me and my wife, whom they also wanted to meet. And the following week, at the beginning of May 1978, I was out on familiar ground in Tehran, setting up the operation on the basis of groundwork already done by a young company engineer. I soon found a flat, and my wife then joined me. So began for me nearly nine years of absorbing work for which my experience as an ambassador served me well in a field different from the diplomatic, but where diplomacy and politics played a part in the commercial negotiations in which I was involved.

18

Iran Again–Revolution–Shah
Out, Khomeini In

I t was 14 years since I had been counsellor at the embassy in
Tehran. But I had been there several times afterwards on
Central Treaty Organization business when I was ambassador
to Turkey; and I was still known to many leading Iranian personalities. In addition, after my service there and my early years in
Shiraz followed by Afghanistan, I was still fluent in written and
spoken Persian. It did not take me long to settle in again now. And
if day-to-day living was not as spacious and cushioned as I had
known it as a diplomat, my wife and I were nevertheless comfortably installed in the Darrous area of the capital and enjoying a
social life that included contact with the British and other embassies, as well as Persian friends.

The British ambassador (an old colleague) and his staff kept me
updated on the background to the political and economic situation
in the country. This was invaluable to me in assessing whether a
given potential capital project was worth recommending to my
head office in London for technical investigation. One such was a
planned naval base at Chah Bahar on the Persian Gulf in which
the Shah was taking a direct interest and which offered scope for
British and American complementary bids. Following my discussions with the naval authorities, my head office set up a
technical investigation team which came out to Tehran over the
next few months. At the same time I was pursuing other potential
projects. But by the autumn of 1978 and the fasting month of

Ramadan there was a growing sense of nervousness and instability in the country.

My chairman had come out to Tehran at that time with the American consultant involved in the naval base project and I had taken them out to lunch. Suddenly, before the meal was over, the restaurant owner in a state of agitation asked us to eat up and leave since he was closing the place. It appeared that a bomb had gone off at a nearby restaurant, much used by Americans, in protest at its being open in the daytime during Ramadan — which had never been strictly observed in the more sophisticated Persian circles.

There were riots in Tehran and some provincial towns; and a succession of attacks on restaurants and cinemas culminated in the horrifying arson of a cinema in the oil refinery town of Abadan in which nearly 400 people were burned alive, unable to get out because the doors had been barred on the outside. Although there were rumours that these activities had been provoked by the Shah's secret police in order to give them an excuse to retaliate, it was generally held that they had been inspired by Muslim fundamentalists on the rampage after anti-state preaching in mosques against the laxity of observance of Ramadan and the prevalence of Western godlessness. It was not hard for religious leaders to make this a rallying point for the millions of Persians with barely a shirt to lose. For the country's oil wealth had still not by any means reached them all; the difficulties of life for the masses in places like the south of Tehran and parts of the countryside contrasted starkly with the affluence of the upper layers of society in the northern suburbs.

In a move to placate religious feeling the government announced that all casinos and nightclubs would be shut down at once for good. And the country would resume at once the Muslim calendar, dating from the Prophet Mohammed's flight from Mecca to Medina in AD 622. This meant abandoning the detested so-called imperial calendar introduced to mark the 2500th anniversary of the founding of the first Persian dynasty by Cyrus the Great. It was a climb-down by the Shah, whose own grandiose idea the calendar was, following the extravagant anniversary celebrations (attended by heads of state and world leaders) in a palatial tented camp at

Persepolis in the south of Iran, capital of the ancient Persian Empire. And in an attempt to maintain his power and position he issued an order prohibiting members of his family from engaging in business — especially any involving the government.

But it was too little too late. We could clearly see a significant new factor in events emerging: ordinary people were beginning to realize that their remote all-powerful Shah was only a man after all and that if they stuck together they could, without being hanged or shot, brave SAVAK, his ruthless security and Intelligence organization, and criticize him openly instead of always having to speak of him with bated breath. In September 1978 Tehran saw for the first time a mass march of the people, estimated at 100,000, in open protest against the Shah — demanding that he should step down and make way for an Islamic republic. It was a demonstration not without casualties as troops opened fire on the marchers.

* * *

But there was more to come, in a development hitherto unimaginable: on a wall in one of the main avenues of the city we read graffiti in high red letters calling for the death of the Shah — *marg bar Shah*. And it was not long before a new pattern of disruption emerged throughout Iran: strikes and boycotts in oilfields, airlines, railways, banks, hospitals, postal and electricity and water services, steel mills, social security and tax offices. The country was becoming paralysed.

Incredibly, there was a single principal instigator of this incipient revolt and he was 2500 miles away near Paris: Iran's leading cleric, the Ayatollah Khomeini. In 1964, as counsellor at the embassy in Tehran, I had seen his expulsion from Iran by the Shah for his part in stirring up the riots against him that had begun in 1963. Iraq had given Khomeini asylum in Najaf, the holy city (south of Baghdad) of the Shiite sect of Islam which is dominant in Iran. From there, uncompromising in his advocacy of Islamic purity, he had continued to pour out propaganda against the Shah, calling for his overthrow and the establishment of an Islamic republic.

This went on until 1975. In that year, at a meeting in Algiers of the Organization of Petroleum Exporting Countries, the Shah and

Saddam Hussein, the strong man of Iraq, discussed the long-standing dispute over the location of the frontier between Iran and Iraq along the Shatt al-Arab, the waterway at the head of the Persian Gulf. In the ensuing agreement on this the Shah undertook to stop supporting the Kurds of northern Iraq in their ongoing rebellion against the Baghdad government. In return Saddam Hussein promised to curb Khomeini's propaganda. But the Ayatollah persisted in this, with the result that in October 1978 the Iraqis ordered him out. By this time he was more bitter than ever towards the Shah, for Khomeini's elder son, carrying messages from him to his followers in Iran, had in 1977 been killed by SAVAK. In his last edict before leaving Najaf Khomeini gave three instructions to his supporters in Iran: boycott all government bodies; withdraw cooperation from the authorities; initiate new Islamic institutions.

For his departure from Najaf, Khomeini was joined by Ibrahim Yazdi from the United States, leader of the main anti-Shah group there. They went to Kuwait but were refused entry and were allowed by the Iraqi authorities to return to Baghdad to take a plane out. In Paris, Sadiq Qotbzadeh, a member of the anti-Shah group, was able to secure French visas for the two, and they flew there — albeit Khomeini somewhat reluctantly at first, afraid of being polluted by infidel Western surroundings. They found refuge in Neauphlé-le-Château some 30 miles east of the capital, in a house arranged by the anti-Shah student committee. (Yazdi and Qotbzadeh stood close to the Ayatollah after his eventual return to Tehran. Khomeini then appointed Yazdi foreign minister, but in 1982 had Qotbzadeh executed for plotting a coup with a number of army officers.)

The government in Paris had not made a point of inviting Khomeini to take refuge there, but it was felt in some quarters that being there might moderate him and make him more reasonable (which of course it did not). And it was believed (wrongly, as it turned out) that there might be a spin-off for France in trade with Iran if and when he came to power there. On expiry of his initial permission to stay the French authorities granted him and his aides temporary residence permits and provided multiple telephone and telex lines. But not before President Giscard d'Estaing had consulted the Shah, who said he did not mind if Khomeini were allowed to remain in France. Presumably the Shah felt that at that distance from Tehran the old man could not do him much harm.

In Paris, however, the Ayatollah found far more scope for propaganda against the Shah than there had been in Najaf, only a few hundred miles from Tehran. He was able to keep in regular touch with the mullahs in Iran. There was the direct-dialling telephone, facilities for recording rabble-rousing Friday sermons for delivery in the mosques, a regular air service for his couriers to carry these tapes there. And there was a constant stream of journalists from many countries visiting him and giving his views free publicity in the world press. It was at a word from him that the first and most serious strikes in Iran — in the oilfields — were organized.

The unrest arising out of this development, spreading country-wide, seemed to put paid to any hope of early decisions by the government or private companies on capital projects which Taylor Woodrow and other British and foreign groups were following up. For one thing, expenditure on defence prospects (including the planned new naval base in the Persian Gulf) no longer lay solely in the hands of the Shah. There was a growing feeling of gloom about the economy, with little business being done. There was almost complete idleness among workers, apathetic resignation in the commercial community, impotence in the government. And there were now powerful anti-Shah demonstrations in the streets by thousands of students — some of them too long in the tooth to be genuine — religious fanatics recruited by the mullahs, more likely. By the end of November there was a widespread rumour that the Shah would be going on an extended holiday with the Empress.

Clearly, drastic developments could be expected. But I felt that, with no actual work in hand yet, Taylor Woodrow was perhaps less vulnerable to these than were companies already committed to contracts. We could therefore afford to sit things out until we saw which way they would go. But I was soon able to see. By November there were bloody riots in Tehran, which the security forces were hard put to control even by firing into the crowds. There was widespread destruction of banks and government offices. British property was singled out and set on fire — the embassy, British Airways office, banks — reflecting the long-standing paranoia that Britain was generally behind the ills of the country, including the continuance of the Shah in power.

Paradoxically, the Shah himself shared the paranoia. This was a legacy of the widely held belief that the country's misfortunes down the years were the result of outside interference; that foreign influence was being continually brought to bear on it; that Britain felt superior about its history of imperial domination of it; that it had been humiliated by the British (and Russian) occupation in the Second World War. The Shah believed, in addition, that Britain resented his postwar move towards closer relations with the Americans. Yet even in these relations he showed signs of paranoia. He saw the rapport he had established with Nixon and Kissinger to be in danger when in 1977 Carter became president. Carter was critical of Iran's disregard of human rights. He took nearly a year after his inauguration to invite the Shah to Washington — and then there were demonstrations against him near the White House, which he suspected Carter of deliberately allowing. He believed that the United States meant to stop supporting him.

At the end of November 1978 he gave an interview in Tehran to a visiting Turkish senator, son-in-law of the late İsmet İnönü and an acquaintance of mine from my time as ambassador in Ankara, who saw me after the interview. He told me that when he asked the Shah how such a serious internal situation had developed, the latter had replied vaguely that he did not know for certain; but he suspected some Anglo-American plot. Senator Toker commented to him that this would hardly be in the interest of these countries themselves — so why should they engage in it? The Shah said he could only suppose it stemmed from their desire to control Iran's oil absolutely again. (Shortly before this — but I only learned later — the Shah reportedly told the Japanese ambassador that he suspected the British were behind the troubles.)

In point of fact, Carter, although lukewarm at first, responded well and showed his support by continuing to supply arms. It emerged later that Washington had underestimated the strength of the growing anti-Shah opposition inside Iran, and so had regarded him as someone to be supported as a safeguard against any en- croachment of Soviet influence in the country. It was this very support that gave Khomeini the basis for some of his most virulent propaganda. Having fanned the people's pent-up hatred of the Shah for the corruptness and extravagance of his regime, he then directed his attacks on what he called the prop without which the Shah could not have lasted so long in power: the United States. The same prop that kept out the Palestine Liberation Organization but gave permanence (and oil) to Israel, arch-enemy of Islam, and with whom the Shah had close relations that went as far as allowing a quasi-diplomatic Israeli representative to set up office in Tehran.

What stood out in the minds of the people, to the exclusion of the good that the Shah had done for the country, was the way he had suppressed all opposition to him. And the way those around him had out of fear and self-interest told him only what they thought he would want to hear. Thus he remained unaware of the resentment that many aspects of his rule aroused. His political and religious opponents saw him as having secured his autocratic position by pledging Iran as an anti-communist pro-Western base. And to keep himself in his position he was being advised by a pro- Western entourage and protected by a powerful and ruthless secret police (SAVAK) trained by the CIA. The gloves were off. For Iranian nationalists the Americans had largely replaced Britain as the main interferers in the country's affairs. From then on it became convenient to blame them for all the ills of Iran — even where these had not the remotest connection with them. It was an attitude inevitably hardened when the American and British governments came out publicly in support of the Shah.

At one point during the riots in Tehran the Shah admitted in a speech that there had been faults in his rule: high-handed autoc- racy, surrounding himself with sycophants, blindness to the reali- ties of the situation of the people. But all this carried little weight against the continuous incitement of the people by Khomeini, still in Paris, who swore publicly to bring him down. And the people, tasting their new-found power, were getting the bit between their teeth. Until now they had gone in fear of uttering a word against the Shah. Now that they realized they could speak out with impunity they were doing so with all the venom of years of silent resentment at his autocratic rule. And they were encouraged by the mullahs, whose power to rally them and intimidate them with the call to return to Islam was now being felt in all its strength.

The government could do nothing about this except continue to keep troops on the streets; and, incredibly, did not allow a word about the unrest into the press, even though it was of course common knowledge inside and outside the country. All news was heavily censored in favour of the government and was put out only on its radio and television. There were now no newspapers except government broadsheets, and Persians and foreigners alike in Iran were getting their news from the BBC World Service.

By now the whole of the country was virtually at a standstill and there was a dusk-to-dawn curfew. The shortage of fuel had become chronic: at filling stations queues of cars were literally a mile long and two abreast, and when the meagre supply ran out drivers would sleep in their cars or go away and leave them in the queue until the next day, in the hope of a fresh supply, however limited, to the pumps. The few litres I still had in the ancient office car I saved against a possible emergency. Meantime when I had to go downtown — in an interval between outbreaks of rioting and shooting — I would take a local taxi (its driver having a small secret cache of petrol) at exorbitant black market rates. I counted poor people in their hundreds queuing for a gallon of kerosene, their only means of cooking. For them, heating in that cold December was out of the question. Our own heating was now minimal as we eked out our little remaining fuel oil. We could supplement with an electric heater but the current was cut off every evening until the next morning, leaving us in the light of candles, which were scarce and expensive to come by. There were no more gas cylinders for cooking but we had an electric ring and my wife prepared food in the daytime while the current was on.

By the end of 1978 Khomeini's long-distance campaign to topple the Shah was in full swing, waged by disruption of the economy and violence on the streets. It was revealing, and frightening, to see how the old mullah, now nearly 80, still operating from Paris, directed the masses over the head of the government in Tehran. He would call for boycotts and strikes and days of mourning, and be obeyed at once. He then ordered striking oil workers to go back to work to meet domestic needs (but not exports), exhorted by Opposition delegations appointed by him. He called on the masses to set up an Islamic Revolutionary Council.

Like all devout Muslims, Khomeini lived by Islamic law. Faith as in Christian practice had no place in this ethos. Laws define Muslim family and social relations, education, diet, morals. Transgression of the law weakens Islam; transgression by default of observance or by deviation to alien practices is heinous and must be stopped by punishment and example. This task falls to the mullahs. And in carrying it out they strengthen Islam by inspiring its adherents.

In his campaign Khomeini knew he had to deal with a middle class and armed forces leaders removed from orthodox observance, as well as devout peasants and merchants. But he was able to use the anti-Shah sentiment in nearly every class as a rallying call. Those who did not like it were killed, or fled, or knuckled under. It served at once his political aspiration of a strictly Islamic state free of alien influence and his determination to punish the Shah. First flight, then death, took the latter from his grasp.

Things had got to the point where it seemed only a matter of time before the Shah left, nominally for a rest but in fact almost certainly for good — given the ominous development that the army, on which he relied to maintain himself in power, now showed signs of being divided in its support for him. On one occasion downtown when I found myself, with others, hemmed in in a side street by a mob rioting at a main intersection, an officer with a truckload of troops guided us out; but instead of then turning on the rioters the troops sat idly by. The mullahs' appeal for a return to the true Islam was beginning to have an effect on the soldiers, who were unwilling to fire on their own people; and there were scenes of the latter sticking flowers into the muzzles of rifles.

In this situation of political instability and economic paralysis thousands of British and other foreigners were leaving Iran. For my own part, however, although I could now see how things were going, and had little ground for hope, I decided that it might just be worth staying on as long as I could, in case, when the Shah did leave, a successor government might restore some semblance of normality in which it would be possible to do business again. My head office, still able to phone me by direct dialling even though it took hours to get through on the jammed lines, agreed to leave a decision on this to my discretion.

There being nothing to do in Tehran at that time, my wife and I went to Bandar Abbas on the Persian Gulf at New Year to stay for a week with Persian friends from my early days in the country at the consulate in Shiraz over 30 years before. We had flown down in an interval between strikes in the airline, but meantime there was another strike and we had to get back to Tehran by road in a small pick-up van loaded with 20-litre cans of petrol for which our friends had scoured Bandar Abbas. My wife and I squeezed in beside the driver, she wrapped in a *chadur*, the long enveloping black body veil of some Persian women, and ordered by me not to open her mouth (albeit she knew the language quite well) if we were stopped by a military patrol or a vigilante group.

On the 1000-mile drive I was amazed to see the extent of the graffiti against the Shah and in support of Khomeini in the smallest villages and on the roadside direction signboards. And in the main street of Qum, seat of the religious leadership, a rough concrete pillar had been put up, on top of which was a dead dog with a dead cat lying on it, and execration of the Shah and the Empress daubed on the pillar. It was a dead city, still sinister. Here and there charred ruins, everywhere shops closed behind steel shutters. Nearer Tehran, huge fires were being stoked in the middle of the road.

A lorry just ahead of us with a load of timber was systematically stripped of it for the fires. Our own main concern was not so much the molestation by dozens of youths surrounding us, and screaming at us to put on our headlights and sound the horn, as the danger of a burning brand or even a cluster of sparks landing on the remaining cans of petrol in the open back of our vehicle. We steered slowly round the menacing crowd as far as we could and finally crawled through. With time to observe the mobs at close quarters as we ran the gauntlet I was struck at once by the organization of them. Youths and urchins obviously enjoying it and getting very worked up were doing the burning and shouting and the menacing of drivers trying to get through. But clearly discernible among them were numbers of responsible-looking leaders and marshals directing groups here and there as the emphasis changed, and acting as traffic police. A truckload of troops by a nearby petrol station watched the proceedings without intervening.

This final part of our journey confirmed my earlier impression that hostility to the Shah now ran the length of the country. Even the most remote village and lonely road was not without some sign of opposition; it was clearly nationwide — not simply a sophisticated urban thing. Yet the Shah could still not accept this fact when it was retailed to him by the British ambassador, to whom I had reported it on my return to Tehran. He suggested to the ambassador that my knowledge of Persian was slipping. He did not deny the evidence of his own eyes and ears in Tehran, and the reports from his representatives in the major towns, that there was a growing revolt against him in urban areas; but he fondly believed that he was revered in the villages, which housed the bulk of the population.

However, by early January 1979 it had become clear even to him that the situation in the country as a whole was out of his control. Riots were becoming more violent and the troops deployed to deal with them were defecting to the mobs; the martial law that had been imposed was becoming impossible to sustain. In a last-ditch attempt to hold on he appointed a new prime minister believed capable of forming a government that could command popular support. This was immediately condemned by the Ayatollah Khomeini, still in Paris; but the Shah declared his confidence in the new government's ability to restore the situation in the country. However, he went on to say publicly that he was tired out bearing so many responsibilities and that he would be going abroad for a rest, leaving a regency council in his absence. But this did nothing to stem the uprising throughout the country, and in Tehran we were surrounded by continual firing.

* * *

Finally, in the middle of January, the Shah and the Empress left the country. In an airport ceremony which we saw on television they reviewed a section of still loyal troops of the Imperial Guard who cordoned off the airport. The royal couple then bade farewell to the prime minister and senior officials and commanders, passed under the Koran held aloft, and disappeared into their aircraft. No members of the diplomatic corps had been invited — as they usually were when the Shah went abroad — and a planned press conference was cancelled at the last minute, leaving a large number of local and foreign correspondents disappointed. The whole operation was conducted under a veil of secrecy and security. While those of us who had known the Shah and had a deep affection for the country shared some of the sorrow we observed on the faces of those who were seeing him off, it was impossible not to reflect on the extent to which he was responsible for his own downfall. The news of his departure brought out hundreds of thousands of jubilant demonstrators on to the streets of Tehran and other cities. Car horns blared and headlights flashed. People sang and danced, showered troops with flowers and festooned their trucks and armoured cars, stuck red carnations into the muzzles of the rifles held by soldiers guarding public buildings and embassies. Statues of the Shah and his father who had led the coup d'état in 1921 that set up the new Persia were pulled down, and everywhere portraits and banners of Khomeini began to appear.

The Ayatollah himself, still in Paris, told a packed news conference that the departure of the Shah was final and it marked the first step towards ending 50 years of the brutal dictatorship of his dynasty and setting up an Islamic republic under an interim revolutionary council. (It was not to be long before the people of Iran realized they now had a new and more ruthless dictatorship over them.) He called on all groups to leave aside any differences they might have and to join together in an effort to reconstruct the country. He dismissed any danger of a military coup to restore the old regime, saying that what he called the ruling clique knew such a move would no longer work now that the whole nation was free; it was not the nation of the past.

Having satisfied himself that his position was now assured and that the Shah would not come back, early in February 1979 Khomeini returned to Tehran after 15 years in exile. On television the old man was shown on the arm of a steward being helped down the steps of an Air France plane (hired by Iranian opposition groups in Paris) into a mass of exuberant supporters — the inverse of the scene three weeks before when the Shah had left. However, we had no opportunity to witness the actual welcome of the Ayatollah; at the crucial moment the screen went black — a symptom of the residual discord in the broadcasting corporation, as in other state bodies, between elements for and against the Shah. But there was no doubt about Khomeini's power in the streets and among the workers, and he used this in his campaign to get rid of the last prime minister — and, by ruthless execution, hundreds of others who had been loyal to the regime, including many of our own friends.

In this the armed forces were to play a key role, the Imperial Guards being still largely loyal to the old government. And the showdown was not long in coming. A Guards battalion tried to crack down on personnel at an air-force base near Tehran who were quietly watching a film of Khomeini's arrival and subsequent doings. To meet the attack the airmen broke into the armoury and armed both themselves and the civilian mobs outside the base: and, after a short but bloody encounter, the Imperial Guards withdrew. But the armed men had the bit between their teeth and joined up with other groups in the city. Army unit after unit laid down its arms or withdrew to barracks. There was then no stopping the revolutionaries: the situation went by default when the bulk of the army, by and large with its officers, turned passive at the very least — and in many cases went over to the revolutionaries.

With the situation on the ground so uncertain, the majority of foreign residents had left the country; there were now hardly any British in my part of Tehran for whom I could continue to act as warden (one of the ambassador's small group responsible for liaison between him and local British residents in times of crisis). And it certainly did not look as if my purpose in sitting it out through the revolution — to see if a new regime would bring some stability in which business could be done — was likely to be fulfilled. Given this situation, Taylor Woodrow phoned me from London (they told me afterwards that a secretary had kept on dialling for the best part of a day until she got a line) and told me

171

they did not want any dead heroes: I should get out without delay.

Just at this time the British embassy announced there would be an RAF airlift to take out any remaining British people whose continued presence was not essential. But that would have meant bringing only a very limited amount of baggage — a situation my wife in particular was not happy about. British Airways would have been our preference, but it had by now cancelled flights and, in any case, had been flying only economy-class flights chock-a-block and with a ban on excess baggage. So I drove downtown in the old office car and, in between street demonstrations, scouted around and found Swissair still open, with reduced staff but usual efficiency. It was going to attempt one last flight the next day; whether or not the plane from Geneva actually came in would depend on the situation report radioed from Swissair ground staff in Tehran to the pilot when he landed at Damascus. But yes, subject to that they could let me have two first-class seats; and yes, I could take excess baggage; about how much would I have?

For a moment I thought about being modest and undemanding and making sure of getting something at least, say about 30 kilograms each. But when I thought about how much we had, I took a header in and diffidently, if not quite casually, said about 100 kilograms. The travel agent did not bat an eyelid; she simply said she would note this on my ticket and reservations. And would we please get to the airport as soon as possible after curfew (5.00 a.m.) — certainly by 6.00 — since although, if the plane came in at all, the flight out would not be before midday, the approaches to the airport might be closed by demonstrations long before then. I could hardly believe my good fortune and bolted out of the Swissair office as if the travel agent might change her mind. But getting home was not easy, for before it had got halfway there the old car developed an oil leak that forced me to a halt and a long wait for a friendly passing truck driver to tow me home. There I had to leave the car in a side lane, since clearly there was nothing to be done about it before we left next day.

19

Flight from Tehran–Market Reconnaissance in Middle East–Return to Tehran

T hat evening we had our landlord and his wife from downstairs, together with Persian neighbours from across the
way, in for a drink. But we did not finish my meagre stock
(alcohol being by now forbidden in the country): I was still hoping
to come back some time. I had ordered a car from a local hire
service for five o'clock next morning; it arrived only after I had
phoned their office repeatedly to waken the driver. Meantime my
wife and I had dragged our assorted suitcases, bags, boxes and tin
trunk downstairs to the entrance, trying not to disturb our neighbours. But our landlord and his wife insisted on coming out to
wish us a tearful farewell.

Getting ourselves and that load into what was a small car took a
great deal of doing. In the event we drove off with suitcases
sticking out of the open boot, the trunk held down on the roof
rack by my outstretched hand, and bags all over us The driver
drove slowly and nervously, as well he might with soldiers dashing
into the middle of the road every so often with loaded rifles
pointed at us while an officer examined our papers by torchlight.

Eventually we arrived at the airport soon after 6.00 a.m. and by
lucky chance got a porter with a trolley. Only the force of the
trolley laden with our baggage got us through the milling crowds
until we could join the Swissair queue, which by then stretched

well back to the entrance to the booking hall. There the porter made to off-load the pile. The prospect of even trying to man-handle this and carry and slide it up to the check-in counter in due course in that crowd was too much even for me, proud of my ability to deal with any adversity. But no, said the porter, there were other passengers who would want him and his trolley. Finally, after an exchange with him in the course of which I mentally blessed my long dead teacher of Persian in Shiraz over 30 years before, I was able to persuade the porter that the money I was prepared to pay him to let me keep the trolley (without himself) would be far more than he could hope to earn from other passengers before the last flight left. So we did at least have that relief.

And not for a minute in the ensuing six hours did we take our eyes off our goods — my wife standing holding on to the trolley, quite relaxed, strung about with jewel box, face case, fur coat, overcoat, raincoat and umbrella. The queue, largely European (by this time most Persian men at any rate were being forbidden to leave the country), was self-disciplined: any attempt to jump it was met with an almost menacing silent approach by several men in the queue at once. Then by nine o'clock in the morning it was an-nounced that the plane had left Damascus for Tehran, and in an hour or so the check-in began. Even though holding tickets, we wondered if there would still be a seat by the time we got to the desk.

However, we got through the usual formalities without difficulty, and into the boarding-gate lounge, where there was another hour's delay while the incoming plane was off-loaded and prepared for the turn round. Finally, well after midday and the six hours' line-up, we were comfortably aboard. Another nervous delay while police came in and carefully scrutinized everyone's documents. Then off. February 1979, fateful month in the history of Iran.

And so to Geneva: a couple of hours browsing round that magnificent airport (making Tehran's cattle-pen only a bad dream). Then British Airways on to London — to find, coming off the same plane, to which it also had been transferred at Geneva, entire to the last item, our baggage. We had feared it might never even get out of Tehran; but with its traditional efficiency Swissair had checked it in right through to London. With such a consignment loaded on a barrow to the height of the porter pushing it, we could hardly hope to walk unchallenged through the Green customs area — though in fact we had nothing to declare. But our answer to the officer's only question, 'Tehran?', was enough to get us through on the nod.

A few days at home was all we needed to recover from our experiences in Iran over the past few months. I then began to reflect on my misfortune. Within a year of retiring from the diplomatic service I had found myself a second career as what was in effect a commercial ambassador, a role that suited me down to the ground and I was fortunate to have landed. Now, just under a year later, events had forced me out and I was back where I had started, with hardly a hope of being able to find other employment. Meantime, however, rather than give me notice of termination, Taylor Woodrow decided to continue to use my services under the existing contract. Early in March 1979 I was sent to the Middle East to survey the markets in Turkey, northern Cyprus and Sudan, and report on planned capital projects in engineering and construction that might be of interest to the company.

* * *

Accordingly, I spent six weeks searching in Istanbul, Izmir, Ankara, Nicosia, Kyrenia, and finally Khartoum. Then, in the middle of April, while out there, I was instructed to join up in Cairo with a COMET mission, a group of leading British businessmen organized by the Committee for Middle East Trade, to explore markets in Egypt. The committee, which advises the Department of Trade and Industry's overseas trade board, is composed of senior private-sector businessmen with long-standing experience of the Middle East, together with representatives of the Foreign Office and the DTI itself. Its main function is to assist in the formulation of British government trade policy for the area and to seek ways of improving British performance there. COMET provides an important interface between Whitehall and the business community already or potentially involved in the

Middle East. In the mission I was now joining I was to represent the British construction industry as a whole, which gave me first-hand experience of the technique of international industrial marketing.

It was a role that was of particular interest to me in that it gave me an opportunity to judge the strengths and weaknesses of British embassies as viewed from the other side of the ambassador's desk. From past experience I knew how far the incumbent there could and should put the local knowledge of himself and his staff at the disposal of visiting British businessmen. I suppose it was only to be expected that on the strength of my past I was given prompt access to the ambassadors in the various capitals I now visited in my new role, and that the briefings I was given by them and their staff answered all my questions. In session with the ambassador in Khartoum, where I had never been before, I realized how valuable must have been my own briefings in past years to businessmen visiting an area for the first time.

But if I personally was now well received, so too was the COMET mission in Cairo — which, as an official body, was efficiently briefed and hospitably entertained. The main weakness in some of the embassies was sometimes the inability of the com-mercial staff to arrange meetings with local officials or bodies at high enough level, with the result that the ambassador himself had to do this. This tended to happen when the staff member con-cerned had not been in his post long enough. Indeed my experience on this tour confirmed the view I had held during my diplomatic career that the Foreign Office often moved staff from post to post too soon. Particularly in the commercial department of an embassy a first secretary might be transferred elsewhere just as he was becoming usefully knowledgeable about local condi-tions. Where a commercial officer did stay long enough to put his knowledge to use, it was all to the good that he was basically a diplomat rather than a Department of Trade official, as advocated by some outside critics. A diplomat posted as a commercial officer for a few years can fairly easily pick up the jargon and basics of the job, whereas a DOT man could hardly be expected to acquire the skills of a diplomat. Visiting businessmen require not only advice on the local market but also a general assessment of the politico-economic situation as background to their operations. And such assessments are part of the stock in trade of the diplomat.

Having reported to my head office on my return from the Middle East towards the end of April I was delighted to be told that, although the company had originally engaged me as its resident representative in Iran, now that foreign construction companies could not expect to find work there again for the foreseeable future, it had been decided that I should go on to be resident representative in Hong Kong. It was accepted that I had never been there before, but it was generously assumed that I would soon find my way around and be able to start following up contract possibilities for Taylor Woodrow. Moreover, in what was a British colony I would have a certain standing which would be an advantage in contacts with the Establishment. I looked forward to this new assignment. I had hardly dared hope that the company would have another opening for me.

I was not expected in Hong Kong for another two months, when the company's marketing director would come there from a trade fair in Peking and discuss with me the modalities of setting up the new operation. I therefore proposed that in the meantime I should go back to Tehran for a few weeks and wind things up there. This meant, first and foremost, disposing of the mass of paper, some of it sensitive, which had had to be left when I simply turned the key in the lock and walked out at 24 hours' notice in February as the revolution came to a head. And the company's house and office furnishings would have to be sold for whatever I could get for them in what was now — with the exodus of thousands of expatriates — a buyer's market. Bills and taxes which could not be paid during the revolution had now to be settled, my own household effects packed and shipped out if that was possible, and the accommodation vacated before the imminent end of the lease.

Management were concerned that it might not be safe for me to go back: dramatic visions of a Khomeini firing squad's first titled victim (a posthumous bar to Taylor Woodrow's Queen's Award?). There was even a flattering opinion that the few thousand pounds to be realized from a second-hand sale were as nothing compared with the value to the company of having their resident representative alive and well in Hong Kong. But I did feel that we should make an orderly final withdrawal from Iran; and, while there would be difficulties, I did not expect there to be any real danger. It was therefore agreed in June 1979 that I should go back to Tehran, wind things up there as quickly as possible, then go straight on to Hong Kong.

* * *

The British Airways flight out reflected the situation in Iran at that time — barely two dozen passengers and only four of these European, plus an overnight journey with a slip crew at Kuwait just after dawn to take the plane on to Tehran then back later in the morning to avoid an overnight stopover there. Tehran airport was even drabber than before and now had posters all over the place exhorting the masses to adhere to Islam, safeguard the revolution, beware of reactionaries and, of course, venerate Khomeini. Contrary to what I had been led to believe, the terminal was not overrun by trigger-happy bearded youths doing vigilante: there were very few of these. But, more significant, there were a couple of knowing-looking individuals examining all passports, asking searching questions in Persian or English as required, and sorting out a number of Persians for further questioning in a room in the corner. At the formal passport control desk there were more questions — particularly of the few Europeans: reason for visit, name of company and occupation in it, past association with Persia, proposed length of stay, scrutiny of work and residence permits; then ostentatious checking of names against a long list held at the desk. I passed muster and went through, with happily no way of knowing whether a suspect foreigner would have been stopped there or allowed through and picked up later, perhaps after he had been in touch with Persian acquaintances.

There were no customs officers as such, only a number of eager young women revolutionaries in ordinary clothes (but not yet veiled) who were harassing everyone, including me. Having told my inquisitor that I had nothing to declare, I was then ordered by her to open the biggest and bottom-most of my suitcases on the trolley. I duly did so, only to see her dash off to some other part of the building for some reason. As I stood awaiting her pleasure I was inevitably holding up a line of passengers behind me. Meantime none of the other young women was prepared to undertake the examination for their colleague who had dashed off, so I just stood there until she eventually returned. After ruffling my shirts and suits and the rest, and finding no arms, or foreign currency, or copies of *Playboy*, or letters for Persians, she waved me through as gracelessly as I had ever seen a Persian woman behave.

But such enthusiasm for the revolution was not shared by the taxi driver who drove me to my apartment. Starting off by telling me that I was his first foreign passenger that day (Persians, he complained, wanted to be driven home for virtually nothing), he went on to speak his mind about the way the new regime was ruining the country — and in particular doing nothing about unemployment. Knowing I spoke the language, he went on to really develop his theme. For the obvious reason that he might have been an agent-provocateur I let him do all the talking while I myself avoided any material comment. But I found the subject of unemployment in particular repeated by the man-in-the-street during my few weeks in the city.

On arrival at the apartment I was greeted warmly by the landlord and his wife (in the flat downstairs) and by Fatimah our servant, whom I had continued to employ throughout our absence to look after the apartment and its contents. The place was sparkling, lunch was ready, the drinks I had left in February were untouched in the cupboard. And in front of the house stood the broken-down old car, kept clean regularly by the neighbourhood dustman for whom I had left a monthly tip for the purpose. The district was eerily quiet after the former noise of rowdy American children and the toing and froing of Germans in their Mercedes. There were virtually no foreigners left. The array of aerials on the roof of the house nearby where the Siemens representative had lived had all been removed when he left. Apartment after apartment that had provided the Persian owners with a lucrative thousand pounds or more a month from American or European tenants was lying empty — with no prospect of being reoccupied.

The neighbourhood shops were still there (many having prudently changed their name to include the word Freedom), as were the newsagent and taxi-hire office — but with stocks running down and barely a foreign customer. And of course no drink, not even local beer, wine or vodka, let alone imported spirits. Shopkeepers and all our local acquaintances were still very friendly and not afraid of being seen talking to me: but they were guarded in their talk, and basically pessimistic and depressed. Our landlord was still without an active job in the oil company (though being paid); our good neighbour across the way was wondering what would become of him now that the foreign bank in which he was a manager had been nationalized. He told me that banking facilities were now back to normal, but applications for remittance of funds abroad were subject to a long involved and tedious procedure with no certainty of being approved. This was a matter of concern to me in view of the fact that I was beginning to sell off the company's property and would have to accept local currency.

The cost of repairing the broken-down car would have been prohibitive so I took what I could get for its sale on an as-is where-is basis to the local taxi-hire company. Selling the contents of house and office was not so easy. The landlord helped by buying some things and bringing his family and friends around. And the maid took in kind the three months' pay I owed her. Others who came to view pressed shamelessly for ever more reductions on the assumption (stated quite openly and impudently by some of them — and regrettably true) that I could not take the goods with me. I could only bluff by saying that I was not desperate to sell; I would be leaving unsold items for my landlord to sell off at leisure on my behalf at fair prices. (In the event of course most of the goods had to be abandoned to him.)

Meantime I spent several days sorting out the mass of paper in the office and destroying most of it. Essential files and papers for return to head office I put into a single suitcase to take with me to Hong Kong and hand over to the company's marketing director who would be meeting me there on his way back to London from a visit to Peking. Basically they were papers relating to the formalities, not the substance, of operations in Iran — company registration, accounts, taxation, insurance, personnel and the like. Nothing sensitive was retained.

About this time I had a visit from the local police station. The

180

inspector started by showing the landlord photographs of my wife and myself and asking if we were still there. When he eventually questioned me I had the impression that this was a routine check on foreigners still in the neighbourhood and not an enquiry into my specific activities now that I was back. Entirely polite and friendly, and apparently satisfied, he left. The more specific enquiry — and confirmation of where the real power in revolutionary Iran lay — came some days later. I had packed my personal household and other possessions and clothes and was in touch with the one remaining foreign (German) transport company about shipping the crates to London for storage. The manager then told me that the customs would not be satisfied simply with a declaration of contents; they had to have clearance for my departure from the country, and for export of my effects from my local *Komiteh* — that is, the Islamic Revolutionary Committee.

Accordingly, I went round there with my landlord, who knew where the *Komiteh* sat: a large house confiscated from some wealthy Persian who had fled the country or been executed. We went in past a couple of villainous-looking youths in the usual urban guerrilla dress who were standing guard with rifles and grenades; then continued into what must have been the main reception room, now bare except for a table in the corner with a couple of armchairs near it and chairs round the walls, which were covered with revolutionary posters. Sitting at the table was a sort of Persian Fidel Castro with rifle propped up against the wall beside him. He was not unfriendly, but clearly suspicious of anything unfamiliar to him — like me. I told him why I had come, whereupon he said I should come back after evening prayers, when someone else (neither I nor my landlord could make out who) would be there. We duly returned to find that the someone was a grey-bearded (but not very old) mullah. He started off by telling the landlord to bring in a professional interpreter through whom the mullah could talk to 'this foreigner'. The landlord knowing none, a younger mullah was brought in who started interpreting preliminary questions and answers.

I had decided beforehand that, to avoid arousing any suspicions my interrogator might have, I would not disclose that I knew

Persian fluently. But the young man's interpreting was so bad that I could not let it go on and I intervened in Persian with the older mullah, whose beard perked up with interest. He condescended to deal with me directly and began to question me shrewdly and searchingly, though politely enough. But religious and revolutionary fanaticism ran through him and I doubted if he would have been so restrained had he been sitting on a formal tribunal. As it was, when he learned of my diplomatic past in his country he could not reconcile it with my current commercial role and wanted to know whether I was not still a diplomat, but operating in disguise so to speak. I had a few distinctly uncomfortable moments; but after about half an hour of his questions and my explanation of all my past and current activities in Persia, he expressed himself satisfied. He said that if I came back the next day with a letter from my landlord confirming that I had been a satisfactory tenant and that he had no financial or other claims against me, I would be given a letter of clearance from the *Komiteh*. This was all duly done and I was given the letter by the man on duty the next day — this time a highly-educated young engineer with good English who went so far as to say he hoped that Taylor Woodrow would one day return and help with the reconstruction that would be needed. Not quite the same revolutionary fervour as his colleagues, I suspected.

This formality over, I was able to start packing my heavy baggage: books, ornaments, rugs, electronic equipment, household effects — about a dozen crates in all. With business of this kind coming in from the many departing expatriates, the German transport company I was dealing with was in full operation and assured me that it could ship my goods to London if I could first get outward clearance through customs. Having hired a truck and taken the crates there, I spent the best part of a day getting clearance papers after not unfriendly officials had thoroughly examined everything and questioned me in detail — a process I could not have gone through by myself without knowing Persian. The carpenter I had brought with me then nailed the crates down and I deposited them, wondering if I would ever see them again.

The young German representative of the transport company was confident that I would, and I paid him in hope. Many months later, and by then well installed in Hong Kong, I was informed by Taylor Woodrow in London of a message to them from Austria to say that my crates had arrived in Salzburg by overland truck from Tehran, some of them damaged, and that it would cost something to have them repaired for the onward journey. Taylor Woodrow undertook to pay, and on home leave later I found the crates stacked under a tarpaulin in my garden, their contents undamaged and only slightly rifled.

Having dealt with the heavy baggage, I then cleared the office and completed the accounts by depositing in the bank the proceeds of the sale of such of the company's furniture and other property as I had been able to dispose of. (It was to be a long time before the bank balance could be remitted to London.) I then began my farewell round of the few remaining British businessmen in Tehran. None had much hope of recovering money owing to them locally. And one of them had just come back from a visit to his establishment at a southern port where he had looked on miserably while vast stocks of liquor, which his company dealt in, were thrown out of warehouses and down the drain — literally. I took leave of the British ambassador and had talks with other members of the much reduced embassy as well. No one was very sanguine about a future for British enterprise in Iran, and all were concerned about the course of political developments. Of Persian friends, few were still contactable. Most of my acquaintances from my year in Tehran with Taylor Woodrow, as well as my many others from years before in the diplomatic service, had fled or been executed by Khomeini's regime.

Tehran's streets were still blocked in a chaos of horn-blowing traffic and there was an air of activity. But this was a superficial illusion: business after business had shut down, and there was repression and intimidation overall. The atmosphere was ghostly and unreal, a feeling brought home to me when I went to the office of a friendly British company to send a package to London through the courier service it used. The lift was not working, and as I puffed my way up eight floors I did not see a single nameplate on any of the landings. All that remained were the clean empty rectangles that had once advertised the dozen major European and American companies which, with 100 others, had hummed with

183

activity in the Great Persian Bonanza. With hindsight, there had been a lesson to be learned. But who wanted to hear it so long as everything was going the way they wanted it to go with the help of Persian friends in high places who were also making a good thing out of it?

Finally the day came in July 1979 when I had done all I could by way of clearing up, and I would leave for Hong Kong and a new chapter. It was only then that the enormity of the occasion struck me. This was how I was leaving the country I had known on and off and become attached to over so many years. I remembered that autumn in 1947, after seven and a half years in the wartime army, when I had ridden 600 miles by bus down the corrugation that was the then road from Tehran to Shiraz. There, streets not paved, a town without taxis, I had climbed into a droshky, the driver with his leather cap Russian-style, and in the pink of a November sunset made my first entrance into the consulate: no need to say British — it was the only one. British vice-consul — the first rung — a moment never to be forgotten. And now that same consulate was the Shiraz local revolutionary *Komiteh* office. *Sic transit gloria.*

My nice landlord and his wife sensed the mood and shared it. Our parting on the evening I now left for the airport was tearful. And on arrival there I found myself faced with a final experience of the new regime. Before any approach to the check-in desk all baggage was minutely examined by Islamic Revolutionary Council vigilantes. A decent-looking polite man took mine in hand and went through my clothing without comment. But when he came to the suitcase of books and papers it was a different matter. He called over a higher-powered individual who took a look, hardly waited for my answer to his questions, and in turn summoned up an obviously unpleasant but intelligent man with a pistol but no insignia of any kind except an air-force tab on his shirt.

He listened to my answers and then proceeded with the help of two loutish ignoramuses with rifles to turn all the books and papers upside down. He seemed to know fair English and could identify some of the material, but he dealt with me in Persian. The most innocent paper seemed for him to hide some damning crime. Why was I taking away copies of the old *Imperial Gazette*? (To

184

have a record of the registration of Taylor Woodrow in the country.) Why had I been around the university? (Attending advanced Persian classes before the revolution.) How much foreign exchange did I have? (Less than I had brought in; there were now no travellers' cheques available locally.) And more. This went on for well over half an hour, until I began to be afraid I would be too late to check in — when I would really let fly at my inquisitor.

Wisely of course I restrained myself and gave him no opportunity to invite me to step inside. His kind of people now had the real power in dealing with the public and were only too ready to exercise it. And I did want to get off to Hong Kong that night by the only, and infrequent, service (Air France) that flew straight there. So I put up with the examination until he was at last grudgingly ready to let me through — leaving me to try somehow to stuff the now disorderly collection of books and papers back into the suitcase. With little time to spare I got aboard. The vast expanse of light that was Tehran faded into the blackness of the long flight ahead. Part of me did not care if I never saw this country again. Part of me dreamed of returning some time. I felt infinitely sad.

20

Transfer to Hong Kong–First Business Visits to China

I n readiness for the move to Hong Kong I had read up its history and development. But nothing had prepared me for the sight of it as the overnight flight from Tehran, barely clearing rooftops, landed on the airport runway built out into the harbour. Later that day I strolled round the tower blocks in the central business district on the harbour side of the main island, wandered in downtown streets, everywhere the endless toing and froing of thousands of pedestrians, mostly Chinese — the picture of Hong Kong well enough known to the world through advertisement and travelogue. But the dynamism of the place was what struck me most, and it has to be actually lived in to be appreciated. British skill and enterprise over nearly 140 years had combined with Chinese industriousness to build up a community of five million people in an area only two-thirds the size of Surrey. At first sight of it I had the impression that every square foot of the small central district had been built up; but I was soon to discover that there was still space for the construction work of all kinds that was going on: roads, bridges, docks, office blocks, an underground railway. My job would be to identify upcoming contracts in these fields that might be of interest to Taylor Woodrow and to send details of them to the company for evaluation.

Meantime, immediately after my arrival, came the prearranged meeting with the company's marketing director on his way back to London from a construction exhibition in Peking. In talks over a few days he gave me a general directive and we discussed how I should operate. Rents being exorbitant, it was decided that as a measure of economy I should in the first instance set up an office at home. He then left me to get on with it. Within a couple of weeks I had taken a lease on an attractive twenty-sixth-floor apartment overlooking Repulse Bay, on the south of Hong Kong island, which included a spare room that would serve as an office; whereupon my wife flew out from London to join me.

I soon began a round of introductory calls to make my presence and my interest known. Taylor Woodrow was by no means a new name in Hong Kong; the company had built the Ocean Terminal some years before. But it had not maintained a permanent presence thereafter; I was now its first resident representative. Although I was no longer a government official, my previous status put me in a senior position in the colony's official order of precedence, and this gave me a useful entry at the highest official and commercial levels. The governor was an old diplomatic service colleague; and I soon got to know a number of heads of department relevant to my work — among them the helpful Scottish director of public works.

My main contacts in the private sector were the heads of leading local construction and engineering companies, nearly all of them Hong Kong Chinese. As did Taylor Woodrow, most British and other foreign enterprises went into partnership with these when tendering for contracts, since their local knowledge, particularly with regard to labour procurement and relations, was essential. Competition was fierce. The days were gone when United Kingdom contractors could expect preference because this was a British colony: Hong Kong, a thriving centre of seemingly endless development, was a magnet for companies from America, Australia, Germany, Japan and Korea, besides Britain.

In the private sector the lowest bid generally succeeded, though before signing a contract the employer might make it known to a higher bidder (whom he preferred were his bid not so high) that he would stand a chance if he brought his figure down. On public projects I tried several times to appeal to the patriotism of senior officials, arguing that Hong Kong was not a sovereign state and could not exist without London, so it was surely not too much to expect the colony to give preference to a British company whose bid might be only marginally higher than a foreigner's. But it was an argument that cut no ice: the government of Hong Kong regarded itself as having a duty only to the people of the colony, and on that basis it would always look for the best price. So far as support of the government in London was concerned, this extended mainly to defence and foreign affairs, in both of which fields Hong Kong shared costs with it. I could see the logic of all this in purely materialistic terms, but I could not help reflecting on the different attitude likely to be adopted by the government of, say, Réunion, when it came to deciding between French and foreign companies tendering there.

However, my thoughts had to concentrate on my own efforts and I set about looking for potential local contracts. I soon found that this was easier than it had been in Tehran where upcoming projects were hardly ever advertised and where details of them had to be ferreted out of individuals, public and private, who often expected some reward for their services. In Hong Kong, invitations to tender in the public sector were advertised in the *Official Gazette*; in the private sector they were sometimes in the press, but more often by word of mouth. Although the government had set up a powerful anti-corruption organization, there were still malpractices in some quarters. I used to avoid these in my searches, which covered tenders for roads and docks, prestige buildings, a racecourse, barracks, the new underground railway and a proposed new airport (later shelved for lack of funds). On receipt of details of some of these projects, with my recommendation, my head office in London decided which ones to bid for, and technical teams came out from there to prepare tenders.

There were also frequent visits by the chairman, managing director and other senior executives of the company anxious to see the situation on the ground for themselves. It was a function of my role as the company's resident representative that I should know the local scene and the senior personalities well enough to be able to introduce the company visitors without delay to the officials and businessmen relevant to projects under consideration and to those others who could brief them on the overall politico-economic situation in the colony in elaboration of my own assessments. Particularly helpful on this, besides the governor, was the diplomatic service officer appointed by the Foreign Office in London as the United Kingdom trade commissioner and head of the only British (as distinct from Hong Kong) government office in the colony. Through him I was able to meet selected ministers on visits from London whom I wished to make aware of Taylor Woodrow's interest in doing business.

Another visitor, in a different category, whom I met in Hong Kong early in 1981, was Julius Nyerere, president of Tanzania, who of course knew me from my years there as British high commissioner. In view of this acquaintance the governor asked me to go with his protocol officer to the airport early one morning to be .with Nyerere during a couple of hours' stopover on his way to Peking on an official visit.

After having been away from Tanzania for nearly ten years I found it absorbing to hear his views on the difficulty of maintaining his policy of *Ujamaa* (familyhood, community living). Tanzanian peasant farmers had not taken kindly to the concept of communal villages; they preferred to go on working traditional smallholdings handed down from father to son. But state intervention in agriculture continued, thus removing incentive, creating inefficiency and fostering corruption where there had been none before.

* * *

When I arrived in Hong Kong Taylor Woodrow was already engaged, in a joint venture with a comparable French company, in bidding for part of the civil engineering works for a nuclear power station in south China not far from the border with the colony. Negotiations over this in Hong Kong with construction companies from mainland China made me keen to make contacts inside that country, which at that time (1979) was being regarded by the West as a possibly lucrative new market looking for technical and financial assistance for development. Japan was already active there, and now American and European industrial and commercial companies, as well as banks, were beginning to set up representation in Peking. It seemed to me that Taylor Woodrow also ought to be looking into the market there; and towards the end of 1980 I was authorized to pay an exploratory visit — on which my wife could accompany me.

It was not easy to get entry into China in those days. A visa could not be obtained unless the foreigner had been invited in by a Chinese state corporation; and obviously, without having been there before, I did not know any to contact. In this situation there had grown up in Hong Kong a coterie of local Chinese business-men with connections in China who set themselves up as China agents. For a fee these would make all the arrangements necessary for the visit of a foreign company's representative — invitation, visa, air passages, hotel, venue for meetings, interpreting. Giving advice to the newcomer on trade with China was becoming big business. There was a bewildering choice of agent open to him: old China hands of good repute, new ones not so good, Chinese middlemen of varying influence and price, and glib enterprising charlatans of various nationalities. Then there were the glossy compendiums, trade journals and reports, the expensive seminars, read-ins and workshops — all geared to a spin-off of the action that was trade with China.

This rash of services was a natural response to the moderniz-ation of China's foreign trade relations. When this first came to world notice in the early 1970s it was immediately — and, as it turned out, wrongly — assumed to be the start of a bonanza for foreign suppliers. Many of these had little if any previous knowledge of China, probably no notion of how to do business there, and no thought of having Chinese expertise on their staff. But El Dorado was waiting somewhere north of Hong Kong; there was bound to be fierce competition; something had to be done at once. For newcomers like myself this meant first finding out how to go about it.

There was no lack of good, authoritative advice from foreign and trade ministries in London; from chambers of commerce and trade associations specializing in China; from big European trad-ing houses and banks with more than a century of experience there. But for the newcomer to translate all this into actual entry to China was another matter; and leaving aside the long-term question of trade itself, there was the problem of reaching the stage of even preliminary discussion with the Chinese authorities. It was to cash in on this basic requirement that the new advisory and consultancy services in Hong Kong began to sprout. And these agents quickly found clients who were prepared to pay well for advice of varying quality, whether it led to business in China or not. And too often it did not. But if this was blamed on a middleman promising more than he could actually deliver, it was perhaps due even more to the revision of development policy by the Chinese themselves, which cut down opportunities for foreign suppliers.

By the end of the 1970s it had become clear to Peking that it had to look at its priorities again in the light of national needs and costs. Also, there was a strong reaction there to the attitude of some foreign businessmen. Too many seemed to the Chinese only to be after the chance of a lucrative contract; too few took account of Chinese intelligence and pride. They were unaware or unconcerned about the Chinese desire to build up mutual trust and confidence with potential suppliers and to cooperate with them. They thought they could simply rush in on a fast sell, and out again with the prospect of a contract.

A revision of Chinese development plans in 1978 on a firmly pragmatic basis had helped to counter such attitudes. It served also to bring some realism into the behaviour of Western firms and to make the newcomers like me among them look critically at the various advisers and consultants competing for our custom. What these offered, charged and actually achieved varied widely according to their experience, influence and integrity. This one would claim to have good connections in China in one sector or another. That one would say he was in business there on his own account and would be glad to share it. Yet another would undertake exclusive commissions for interested Western firms. And some of them would straight away ask for a retainer, fees, expenses, even a binding promise of a commission on an eventual contract.

It took me days of negotiation in Hong Kong with the agent I had engaged before he would reduce the exorbitant fee he had at first demanded to a more reasonable figure acceptable to me. Even that, I knew, was far too high for the work that would be involved; but I had to make a start somewhere and without his help I could not get anywhere. And if I did not accept his services he would have no difficulty in selling them elsewhere. At the same time as I was making arrangements with him I was in touch with the director of the Hong Kong office of a leading British merchant bank interested in financing capital projects that might be undertaken in China by reputable British and foreign contractors. We decided that it would be to the advantage of both of us if we went in together as complementary partners, neither with a commitment to the other at that stage but both with a view to getting some idea of the potential for business.

That this would not be easy was soon clear to us from the information we got from British and foreign representatives in Hong Kong who had already been there. It was going to be a hard footslog all the way, and the training manual had not yet been written that incorporated all the experience of the companies that had done the march and the others that had fallen by the way. The centralized control of even the smallest Chinese commercial or industrial enterprise — all of them of course state-owned — involved endless red tape that could tie up even the simplest of negotiations inordinately long, whatever the eventual outcome. This tended to lay a dead hand on the proposals of what were often highly-skilled Chinese engineers who, if allowed to use their own initiative, could have negotiated through to an outcome, whether successful or not, without undue delay. That was always assuming the negotiating table had been reached. For there was a major problem not generally highlighted in the words of wisdom heaped on the foreign newcomer by his advisers and consultants.

Normally a Western firm looks for a capital project contract overseas in response either to a specific invitation or to the country's stated desire for particular development. But this was not the case with China, where nothing was published. So the newcomer was hard put to know where to start. If he asked the authorities there what projects were being planned in his company's field of interest, he generally received the counter-question: What projects could he offer for consideration? It was a situation I encountered in each of the several fact-finding visits I made to China during my four and a half years in Hong Kong, visits that gave me valuable experience for when, a few years later, Taylor Woodrow appointed me to Peking. By that time conditions there for foreigners had changed for the better: there was more accommodation available, police surveillance had greatly relaxed, state corporations had been given some autonomy.

But on that first visit from Hong Kong to Peking in 1980 my wife and I found ourselves in an atmosphere of the typical orthodox communist state of those days. The one undeveloped old hotel, an amalgam of successive British, French and Russian designs over half a century, had (as my wife described it) wall-to-wall floorboarding with hot and cold running cockroaches. It was run by a government department whose prior allocation of a room to a foreigner was a prerequisite to his application for a visa. The only traffic on the streets, besides bicycles and horse-drawn carts, were military and civilian trucks, curtained Russian limousines carrying senior officials, and some taxis. To hire one of the latter at the hotel it was necessary to fill in a detailed application form; and then the vehicle would be tailed by an unmarked police car trying not to look like one.

Conversation with foreigners was forbidden to Chinese except on official business; but the man-in-the-street would stand and stare wonderingly at the comparatively few foreigners around. On one winter's visit my wife's fine leather boots aroused constant interest. Getting into official contact with the state construction and engineering companies in which I was interested was a slow and laborious business, which even our Hong Kong Chinese mentor could not speed up. And with my banker associate I found myself sitting around waiting for hours, sometimes a day on end, for a promised meeting.

Most of my exploratory visits lasted from five to ten days and targeted port development, which was high on Peking's list of priorities and on Taylor Woodrow's specialties. In cooperation with the company's energy subsidiary I also investigated possible openings for work in the offshore oil industry, which was being developed at that time.

It was not expected that any of these short visits would lead to a contract; but they were invaluable as reconnaissance of a difficult and complicated market which was beginning to attract Western interest more seriously than it had done in the past. Equally important, the visits enabled me to learn my way around the corridors of Chinese commercial and administrative institutions and to get to know, and become known to, key personnel there in the fields in which I was interested.

In the light of this I was gradually able to get myself into China and arrange business meetings there without having to call on the expensive services of the Hong Kong agents on whom I had had to depend on my first visits. The culmination of this process was that, with the sponsorship of the state construction company in Peking, I was able to get a multi-journey visa that enabled me to move in and out of China as often as I wanted over a period of six months, and could then renew it. This was a prized achievement at that time and one that enhanced my standing in the expatriate commercial community in Hong Kong doing business with China, many of whom still had to apply for a visa for each visit.

Soon after my arrival in Hong Kong in the middle of 1979 I found myself embarked by chance on a spare-time activity that was to occupy me intermittently during my time there — and beyond. The deputy head of the government information department was a retired colonel who had been my military attaché in Jakarta when I was ambassador to Indonesia. When Mountbatten was murdered by the IRA in August 1979 the editor of the *Asian Wall Street Journal* wanted to publish an appreciation of him. Having learned from the colonel that I had been on Mountbatten's staff when he was viceroy, the editor asked me to write it — which I did. I of course declined the fee that was offered to me afterwards, whereupon I was invited to write occasional articles for the paper, for which I would be paid, on international political and economic affairs, both topical and historical. I enjoyed doing this, and the research that was often needed for it, as a break from my work. It was an activity that continued for some years after I had left Hong Kong for other posts, and it became easier with practice. The journal especially welcomed my contributions on problems concerning Turkey and on doing business with China.

By the end of 1983 I had been four and a half years in Hong Kong and in that time had put Taylor Woodrow on the local map, sending back to head office details of a variety of civil engineering projects planned for the colony. As I mentioned earlier, tenders for these were not of course all successful; competition was severe, especially from Japanese and Korean contractors who regularly undercut Western bids. On public sector contracts the Hong Kong government in its desire for the lowest price continued to deny any concession to British bidders. But the private sector was more flexible, with many local contractors anxious to maintain their established links with British companies.

21
Bahrain

By now it might have been logical for Taylor Woodrow to
have had me transfer my activities to China as their resident
representative there, to take advantage of the basic knowledge I had acquired of that market. But that was not to be for
another couple of years; for the meantime it had been decided to
post me to Bahrain, in the Persian Gulf. The government there was
planning a number of construction projects that might be of
interest, and I was to explore the possibilities in these. Meantime,
when I arrived at the beginning of 1984 the finishing touches were
being put to the prestigious Sheraton Hotel that Taylor Woodrow
had built, together with a related office block. The hotel contained
a number of self-contained suites in oriental decor where the
ruling Emir of Bahrain could accommodate in style his fellow
rulers in the Gulf Cooperation Council — Kuwait, Saudi Arabia,
Qatar, the United Arab Emirates and Oman — when it was his
turn to host their annual meeting.

I was gratified to find that I was remembered by the Emir (who
received me warmly) and a number of local businessmen I had
known during my time in the political residency in the 1960s. This
had of course given place to a British embassy when the island
became fully independent in 1971. Contract search here was not
difficult, nor was negotiation if things reached that stage; the
public sector in particular still followed traditional British procedures. It was a matter for regret that by the time I arrived the
contract had long since been let for the construction of an elevated
causeway linking Bahrain with the Saudi Arabian mainland

opposite. So I concentrated on smaller planned projects on the island itself. It was an agreeable environment to work in, disturbed only by the echoes of the nearby war between Iran and Iraq.

Bahrain is the smallest political entity in the Persian Gulf. But lying midway as it does, and little more than 20 miles off the coast of Saudi Arabia, it has a regional importance out of proportion to its size. There was a steady coming and going of delegations from the other members of the Gulf Cooperation Council. This had been set up in 1981 as a non-aligned organization to develop cooperation and coordination in the political, economic and defence fields. Bahrain slipped into this new role easily from its former political insularity. It was an insularity which was to some extent the legacy of a century and more of treaty relations with Britain whereby the latter handled the island's defence and foreign affairs. But by the end of that relationship and the assumption of full sovereignty Bahrain had acquired a sophistication and a knowledge of the outside world, and the West in particular, that made it easy for it to take its place in the international scene.

It achieved this without being one of the oil-rich. There is some oil in the south of the island — it was the first discovery in the Gulf, in 1932. But this has never matched its neighbours' resources and it is expected to run out by the turn of the century. This will leave Bahrain dependent for its income on new discoveries of gas, on the refining of crude oil from Saudi Arabia via an underwater pipeline, and an aluminium smelter and diverse other industries.

Parallel with these activities was its development as an offshore banking centre, gradually replacing Beirut in that role as the latter continued at that time to suffer destruction in the civil war. With English spoken everywhere on the island, good air services and telecommunications, no taxation, a free-currency market and the most liberal and sophisticated living environment in the Gulf it was well-placed to fill that gap. I found the Bahrainis preoccupied with profitable trade, going about their daily lives outwardly unperturbed by the Iran–Iraq war and its extension to the waters around the island. But there was an undercurrent of concern. Bahrain saw itself in the front line, something of an advance Saudi base — an impression strengthened by forthcoming completion of the causeway between the two countries, financed entirely by the Saudis. This was a link seen by both as giving confident reality to their *de facto* alliance over and above their association in the Gulf Cooperation Council. It was an alliance that as a result of Saudi generosity had already brought Bahrain real advantage in the conomic and military fields.

22

China–Problems of Doing
Business–Retirement Again

B y now it had been decided to transfer me to China to set up an office for Taylor Woodrow in Peking. But before that I was called back to London for briefing as a member of a company team that was going out to Peking at the beginning of 1985. We were to meet up there with our joint venture partners, a French construction and engineering group, for the start of substantive negotiations with the Chinese state corporation concerned in construction of the Daya Bay nuclear power station in south China near the border with Hong Kong. I of course knew something about Chinese business methods from the visits I had made to the country during my years in Hong Kong. But this was to be my first experience of negotiations, as distinct from exploratory discussions. It introduced me to what I was to come to know well: the Chinese propensity for squeezing all they could out of their foreign partners in any joint venture while themselves putting in a minimum, yet insisting on being the majority partner.

Thus they would expect the foreign company to put up, say, £100 million by way of equipment, management and technical expertise, while they themselves would what they called match this with land (all state-owned in any case), buildings and local labour at low rates of pay — worth in all a fraction of the foreign company's investment. And when, on highly technical projects such as the nuclear power station, some foreign labour (in this case British, French and Hong Kong) had also to be used, the

Chinese tried to insist that their own labour should be charged to the project at foreign rates — even though actually being paid at local rates. This was an attempt that was firmly resisted.

These negotiations were only the first step in what was to be a long drawn-out process during my forthcoming stay in China before the subcontracts for the civil engineering works were signed. The negotiations were slow not only because of the intrinsic difficulties but because there had to be three-way translation of the proceedings (English–French–Chinese) step by step, and frequently English–French, where I acted as interpreter. On conclusion of this stage, which lasted a month, I went back to Bahrain to close down the office and house, then left in April 1985 to set up in Peking.

Despite the expense of keeping a representative there, many foreign companies and banks were doing so. For they believed there to be growing prospects of doing business, particularly in the fields of construction and engineering: roads, railways, ports, oil installations, power stations. And there was special interest in hotels, commercial complexes and apartment blocks to cater for the growing foreign population. A number of modern three-star hotels had already been built, designed by foreign architects — often to the specifications of major international hotel groups who would manage them. These were financed as joint ventures between local enterprises or municipal authorities and foreign construction companies, mostly from Hong Kong.

Meantime there was still virtually no private accommodation apart from blocks of state-owned apartments for diplomatic personnel and journalists. My wife and I had therefore to live throughout our stay in China in a small but comfortable suite in one of the new joint-venture hotels — a far cry from the old Peking Hotel we had lived in on our first visit from Hong Kong in 1980. But even this was hard to come by and I had to live first in a small single room until a suite was available, when my wife came out to join me. The ground floor of the hotel housed the offices of a number of well-known foreign banks and companies — mostly American and Japanese, then British, French, German and Australian — and Taylor Woodrow now joined them.

The costs to the company of living and office accommodation, as well as entertaining, communications with London and taxis (it was exorbitantly expensive to import a car) were very high. I was therefore anxious to get some return for this outlay by following up every possibility of a contract. I set about making myself known to state construction companies, as well as banks and other financial institutions likely to be of use in my search. In parallel I sought discussions with senior officials in various relevant ministries. This was not always easy to arrange. At first I often waited for days, at times more than a week, for an appointment I had phoned for to the English-speaking foreign liaison official (often a young woman) who was on the staff of most ministries.

In the course of time I got tired of this and, once I had learned my way around, would if necessary just take a taxi to the ministry and talk my way past the guard at the gate. This I did by producing company description brochures in Chinese and using the basic Mandarin I was acquiring by lessons from a local teacher. I would then ask to speak to the liaison official. Phoned by the guard, she would obligingly come to the gate and greet me politely. Thence when I had explained what I wanted and the reason for the urgency of it, she would take me into the ministry and do her best to get a meeting for me with the official concerned, or another acting for him. Meetings always took place in special meeting rooms, which every ministry had; no outsiders were ever admitted into offices. Whether or not a foreign visitor brought an interpreter or spoke Mandarin well enough himself the ministry always provided its own interpreter. This of course meant that meetings took twice as long as the actual substance of them.

I would usually bring to a meeting an illustrated brochure I had put together in English and Chinese to describe Taylor Woodrow's experience and achievements in the field under discussion. There was no point in presenting a thick glossy general company brochure in English of the usual European kind: the road to any desk in Peking was cluttered with piles of these lying around unopened and gathering dust. It was important to make a specific presentation that would attract Chinese technical and commercial interest — and one that would reflect a sympathetic approach to Chinese aspirations.

This meant I had to compile separate presentations for each of the various projects I was interested in. China was altogether too big for a haphazard search for business. A foreign company had to decide in which fields to concentrate its effort, seek out the most likely possibilities and stick with these, then get down single-mindedly to the tactics of approaching them. Identifying the possibilities was a major task which justified the presence of a resident representative. Japan's outstanding success in China could be traced to its, at that time, nearly 500 representatives, the majority in Peking with the rest spread over a dozen other cities. The United States trailed a far second with fewer than 100 men, followed by the major European countries with a mere score or two each, almost all of them in Peking.

Being based there meant considerable travelling around provincial centres, mostly on the extensive railway network but occasionally on roads that could be lethal. I came to enjoy Chinese long-distance overnight trains, hauled by great steam locomotives. As a foreigner I travelled what was called soft-berth, while the majority of Chinese had to put up with hard-berth. In the four-berth sleeping compartment my fellow passengers were usually Chinese officials or state corporation executives, friendly and often interesting, communication between us being a mixture of basic Mandarin, elementary English and sign language.

In the course of two years I went on business visits (some several times) to Canton, Shanghai, Tientsin, and a dozen other provincial centres as far north as Harbin and south to Chungking. I had to be cautious in approach to the authorities there, for there was as yet no clear-cut division of responsibility between the centre and the provinces. It was largely in the latter that the end users of processes and the consumers of goods and services were to be found. But it was at the centre that policy planning, financial authority and operational decision usually lay, particularly where infrastructure projects were concerned. It was true that the government had recently announced economic autonomy for a number of regions and cities — but with provisos on the cost of a project and the relation it bore to national planning.

Unless the foreigner was confident that a regional target he was aiming at met these criteria he was well advised not go rushing out to the provinces without first consulting the appropriate central authority. The local end users, perhaps over-confident of their autonomy and anxious to get on with the job, might go far down the road of negotiation with a foreign partner — only for both of them to discover obstacles at the centre. The province or municipality might not be able to get the additional funds it had hoped for. The ministry might have cancelled an infrastructure improvement on which the local body was relying for supply or transport related to its proposed project. Or national planning might have given priority to a similar project elsewhere.

In my discussions, whether at the centre or in provincial capitals, I soon learned that the Chinese had a wide range of technical skills themselves. On a visit to Nanking I was taken to see the impressive six-and-a-half-kilometre-long combined road and railway bridge over the Yangtze. The designing of this had been abandoned halfway through by Russian engineers when Sino-Soviet relations were broken in the 1950s. The Chinese, unaided, had then completed the design and built the bridge by 1968. When they turned to the West for assistance in a project involving higher technology they knew exactly what they wanted and on what terms. And the basis of any Western response had to be cooperation, friendship and mutual trust. Chinese negotiators reacted sensitively to a visitor's manner. They preferred confidence with quiet courtesy to bluster or effusiveness. The stock foreign assertion of desire to cooperate with China for mutual benefit was listened to politely. But they knew that the foreigners were in it for the money; and they accepted that — provided China also got what it wanted out of it.

They wanted foreign assistance for three main reasons — technological, managerial, financial. They were competent to build a five-star hotel or a commercial complex themselves. But to do so, and then maintain and run it to a standard that would attract the international clientele whose hard currency would make the project profitable, required expert foreign management until their own people were adequately trained. To get such projects off the ground they needed foreign assistance and investment. Indeed, I found that the subject of finance was often raised even before talk got round to the technicalities of the project. I therefore usually arranged to be accompanied at meetings by the local British repre-

Envoy Extraordinary

sentative of a major London bank who spoke fluent Mandarin. By
his very presence he strengthened my position in the eyes of the
Chinese, while for him there was always the prospect of business
for the bank if and when Taylor Woodrow secured a contract.

* * *

Yet despite all this careful preparation we could never expect a
predictable pattern to negotiations. A scheduled meeting might be
cancelled at short notice or suddenly adjourned. An important
member of the Chinese group might be called elsewhere and disappear from the proceedings. A provincial authority might
suddenly cancel negotiations on instructions from the centre, the
details of which were never disclosed to us. Success was not to be
expected easily or quickly. A foreign businessman might be
encouraged by a favourite Chinese gambit — signing a so-called
letter of intent — and produce this triumphantly to his head office.
I soon learned that this might not be exclusive to one company,
and would in any case do no more than place on record the desire
of both sides to continue negotiations with a specific aim. Still, it
was a mark of progress that enabled the foreign company to plan
future meetings and gradually make itself and its representative
known. Continual personal contact was all-important to the
eventual outcome. So too was the state of political relations between China and the foreign country involved in the negotiations.

Britain's relations had gone through many vicissitudes over the
years and happily were on an upturn during my time in China.
This was heightened in 1986 by a state visit by the Queen, the first
British sovereign to pay one. It had been nearly 400 years since her
namesake had sent a letter to Emperor Wan Li with a group of
English merchants — who in the event never reached China.
Thereafter Englishmen started trading successfully, if restrictedly,
with Canton, without the backing of their sovereign. It was not
until 1793 that another attempt was made to contact the Chinese
emperor, when George III sent Lord Macartney, career politician
and one-time ambassador to Russia as his emissary. Macartney
arrived with a party of nearly 100 including a German band, and
bearing many gifts. But the emperor was not impressed by what he

204

regarded as a mediocre tribute from an inferior. And when Macartney refused to kowtow he was sent packing. He was succeeded in 1816 by Lord Amherst. But he was denied an audience of the emperor when he refused to appear before him without being given time to wash, shave and dress as he considered an Englishman should for such an occasion.

After these rebuffs Britain's interests in China were given no official support in London but were upheld instead by its traders in Canton. Their lucrative sales of Indian opium (much of it in exchange for tea), despite all Peking's efforts to suppress the trade, led to a war that Britain won in 1842. As a result of this, Hong Kong island was ceded to her 'in perpetuity' and extraterritorial rights were granted in a number of so-called treaty ports on the mainland of China. Only in 1858 did the emperor finally agree to the opening of a British diplomatic mission in Peking. But when his mandarins were tardy over implementation of the agreement, a British force aided by a French, with a show of impatience incomprehensible to the Chinese, marched into Peking and burned down the Summer Palace. In London this raised hardly an eyebrow. For this was imperial Britain at the height of its world power.

The great British public thought of China as some kind of dependency. Britain was sovereign in Hong Kong, managed great trading warehouses in Canton, maintained a diplomatic and consular establishment of nearly 70 officials throughout the country (many of them fluent in the language) and a Supreme Court in Shanghai, virtually ruled a number of ports, and ran China's maritime customs service with a corps of British officials whose career it was. In this situation it was not surprising that Britain's relations with the country up to the end of the nineteenth century should have been so bad. What is surprising is that by the 1930s, despite Britain's refusal to respond to pressure for revision of what the Chinese called the 'unequal treaties' which gave Britain Hong Kong and the coastal concessions, the Chinese should have been receptive to the idea of a new relationship.

But it was still not an easy one. Even by the Second World War, when virtually free of foreign influence, the Chinese were not unnaturally still reacting against the iniquities suffered while that influence had lasted. Economic aid from abroad might be sought, but this did not inhibit the expression of a nationalism that at times bordered on xenophobia. Even Britain's recognition of the new republic within months of the communist takeover in October 1949 was received with bad grace. Peking believed London had taken the step not out of goodwill but in an attempt to salvage some of its still remaining commercial interests in the country. This, together with Britain's continuance of relations with Taiwan, led the Chinese to peg diplomatic representation at a low level and refuse to exchange ambassadors. It was to be 1972 before an exchange was achieved, after Britain had cut its remaining links with Taiwan and voted for China to replace that administration as a permanent member of the United Nations Security Council.

In the intervening period, however, the Cultural Revolution had seen the arrest of British subjects in China and the humiliation of British diplomats there, culminating in the sack of the embassy in August 1967. (In 1971 the Chinese government agreed to pay for reinstatement of the buildings.) Despite public clamour in London for retaliation against these actions the government refused to yield to it. There was concern for residual British commercial interests in China. But there was also understanding of the Chinese reaction to the memory of past foreign impositions, and reluctance to force the country into a corner. It was an attitude that paid off with Peking after the Cultural Revolution was over. Once ambassadors had been exchanged the way was clear for a new era in Anglo-Chinese relations.

In a succession of exchanges by foreign ministers and others the high point was the visit of Mrs Thatcher, when prime minister, to Peking in September 1984 to initial the agreement for the return of Hong Kong to Chinese sovereignty in July 1997. The Queen's arrival in 1986 was therefore more than just a courtesy state visit. It set the seal on the progress of the two countries towards outliving the bitter memories, the injustices and hostilities between them of more that two centuries. On both sides the arrogance of great empire seemed at last to have given way to tolerance borne of lesser greatness.

This improved atmosphere, however, did not invariably ensure a smooth ride for British commercial negotiators. In 1983 Peking refused to ratify a major defence supply contract with Britain which had taken nearly three years to arrive at before it was finally signed by the organizations concerned. The reason put forward by the Chinese government was that it was not satisfied with the price, technology and delivery dates. Behind this statement were whispers of internal political disagreement over the contract. But what stuck in London's throat was Peking's simplistic excuse that it discovered defects in the contract when it first examined it *after* it had been signed by the British and Chinese negotiating groups. The British government found it hard to believe that the Chinese authorities directly involved in a deal of this kind would not have been working to a brief that took account of criteria set by the central government, and referring back doubtful points as they arose.

As my own activity in China developed I became conscious of the possibility that I might be wasting time, effort and money in negotiating with state corporations whose decisions might be repudiated by higher authority or challenged by other organizations. I did what I could to guard against this by spreading my net wide over all the groups likely to be involved in a project. I was able to have friendly discussions with the principals both in Peking and in provincial centres where these had an interest in the project under discussion.

I soon discovered that the Chinese are not the inscrutable humourless people so often portrayed in the West. On the contrary, they showed pleasure or disappointment without dissembling, and laughed easily when amused. But they tended to be inflexible in negotiation and to weight the balance of equity in their own favour. I sometimes had the impression that they negotiated in the confident belief that if they could not get what they wanted from my company they would get it from one of the many others lining up to do business with them. And chief among these were the Japanese and Koreans, who undercut most Western bidders for contracts by profiting from lower production costs, more generous financing, proximity and a wider knowledge of Mandarin.

In nearly two years in the country I pursued, to varying lengths, many possible openings in a number of fields (ports in particular) for all of which, bearing in mind the competence of the Chinese themselves in actual construction, I generally proposed project management and finance, particularly where high technology was involved. But, apart from the small subcontract with our French partners in the nuclear power station project in the south (in which I was only marginally involved), none of my efforts resulted in a contract. In many cases the Chinese wanted more than Taylor Woodrow was prepared to give them, in others the competition was too strong. It was poor consolation to me that other Western contractors (including leading Americans and Germans) had not done any better. None of us could see any clear prospect of work, and meantime the cost of maintaining representatives in Peking was going steadily up.

I was by now accustomed to China and was enjoying living there, with my knowledge of the language growing. But towards the end of 1986 I felt that I had in all honesty to tell my chairman that there seemed to be little prospect of a return for the company on its vast outlay on keeping me in the country. I knew I was in effect talking myself out of a job; but the way things were this was unavoidable — and the chairman agreed. Unfortunately there was no other post abroad in the role in which I had served the company for the past nine years nearly. So I took retirement for the second time, approaching my seventieth birthday.

* * *

I could not really complain. Following my 30 years in the diplomatic service I had enjoyed a second full-time career, one that I had been fortunate enough, at 60, to find for myself in a completely different field from diplomacy, but for which my diplomatic experience suited me ideally. It was a career of nearly nine years. As a member of the Taylor Woodrow team I had worked with friendly and helpful colleagues from whom I learned a great deal. I had gained first-hand experience in the technique of contract search and negotiation in the engineering industry. As did my diplomatic service, it was a career that gave me complete job satisfaction. And it had been a pleasure to serve someone as considerate and inspiring as Frank Taylor.

In that role in Iran I had lived through the overthrow of the Shah and the revolution that brought Khomeini to power — the climax of a period of history that had begun 16 years before in Tehran when I was deputy to the ambassador there. I had served Taylor Woodrow in Bahrain when it was touched by the war between Iran and Iraq, but not to the extent of limiting the scope for contract search. And in six years in Hong Kong and China, my first stay in the Far East apart from my army experience in Singapore, I had come to know something of a part of the world far removed in distance and culture from the Middle East where I had spent so long. Apart from two years in the Foreign Office in the 1950s, I had served abroad continuously, in war and peace, for nearly 50 years. Now I would be setting out for home.

23
Slow Train to Hong Kong

I decided that the first stage of the journey should be, with my wife, an exotic train ride from Peking to Hong Kong. I asked the hotel, well in advance, to make reservations for us on sleeping-car express (so-called) No. 15 leaving the capital at 10.55 every evening and arriving in Canton (for the connection to Hong Kong) at 7.42 on the second morning following: two nights and a day, just under 56 hours in all. There were only four-berth compartments, so I asked for a whole one of these to ensure some marital privacy. The fare was modest enough for me to pay for all four berths. But however willing I was to do this, I could only have two. The train was heavily booked and I was told it was antisocial not to have all the berths actually utilized — unless of course you were a leading politician, official or officer, in which case an exception could be made.

Being none of these, I now began the agonizing speculation about our likely fellow travellers. Sex discrimination is not a feature of Chinese trains, so there was a wide choice for specu- lation, and the mind ran the gamut of male, female, old, young, smoker, spitter or hawker (or both). By this time I had begun to ask myself what the particular virtue of train was over aeroplane and whether my wife was going to thank me for allowing her to share my middle-aged itch for the unusual. Then suddenly it began to look as if I would perforce be getting out of the situation; for the hotel agent brought us the news that when he actually went to buy the tickets he was told that he couldn't — unless he had authorization from some official sponsor. Ah yes, it was true that reservations had been made. But that was irrelevant. Anyone could make a reservation. What mattered for a foreigner was the authority to move from A to B. No authority, no ticket.

However, I decided not to take this easy way out. I casually mentioned the problem to officialdom. Eyebrows were raised in curiosity (and suspicion?) at such masochism when there were jet planes doing the journey safely and comfortably in a couple of hours. But it was finally accepted that the ways of the British are no less inexplicable than those of the Chinese — and equally inoffensive; and my request was politely noted. Behind the scenes some administrative machine got slowly into gear and next evening the agent turned up with two highly complicated pieces of paper, which were simple train tickets from Peking to Hong Kong for two nights later.

The price on the tickets was less than I had been told they would cost. I at once concluded that we had been given hard berths instead of the soft that are the norm for foreigners. I sent him back to enquire. By now it was of course too late for him to do anything, so it was the next day before he returned with confirmation that they were indeed soft berths. I could only assume that through sponsorship by the ministry there was some discount. At all events I took the tickets without qualm, since the saving would offset the cost of our hotel room for an extra full day to enable us to stay in it until 10.00 p.m., when it would be time to leave for the station.

Getting a taxi at the hotel was no problem; and having loaded the baggage mostly into the interior (for want of a big enough boot), the driver dashed off along streets now largely empty of the usual procession of vehicles. Peking railway station loomed up ahead in the crisp November night air, as unmistakably what it is as are Victoria, Grand Central or Dar es Salaam, that monument to the Chinese themselves. The difference here was that the cab could go only so far. None of the smooth convenience of a drive up to the entrance, with porters or baggage carts abounding. Taxis had to stop in the parking area well in front of the building while passengers descended, got their own baggage out and dragged it into the station through what looked like half of Peking either coming or going.

211

Into the station, but not straight into the station. Here were no grand porticos. The crowd narrowed into several single files admitted through narrow openings where tickets or other forms of pass had to be shown. Once inside, it was no good looking for human or mechanized help with our mound of cases. These had to be toted or dragged or otherwise moved along by ourselves as best we could. And it was not just a step from entrance to platform. Across the hall over dozens of supine bodies waiting for trains who knew when, up an escalator (it might have been worse — a staircase), along a passage, into a waiting-room and received by a nice female official for all the world like an airline ground hostess.

There we got the first sight of our fellow passengers, in hard berth and soft: good solid citizens, family groups, peasants, workers, soldiers, officials. Surrounded by parcels, boxes, small cases, a birdcage or two: but few if any burdened with 40 to 50 kilograms of baggage meant to be handled on an airport conveyor belt. Clearly they knew the form: why didn't someone tell *us*? And we were not through yet. The girl gave the NOW BOARDING nod and we steeled our aching arms and shoulders to drag the load back along the passage, through the ticket check and downstairs to the platform. The train at last. Relief. But wait: was our carriage really the one that looked as if it was half a mile down the long train? How to steer ourselves and baggage to it through the milling crowd? Desperate needs called for desperate remedies.

The heavy baggage trolley in front of us was obviously intended for official use; but, since my rudimentary spoken Mandarin did not extend to understanding what must have been a warning on the trolley, we loaded our bags on to it, confident of being able to plead foreign ignorance if it came to that. Happily it didn't. Trying to keep the wobbling thing on a straight course down the platform, we piloted our way unchallenged through a sea of official and private faces incredulous, impassive or openly amused at the sight of obviously capitalist foreigners doing their own coolie thing. But it did get us to the appointed carriage with a minimum of further sweat, and there a helpful conductor had someone take the baggage aboard.

At first sight the four-berth compartment seemed impossibly cramped. But perhaps it was only the effect of the lace curtains, window-table cloth, headrests, all demurely Victorian. On the table a small plant in a pot. A flask of boiling water. On the berths, clean linen and soft duvet. And the heating made us forget that it was nearly zero outside. Everything seemed comfortable: it only remained to be seen who else would be sharing the compartment. A last-minute approach to the conductor confirmed that there was no chance of being able to have it all to ourselves: the train was packed.

As we sat in speculation, they appeared: two charming, lively young women from Hong Kong, sisters, returning from a visit to the land of their fathers far north — Mongolia. And they wondering a little apprehensively, no less than we were, who they would have to share the compartment with. Their English was fluent. And when it turned out that one of them was a secretary in an office well known to me, I began to wonder whether an all-knowing ministry in Peking had not arranged the whole thing. Then I dismissed the idea. You just never know your luck.

By now there was the bustle that marks the departure of long-distance trains anywhere. On the dot, with a whistle and a hoot, this one pulled out — to the accompaniment of music throughout its length. This soon gave way to a female voice listing details of the train and its facilities, loud and clear through the loudspeaker in every compartment. The voice, and the music, would become well known to us; ordering our day from morning call to lights out, from meal-time to siesta-time; waking us up and putting us to sleep; regaling us with musical requests, the latest news, revolutionary marches, Mongolian love songs; to say nothing of more practical items like the length of the Yangtze and the span of the bridge over it at Hankow.

There was an amicable togetherness throughout the train — even in the hard-berth carriages — and the handful of foreigners were shown special consideration by the people of the country. The train officials were polite and attentive. One worker spent all his time keeping corridor and lavatories scrupulously clean. This did nothing to shorten the wait for these at peak times; and the tiny washbasins were good reason for growing a beard and using eau-de-Cologne liberally during the journey.

On the other hand, eating and drinking were no trouble at all.

The train was barely under way when a perky little country girl in off-white white bounced into the compartment, introduced herself as our restaurant-car attendant, sat down at ease and proceeded to discuss our likely wants for the following day — breakfast, lunch, supper and anything in between. And the menu she showed us was astounding: we counted 52 dishes and were assured that every one was available. In my mind I was already composing a letter to *The Times* inviting the attention of British Rail's catering manager to the alternatives available on Chinese trains to tepid brown Windsor soup and plastic scrambled eggs.

Tomorrow's order being placed, the compartment prepared to bed down for the night. Sophisticated Hong Kong girls though they were, our travelling companions in the top berths made demurely to creep under the duvet almost fully dressed. Quickly realizing that a gesture was called for, I told the ladies I would pace the corridor while they slipped into something more comfortable — like pyjamas. I did the same in the lavatory, like a contortionist. And I congratulated myself on having remembered to pack night things and toiletries in a small bag because, once four occupants' heavy baggage was stashed in our small compartment, there was no getting at it *en route*. And so to sleep when the lights were turned out throughout the train, which rocked its way gently, if slowly, southwards, with only the occasional technical stop.

Suddenly the dawn silence was broken by a crescendo of reveille music centred round 'The East is Red'. One of the young women, with the loudspeaker almost in her ear, was the first to react, but with the stoicism of her fathers she pulled the quilt up around her head and tried to ignore this 6.30 summons. There was no ignoring it. Within minutes the corridor was a busy thoroughfare echoing with voices and there was clearly a run on the lavatories. Besides, it was getting light outside and the China we were travelling by train to see was coming into view. Once again I politely left the ladies to their cramped dressing room, and soon we were all sitting down to a satisfying hot breakfast.

By this time Zhengzhou, the first scheduled stop, just across the Yellow River, had come and gone on time. The country alternated between arable land and barren stretches, with higher ground to the west, where Xian lay. The air was milder, the scenery grew more varied; and lunch was convivial, with recognition and many a glass raised in toast from table to table. Immediately after, the blinds in the corridor were pulled down and silence imposed for the afternoon rest. By the time the music woke us the train was pulling into the industrial complex of Wuchang-Hankow, across the impressive two-tier rail and road bridge over the Yangtze, designed and built (the loudspeaker reminded us) entirely by Chinese enterprise. Here we stretched our legs along the platform, watching the coming and going, the soft-drink and hot-bun vendors, seeing the people as ordinary as people are on a railway station anywhere.

Back on the move, over afternoon tea in the compartment, we were visited by a posse of officials inspecting tickets. Friendly, polite, but insistent, they asked for my fare. I pointed out that I had paid it — as stated on the tickets. Well, they asked, did I pay it, or the ministry? An important point, this. But my Mandarin cannot cope with it, and our travelling companions, who could surely help, are visiting some acquaintances from their Mongolian trip further down the train. Happily at that moment they returned — and all was revealed.

As foreigners, we had the privilege of paying more for our tickets than a Chinese, and since it turned out that I had only paid the Chinese fare in Peking I had now to hand over the balance. I now realized why what I had paid in Peking was less than I had expected; but the agent had not told me (or I had not understood). With smiles and apologies the inspector took the excess fares from me and made out a receipt. The girls jokingly suggested that we should have contrived to travel as guests of the ministry, who no doubt got a preferential rate.

So the journey continued, the scenery slowly changing to sub-tropical; and everywhere on the land, activity. Over an excellent piping hot meal made in the kitchen we watched Changsha go by in the darkness. Mutual toasts with our travelling companions and seemingly half the restaurant car; request music over the loud-speaker; a nightcap in the compartment, and so to bed again. And at 7.45 next morning — a bare three minutes behind schedule — Canton. Come hell or high water, I was going to shave and change shirts for the arrival — and I did.

It had been an experience (even my wife agreed) well worth some minor discomfort and initial qualms. At an average 70 kilometres an hour over 2500 kilometres (give or take a few) we had been able to see more of China and its people than would ever be possible by air. And we had seen them in an entirely Chinese environment. With a few words of the language we found them polite and friendly. They had gone out of their way to be helpful. And at Canton there was someone to carry our baggage.

24
Third Career–University Lecturer in Turkey

B ack in Wimbledon, I did not take kindly to my second retirement. I did not feel my age and still wanted to do something. Not belonging anywhere, without the discipline of a regular job, I was restless. I filled in the rest of 1987 as best as I could: brushing up my Turkish, putting in order papers and books I had never been home on leave long enough to attend to; taking short holidays abroad with my wife. Then in the autumn I drove out by myself to Turkey. The consulate-general in Istanbul was still holding in store for me the household possessions salvaged from my Taylor Woodrow car that had been involved in a collision with a tractor near Ankara nine years before when I had been driving to Persia. Now was the first opportunity I had to collect the goods and bring them back to our house in London.

All these, however, were merely ephemeral activities to fill in time: I had to have something more regular to do. Early in 1988, therefore, I decided to enrol in a course of Turkish for foreigners at Ankara University in order to keep up my knowledge of the language. Before driving out there I wrote about my plan to a Turkish friend from my years as ambassador, who was doyen of the higher education establishment in Turkey, and told him I looked forward to meeting again in Ankara.

In reply he phoned me from there to say that I would be wasting my time enrolling in that course, which he knew to be on a far lower level than I had already reached in the language. Instead, why did I not come out and teach at Bilkent University just outside the capital, which he had been instrumental in founding a few years before? A department of international relations had been set up, which required someone to teach the history of diplomacy and diplomatic history, and he was confident that the faculty search committee would endorse his nomination of me. True, I had no formal qualification as a lecturer, but he believed that my many years of practical experience in the field of international relations more than made up for that. And English being the medium of instruction in the university, a native English speaker would be an asset. I was delighted at this opportunity and I accepted his offer without hesitation.

A few weeks after this conversation I received a letter from the rector confirming the committee's acceptance of me and setting out the terms and conditions. I would be designated assistant visiting professor, accorded all the facilities of the university, and accommodated rent-free in one of the furnished staff apartments on campus. The salary was the local currency equivalent of only a few hundred pounds a month, which in the first year I was there could not be converted into sterling — though in later years it was. Any of the very few foreign staff depending on their salary to meet commitments in their home country would have been hard put to make ends meet. I, fortunately, with diplomatic and old-age pensions, was not dependent on the salary. For me the most important consideration was that I had a job again. It was agreed, however, that I would attend for only one of the two four-month terms in the year (September to January), since I did not want to leave my wife on her own in London for the best part of a year.

She could of course have accompanied me; the lodgings were adequate. It was not that she did not like Turkey. On the contrary. But — as she put it (and I had to agree) — she had followed me loyally round the world for 40 years, living out of packing-cases, and she felt it was now time to put roots down in our own house. Besides, what would she do by herself all day in the lodgings while I was at work in the faculty at the other end of the campus? There would be a limit to the number of times she could go and play bridge with Turkish ladies who might still remember her from our embassy days over ten years before.

218

Third Career—University Lecturer in Turkey

This having been decided, I had now to get down to preparations for the job. There were as yet no standard books on diplomacy in the university, or prescribed for students. And in any case it seemed to me better that I should write my own lectures in a form that I knew would suit the pattern of instruction that I had in mind on the basis of my own knowledge of the subject. Since that knowledge, however, was not comprehensive, it was clear that in the ensuing four months before I went out to Ankara I would have a great deal of work to do, briefing myself from a wide range of published books and other material. I spent weeks in public libraries and private. Finally I had enough material to sit down at home and type out several dozen lectures linked in logical and chronological sequence, each with a one- or two-page summary, which I intended to hand out to the students to help them absorb the facts.

The lectures, in two fat loose-leaf volumes, were packed in a hand-case, which I planned to take out of the car on each overnight stop on the drive to Ankara, even if the car were garaged. Whatever else of my belongings might be stolen, I could not afford to let this item be. I was now ready to leave, the car loaded with my things, including heavy clothing and footwear for the severe Turkish winter that lay ahead, a selection of kitchenware to supplement what would be available in the apartment, a powerful short-wave radio and classical music cassettes with a player.

In the middle of September 1988 I set off on the seven-day journey over the Alps into Italy and down to Brindisi for the 24-hour ferry to Patras in Greece. (On subsequent journeys it was possible to sail from Ancona in the north of Italy: 36-hour ferry, but shorter road haul.) I then drove along the Gulf of Corinth to a point short of Athens, turning north through Thebes, Larissa, Salonika, then east to Kavalla and on to the Turkish frontier for Istanbul and Ankara. It was a 2500-mile journey from London that I had done several times before and the route was becoming as well-known to me as to the drivers of the many heavy trucks of different nationalities who used it to and from the Middle East.

I was of course quite familiar with Ankara, but did not know where Bilkent University (new since my day) was. So I had by prior arrangement with the dean of the faculty put up for the night of my arrival in the capital in a small hotel on the main avenue. Next morning he called personally as a gesture of welcome, and guided me to the university. He and the head of the department of international relations then showed me round the campus and installed me in my comfortable lodgings there.

* * *

Bilkent (an abbreviation of the Turkish for City of Learning) was the first private (fee-paying) university in the country, opened towards the end of 1986 as a purpose-built institution on a green-field site set back a couple of miles from a main road five miles out of Ankara. It covers 1300 acres about 200 feet above the city, which itself is nearly 3000 feet high. Besides spacious faculty and administration buildings, music rooms, auditorium, students' union, library, sports arena and restaurants, there are extensive dormitories for students and residential apartments for faculty staff and families. This whole remarkable establishment is the brainchild of one man, Ihsan Doğramacı, the man who had invited me to join the staff. He was born into a well-to-do Turkish family in Kirkuk during the First World War when what is now Iraq was still under Ottoman rule in its final stages. His future wife's background was similar, with a family association with the Turkish Petroleum Company of those days.

He graduated in medicine at Istanbul University in 1938, and after the Second World War used his family wealth to set up what was called the Hacettepe Foundation, which eventually financed the establishment of a hospital and university of that name. Apart from his role as executive director of the International Paediatric Association in Paris, his main interest was in the development of higher education in Turkey. It was in this context that he set up Bilkent University, which opened in October 1986 with 500 students, the first of the 5000 for which it was designed — increased to over 6000 by the time I joined. Academic staff were head-hunted from the faculties of a number of Turkish universities and recruited among Turkish academics on postgraduate study abroad, mainly the United States. I was one of the few non-Turkish English-speaking lecturers also engaged.

220

Fluent English is an essential requirement, since it is the medium of instruction in all faculties — though Turkish is used for some Ottoman subjects. All potential students must take an English proficiency examination; those who qualify are admitted directly to faculties as undergraduates, those who do not are required to complete successfully a one-year course at the university's English language preparatory school. This is staffed largely by over 30 young Englishmen and women (with a few Americans) recruited through the Centre for British Teachers in London and administered by a manager appointed by that body.

The faculties embrace science and engineering (electrical, electronic, computer and industrial), economics, management, administration, international relations, letters, music, fine arts and design. In addition there are vocational training schools for tourism and hotel management, secretarial skills and computer technology. Undergraduate courses last three years and lead to BA or B.Sc. degrees; graduates may then read for a Master's degree, but only if they intend to go on to a Ph.D., which is expected to take four years after initial graduation. Suitably qualified Ph.D. candidates may be granted full tuition fees and a monthly subsidy, or be given a salaried appointment as a research assistant.

The university is a non-profit-making organization supported by the endowments of the Hacettepe Foundation, which is funded by the Doğramacı family. When I arrived the fees (revised annually) were around US $4000 a year for tuition, towards which the Hacettepe Foundation paid the students a small subsidy. Besides this there were local charges for board and lodging. There were a number of scholarships. And substantial tuition and lodging grants were given to students of music and engineering, the two subjects that had priority in Doğramacı's plans. Promising children were admitted to the music department from the age of 11 and given academic education as well.

I found myself the only non-Turkish member of the staff of the international relations department. The Turkish staff (some of them women) almost all had doctorates from leading American universities; they were also all completely fluent in English and a number of them had written an impressive list of internationally-recognized academic papers. They were most agreeable colleagues.

221

My own students, of which a quarter were female, were second-and third-year undergraduates aged between 19 and 23, whom I taught in classes of about 65. Only 50 or so in each class were reading international relations as a major subject; the rest were from other departments who chose my lectures as an elective course. When I first arrived I was flattered to think this might be because lectures by a native English speaker were sought after. But my ego was soon deflated when I realized that the real reason was that my lectures coincided with empty slots in their own degree programmes, which they had to fill.

Faculty staff had to lecture for six to nine hours a week. Regular tutorials were not known, but lecturers were always available to students who wanted to discuss particular aspects of lectures. After my first winter of lecturing on diplomatic history and the history of diplomacy, I was invited to return the following year to lecture, in addition, on international organizations. For this, as for my first course, I spent weeks in London writing a further set of lectures, then drove back to Bilkent in what were by now familiar surroundings.

Although all students had to qualify in English, I did not find all of mine entirely satisfactory in the language. The top range were very good in both written and spoken work, several of them having studied at language schools in England or the United States. The majority were adequate to a greater or lesser degree. But there were some at the bottom end who were less than adequate, which showed up clearly in their examination papers. Bilkent is modelled largely on American lines — two four-month semesters a year (fall and spring); elective courses to supplement major degree programmes; and two mid-semester examinations in addition to a final. Overall results are measured in terms of the coefficient of a grade point average, with a minimum pass mark of 60 per cent. And there is an end-of-semester evaluation of lecturers and courses by the students — which I passed well.

I was warned beforehand by the Turkish staff that there was likely to be some cheating (or attempts at it) in the examinations. I was amazed therefore to find that all students brought in their own writing paper and that some left their books and notes on the chairs that separated students one from the other. I soon changed all this. On one occasion, on marking scripts after I had taken all precautions and invigilated closely with the help of a research assistant, one young woman's paper appeared more and more familiar until I realized that much of it was word for word my own lecture (texts of which were given to the students after the lecture). I called her into my office and challenged her. I was careful not to accuse her, but she got the message and in a flood of tears assured me that she had not cheated. It turned out that she had memorized several pages — to me a remarkable feat, though there were instances of other students memorizing individual paragraphs or lists of events from texts.

I lectured this particular student on the difference between learning and memorizing and, of course, could not give her any credit for her paper. I made her take what was called a make-up. This was an alternative set of questions composed for students who for one genuine reason or another (usually illness authenticated by a doctor or a hold-up in the snow on a mountain pass on returning from a weekend in Istanbul) could not take the original examination. As well as genuine reasons there were of course the try-ons — like one of my students who took the original examination but, on coming out of it, told me he knew he had done badly because he had not been feeling well, so could I not scrap his paper and give him a make-up? He really believed his request was reasonable and that I could be persuaded. He left a disappointed young man.

On average, the majority of the best performers in class and examination were the young women. Although in modern Turkish society there are no restrictions on female students, they still tend to be conservative and reserved; on campus the occasional hand-holding or waist-embracing, but none of the unseemly ostentatious necking in public so prevalent in the West. Out of classes they seemed to spend more time on study than social cavorting and came well prepared to lectures. They were generally earnest students, concerned about their progress towards a degree. Occasionally a less gifted one who had not done too well in an examination would come and ask me to reconsider her grading, bemoaning tearfully the fact that her marks in other course subjects were such that if she did not come out of my course with a

223

better mark her average would set her back a year for repetition. Notwithstanding pleading Turkish eyes I had to harden my heart: all I could promise was that I would consult with her other teachers and see whether she had enough potential to do better the following year, and so avoid being relegated now.

The young women were generally well-groomed. Among them, however, were a couple of dozen, mainly scholarship girls from rural families, who wore a headscarf and long coat — a throwback to the days before Atatürk founded the secular republic and outlawed such relics of the sultanate that are today the dress of Islamic fundamentalism in neighbouring Iran. There had been demonstrations in a number of Turkish schools and universities both for and against the wearing of headscarves. Some of the fiercest critics against were women teachers and professors, who felt apprehensive about any movement that might relegate Turkish women to their earlier position of inferiority. In wider terms it was seen as possibly the thin end of a wedge opening the way for Islamic fundamentalism in Turkey.

At Bilkent the question came to a sudden head when a Turkish male lecturer in the international relations department ordered a student in his class who was wearing a headscarf to take it off or herself out. She chose to take herself out — and went straight to the head of department to complain. The result was a faculty meeting called by the dean. Fierce discussion there centred on the rights of an individual in a free country, which was felt to be more important than any fear of fundamentalism — considered in any case a groundless fear in Turkey. So objectors (including women staff) found themselves in the minority and the headscarf wearers won the day and they continue their practice. But they keep a low profile, helped I think by the fact that they tend to be among the drabbest of the girls, overshadowed by the many attractive ones in stylish modern dress.

It might be thought that because Bilkent is a fee-paying university it would be resorted to by wealthy parents whose children cannot make the grade into a state university. But in fact aspirants to Bilkent have to take the national university entrance examination. Clearly of course those who put Bilkent at the top of their list have parents who can afford it. There is some evidence of this in the great number of cars, many of them Mercedes and BMWs, in students' car parks, belonging to those (or to the fathers of those) who commute from Ankara rather than live in dormitories.

I had the impression that not all students were anxious to acquire knowledge for its own sake — though those who did were the best. For many the aim seemed to be simply to pass their examinations well enough to get a degree and take it out into the marketplace in the hope of landing a job. For others this was not the end objective; they would be going into a family business, where having a degree would enhance their status. Of the many students in my classes only two had their eye on a degree in international relations as a way into the diplomatic service. There is a students' advisory service (run by the rector's wife) which helps with career placement; and leading Turkish companies head-hunt for graduate trainees at Bilkent among other universities.

From time to time guest lecturers are invited to address the university as a whole or specific departments. They come from a wide range of international organizations as well as from the upper echelons of the Turkish civil and military establishment. In the question-and-answer sessions that follow, postgraduate students in particular show a good understanding of world and regional problems. They have clear views about Turkey's European vocation.

So too indeed did my undergraduates in class discussion on the subject. Few of them had any doubts about the correctness of Turkey's orientation and its key situation between Europe and the Arabs — though they suspected that the majority of the population east of Sivas, in Anatolia 275 miles east of Ankara, had little if any idea of what all this meant. But I found that many students had doubts about their country's chances of full membership of the European Union in terms of political, economic and social progress. For some these doubts were rationalized in bitter expression of the view that while the West was glad enough to have Turkey enter the war against the Axis in 1945, to enlist its military strength in the Korean war in 1950, and then add it to NATO two years later, it was in no hurry to admit a Muslim country fully into its circle.

This was seen to be borne out by the fact that Greece, an associate member of the Community since 1962, only a year before Turkey, was admitted as a full member in 1981. The students had no doubts about the hostile part played by Greece in the European Union in extension of its vendetta with Turkey over Cyprus and the Aegean. They felt that to counter this Turkey needed to strengthen its public relations apparatus and make its own case better known. While I was of course interested in such views I was careful not to initiate class discussion of Turkish internal affairs. But discussion of wider international problems — Cyprus, the Persian Gulf, Arab–Israeli relations — inevitably touched on Turkish government policies. On this subject the students were as outspoken, for and against, as young people in the West. While they deprecated what they saw as shortcomings in Turkey they emphasized their freedom to talk about these without fear.

They took a realistic view of their country's place in the world and were as ready to support their government as to criticize. They approved the prompt closure of the oil pipelines to Turkey from Iraq in the lead up to the Gulf War in 1990 and the use of the air base at Incirlik in the southeast of the country during the war. On the other hand, two years earlier they had disapproved of their government's precipitate recognition of the Palestine Liberation Organization's so-called State of Palestine while there was still no international recognition of Turkish North Cyprus as a state. They felt that their government had thrown away a bargaining counter.

In 1990 I accepted an invitation to come back to the university for a third winter term; I enjoyed teaching and looked forward to following the progress up from class to class of the students I had first taught in 1988. It was an interesting and challenging new experience for me after my two earlier careers and I found a great deal of satisfaction in the response I had from those who were anxious to learn and set themselves to absorb my lectures. And to be surrounded by enquiring young people kept a man of my years on his toes; he could not get away with verbosity. A salutary warning for any ambassador.

Index

army service, 8, 12–13
Bahrain, deputy political
  resident, 64
Bilkent University, lecturer at,
  218
civil service examinations, 5,
  6
consular service
  examinations, 7
counsellor, 18–19, 20, 28,
  30–1, 49
diplomatic service, 141
Doctor of Laws, 153
employment after retirement,
  153–4, 156; *see also* Taylor
  Woodrow plc
family circumstances, 5
grandparents, 1, 3, 4
Hillhead High School, 5, 19
Ibn Saud, audience with,
  38–40; *see also* Saudi Arabia
Imperial Tobacco Company,
  5–6
Indonesia, appointed
  ambassador to, 67; *see also*
  Indonesia
Inland Revenue, 6, 7
intelligence training, Karachi,
  14
Japanese, qualifies in, 13–14
Jedda, first secretary and
  deputy ambassador, 36
job-hunting, 155–6
Kabul, oriental secretary, 31–
  2
KCMG, 123

marriage, 15
Mountbatten, Viceroy, 16,
  20, 23; *see also under*
  Mountbatten, Viceroy
Nyerere, President Julius, 89,
  90, 92, 93, 94, 99, 102, 104
Obote, Milton, 102, 104
officer training, 11, 13
Owen, David, 137; *see also*
  uner Owen, Dr David
Saudi Arabia, *agrément*, 82;
  ambassador, 80; appointed
  first secretary, 36; opposition
  to appointment, 81–5; *see*
  aslo Saudi Arabia
Shah of Iran, 63; *see aslo* Iran
Shiraz, vice-consul and consul
  in, 24, 25, 27, 29, 31, 137,
  159, 168, 184
Tanzania, appointed high
  commissioner, 95; *see also*
  Tanzania
Turkey, appointed
  ambassador to, 107; *see also*
  Turkey
Phrygians, 110
Poland, 1–2
Poona, 13
Provisional People's
  Consultative Assembly, 74
Prussia, 1
Punjab, 108; *see also* 1st
  Punjab Regiment

Qashqai, 26
Qatar, 196

Qotbzadeh, Sadiq, 162
Qum, 168

RAF, 10, 14, 24, 50, 55–6, 66, 172
Rashidi tribe, 39
Red Sea, 38, 49
Rediffusion Television, 75
Republican People's Party (RPP), 112, 114–15
Repulse Bay, 187
Réunion, 188
Revolution Council, 106
Rhodesia, 88, 94–5
Ribbentrop, 119
Riga, 3–4
Riyadh, 38–9, 43–6, 48
Roman Empire, 110
Roubaix, 9
Rowland, Tiny, 91
Royal Navy, 55, 128, 138
Russia(n), 1–2, 4, 12, 25–8, 32, 95, 97, 102–3, 112, 125, 164, 204; *see also* Soviet Union; USSR

Sa'adi, 24
Sabah, 70
St John, 110
St Paul, 110
St Petersburg, 3
Saint Sophia, 109
Salalah, 57
Salonika, 112, 219
Salzburg, 183
Sarawak, 70
Sardis, 110

Satow, Sir Ernest, 152
Saud, Crown Prince, 40
Saudi Arabia, 35, 36–7, 39, 40–2, 44–7, 48–51, 56, 67, 80–3, 85, 89, 102, 149, 196–7
Saudi Arabian Tanker Company, 40
SAVAK, 64, 161–2, 165
Second World War, 26–7, 39, 49, 59, 78, 119, 125, 141, 157, 164, 205, 220
secret Intelligence service, 21
Sejny, 1
Seljuks, 110, 112
Select Committee on Overseas Development, 150
Semarang, 78
Serengeti plains, 106
Seychelles, 125
Shabwa, 50
Shah, Reza, 26
Shanghai, 202, 205
Shatt al-Arab, 162
Sheikh's Garden, 25
Shiite, 63, 161
Shibam, 50
Shiraz, 24–7, 29, 31, 59, 137, 159, 168, 174, 184
Siberia, 3
Sicily, 112
Siemens, 179
Simla, 14–15
Simonstown, 97, 101
Singapore, 16, 19, 53, 69–70, 75–9, 103, 209
Sivas, 225

Index